Personal Sovereignty

'a journey to freedom'

The Temple of Understanding
Volume I

Adrian Emery

Wisdom Press

First published in Australia 2019

Copyright c 2019 by Adrian Emery

All rights reserved

No part of this work may be used or reproduced in any manner whatsoever without written permission from the publisher except in the case of brief quotations embedded in critical articles or reviews

Wisdom Press
34 Johnsons Rd
Bilpin NSW Australia 2758
www.wisdompress.com.au

ISBN: 978-0-6485106-0-4 (pbk)
ISBN: 978-0-6485106-1-1 (ebk)

Printed and bound in Australia on paper from responsible sources

*dedicated to humanity
in the hope that we may find
our way back to our rightful place and destiny*

THE TEMPLE OF UNDERSTANDING

The word temple derives from the Latin word – templum, meaning a sacred precinct or the dwelling place of a god or gods: the house of the deity. In ancient times, the temple was not so much one building as in a church but more of a cluster of buildings with varying degrees of access for different ranks of people or strata of society. These precincts would typically have one main building and many smaller out-buildings. The sacred ruins of Machu Picchu or the Pantheon in Greece typify such a complex temple structure over a vast geographic area.

In modern terms the word temple signifies a place of worship for all faiths as opposed to the words church, synagogue or mosque where each pertains to a specific religion. I am using the word temple in both these senses. On the one hand, it is agnostic in the true sense of the word - not that one is an atheist who does not believe in a Supreme Being or God but rather that it is impossible to know the nature of the ultimate reality from a limited, rational and totally logical view point. So, one does not try to define God but accepts it as an unknowable and ultimate state of being.

In the other sense, *The Temple of Understanding* is a composite structure just as the original Roman word templa (the plural of templum) was a composite structure of buildings. Moreover, just as any building, and especially one as grand as a cathedral or temple, is a complex structure requiring much planning, design and ultimately construction, so too, *The Temple of Understanding* is not just one simple thesis but has many facets to its construction.

The central theme of this structure is that modern humanity exists historically within an all-encompassing and pervasive misunderstanding of who we are, why we exist, where we have come from and where we are going to. This misunderstanding is a virus that has invaded every aspect of our lives, culture and society creating chaos and confusion down through the ages. Like a computer virus that creates havoc with our software or a biological virus that creates ill-health within the body, this virus resides within our meta-belief system or the operating system of our mental makeup.

Like a fish being unaware of the water within which it lives or humanity being unaware of the air we breathe, this misunderstanding has become so pervasive in every area of our lives that we are not only totally unaware of its existence, but vigorously and illogically defend any attempt to shine a light upon that existence and the destructive effects it is having upon our very being and ultimate survival.

It is also my thesis that this misunderstanding is rendering humanity, as the current form of homo sapiens, extinct because the principle of evolution demands that all beings and all species adhere to the Universal Laws of Life through knowing and understanding precisely how life works. This misunderstanding separates us from the flow of life causing blockage and limitation of our energy sources. We have become weak and vulnerable as a species and are no longer plugged into and connected with the divine principles of life.

The Temple of Understanding is not a religious thesis – there are far too many religions in the world already causing enough mayhem, conflict and misery. Nearly all wars, conflict and bigotry revolve around religion which is a direct descendant of this misunderstanding. This temple is not erected to pay homage to any god or gods but to honour life. We may not be able to define or know God, but we can study, know and define life. Humanity is an integral part of life and it is the exploration of our rightful place within the Infinity of Being that this temple seeks to address.

One of the fundamental aspects of intelligence is curiosity – a desire to know how things work. Indeed, humanity has spent most of its history seeking answers to the questions, both metaphysical and physical, as to how life works. But in any epistemology, we need to ensure that our foundations are true and correct. The most important part of any large building or physical structure are the foundations. These must be capable of supporting the eventual structure or it will inevitably collapse. So too, if our founding premises are not correct then the ensuing structure of knowledge will be erroneous opinion rather than justified belief. How do we know if our beliefs are correct?

There is only one sure way and that is the test of time. Similarly, we can only know if a building will survive the ravages of time and weather long after it is built. If our working body of knowledge is correct, we will live and prosper; if not, we will not withstand the evolutionary dictates of time. It is my contention that humanity stands at the crossroads and needs urgently to reassess its fundamental premises or assumptions of how life works because plainly our lives do no longer work.

Whether we examine our lives as an individual human being or as an entire species, something is definitely not working. We are on a collision course with the Earth – the only home we have. We are the only species that wages war on each other to the extent that we endanger not only our own survival but that of the very planet and indeed the neighbouring solar system. As I write, we have two megalomaniac leaders (if indeed that is what they truly are?) threatening us all with their egoic posturing. We are the only species that pollutes its nest to the point where our ecosystem and environment can no longer support us. Our current lifestyle is inherently unsustainable. As individuals, we have lost the meaning and purpose of life and we seem to be at odds with the process of life itself.

We are fundamentally divorced from reality which leads to the inevitable conclusion that our basic premises are incorrect. They have not withstood the test of time. Life on planet earth is 4.6 billion years old. In that context, humanity is merely a few hundred thousand years old and our particular belief system is but the twinkling of an eye. The overriding paradigm within which western man lives is at most two thousand years old. This is nothing in the grander scheme of things. If we narrow our focus onto the current reigning meta-belief system, it is perhaps at most five hundred years old and the current economic system would be no more than three hundred, born in the Industrial Revolution of the seventeenth century.

So, we can see that our foundations have NOT withstood the test of time. In not even one hundred years, we have created a lifestyle, an economy and a society that is at odds with the basic principle of life, that is inherently destructive on all levels and that is unsustainable. This structure is based upon a set of beliefs that are faulty. And as rational, intelligent beings, we need to urgently acknowledge this fact and make an immediate about turn adapting to the reality that confronts us. This is the dictate of the evolutionary process.

Life on planet Earth has been evolving for 46 thousand million one hundred-year periods. In just one of those one hundred-year periods we have almost destroyed the lot. It is absolute arrogance, insolence and blatant stupidity to not acknowledge that something is fundamentally wrong and what is wrong is our foundation. The basic building blocks of our entire edifice of knowledge are faulty. We live within a monstrous misunderstanding that precludes us from seeing clearly and understanding the sacred processes of life.

As previously mentioned, we do not need to concern ourselves with trying to define or understand the nature of God – the Ultimate Reality. But we do urgently and desperately need to concern ourselves with the nature of life that surrounds us in our own ecosystem or very soon we will not be a part of that life much longer. In this sense life is not negotiable.

One of the intrinsic errors in this misunderstanding is the arrogance of man: that somehow, we are more intelligent than life, that we can bend and dominate life and its natural processes, that we are the crowning glory of creation at the top of the tree of life; that we are the supremely intelligent being on the planet and that life is subordinate to us to do with it what we choose. And nothing could be further from the truth. All forms of life are inherently equal, and all forms of life are beholden and subject to the Universal Laws of Life. These laws do not just pertain to life on Earth but are truly universal, regulating life throughout the omniverse; for we now know that our universe is just one of many and that life is truly infinite.

Again, it is the complete arrogance of man to believe that he is alone in the far reaches of the cosmos and the only 'intelligent' species in creation. Life is far superior to man and life will decide whether the current form of homo sapiens survives or not depending on our choices and our behaviour. Our current trajectory is certain extinction. We need to change our direction, our lifestyle, our modus operandi if we wish to survive. And to make this drastic change we need to change our meta-data fields of who we are, why we are here and where we are going.

This complete software rewrite is essential because we exist within the misunderstanding which as a virus has played havoc with all of our operating systems. We need a complete reboot! This will not be easy, and humanity will be dragged kicking and screaming because it wants to hold onto the comfort zone of the known even if that known is wrong and injurious. Humanity has never given up the *status quo* easily – witness the Inquisition, the Reformation, the Fundamentalist and Fascist mentality that always rules the world. The negative ego holds onto the power it has accumulated. We exist dictated to by our past not our future.

We have a fundamental identity belief that is outdated and outmoded and is no longer serving our evolution or the process of life on the planet. The real question is whether we can make that identity shift in time before it is too late or will the inevitable evolutionary shift to a newer and more noble species of homo take our place. Whether we like it or not the storm clouds of change are upon us now. We will need to go through the eye of the storm in the foreseeable future and we are talking years, not decades.

The real question is whether you, as an individual, will be ready: physically, emotionally and mentally, to ride that wave of change for this will be decided on an individual basis and no one can go through the storm or ride the wave for another. Neither can you do it holding hands! As in any major evolutionary adaptation, those individuals with the required superior genome that is more suited to the emerging epoch will survive and thrive and those that do not mutate will perish and die out.

Obviously, the million-dollar question is: what is the superior and appropriate genome? What are the traits or characteristics that are essential to cultivate to survive into the 21st century and beyond? Moreover, it is not just a matter of following some recipe nor having some genetic surgery to implant the missing gene. We need to redesign ourselves at the core and to do this successfully we need to move out of the darkness of the misunderstanding and into the light of true knowing. We need to establish ourselves with a new identity at our core.

This will be the New Human!

So, the real question becomes – how attached are you to Being You? Can you envisage a totally different way of Being? Are you prepared to give up, to walk away from the structure that you have built around yourself, to dismantle the edifice of you? This is the *Temple of*

Understanding. In that temple the old you, the current version of you simply does not exist.

We need to accept that who we are is merely a construct; there is nothing sacrosanct about our definition of being human. It is merely one design and a faulty one at that. But we are attached to the design; we like it even though it really does not work and makes us miserable. We would rather put up with the pain than go to the dentist or doctor or do the work required to make us healthy. Moreover, there is no quick fix here. It requires years of training, discipline and work. We need to fundamentally retrain our brain and the way it works. Our operating system has a virus which makes our thinking process faulty.

Are you attached to your ego? Do you like your toys? Can you exist without your material and egoic accumulations that define who you are? You see you are **not** who or what you currently believe you are. You are a soul housed in a body. You are a multidimensional being preoccupied with a one-dimensional reality. Even your mind is not just your linear, rational thinking brain. You do have feelings; you do have an intuition; you do intuit; you do have gut knowing and so on. We all experience déjà vu and premonitions. We all work with our sixth sense. We all know these things exist even though they are denied by mainstream media and the scientific establishment.

You are so much more than your currently limited definition. And precisely because we deny these inner riches and wealth of our real spiritual being, we cling to the outer trappings of material and egoic accoutrement: the clothes, the car, the house, the job, the image, the ambition and the social standing. These seeds have been planted for millennia and are now in full bloom. But they are weeds in the garden of our soul smothering the flowers of our real self.

Our true nature can no longer breathe freely but is trampled under the weight of our accumulation. It is so heavy being you! It is unbearable. We are all exhausted from carrying the burden of our negative ego. It will not let us go even for a moment. The eternal and exhaustive inner dialogue of nonsense and mayhem. It is on-going, and it is insane.

We do not need to understand the nature of God. We do not even need to ponder the wanton destruction of the planet. Merely be the witness to your own mind; simply observe the daily ritual of your thinking and your obsession. Witness the haste and the activity that surrounds us - for what? What are we creating as a society? Where is our legacy – what will our great grandchildren inherit? How will they judge us? It will not be pleasing. In a single generation we have squandered the blessings bestowed upon us by the bounty of nature.

The age of mass consumerism and conspicuous consumption. Our current temple has as its altar the greed of materiality and the priest is the alter-ego of our mind. We produce and consume trinkets of triviality. He with the most toys wins. But wins what? What is the purpose and meaning of a life spent pursuing an exterior image that others can be envious of? What are we creating of worth, of sacredness, of lasting value?

Where are our values and what are they? Are we a valued being? Do we value ourselves? Does this question even make sense to you? If I were to ask you: do you really value yourself and how do you do that? If you truly valued yourself would you waste your life, your time, your energy and the precious gift of life in the pursuit of the inessential?

Is your life committed to building something of consequence even if that is serene happiness and inner contentment? It need not be external, although, to accomplish for the good of the world and for others is the highest good and its own reward. More and more studies are now finding that being altruistic creates the greatest happiness. It is not the pursuit of our own pleasure that delivers lasting value but being of service to others. Other studies are also now finding that this is an essential ingredient to living a long and noble life. Those who contribute to society in some meaningful way enjoy robust health into a ripe elderly age. Giving is receiving. Taking leads to emotional bankruptcy and personal depletion.

Life is a gift and it is given freely, but it does bestow upon us the obligation and the necessity to give back. This is a part of the circle of life. All of nature understands this cycle; it is only modern man who has lost the inclination to give but is obsessed with taking. As we deny the inner depth of our true nature with all its spiritual wealth, we crave the trappings of a false idol.

But this is all just a part of the misunderstanding that we suffer under: the grand delusion! We need to redefine who we are and where we came from. If you are on a journey and come to realise you are lost, you must first reflect on when you last knew where you were and where you went wrong. Only then can you find the right path to get you back on track.

Our creation myths are wrong. Our basic cosmology is erroneous. The story of who we are and how we came to be here is a children's fairy story that is filled with improbable events at best and downright misleading lies at worst. We have been misled deliberately to keep us asleep, to keep us afraid, to keep us compliant. A sleeping humanity choosing not to think seriously, not to wake up, not to take responsibility for its destiny and not to take its rightful place in the Infinity of Being.

Far easier to create the antagonists of God and the Devil as the perpetrators of our reality and we the hapless victim in their eternal struggle between good and evil. What a convenient cop out. No accountability; no personal responsibility; no sovereignty.

These are large topics and need detailed analysis if we are to come to a better understanding of who we truly are and why we are here on planet Earth. *The Temple of Understanding* consists of three titles: *Personal Sovereignty, TaoTuning* and *BeComing One*. They form the three pillars or foundation stones upon which the temple stands. Each one addresses a separate and specific condition of the misunderstanding.

Personal Sovereignty deals with the ability to be truly sovereign: to make our own decisions, to be free from external influence and free to be true to ourselves; to live our lives authentically. To be independent, self-reliant and autonomous; to be a sovereign being. To end the dominance of the altered negative ego and to live holistically with intuition and grace. To experience the real intimacy of sovereign love.

TaoTuning then explores the ability to flow with the cosmic currents of life. To be able to ride the wave of your own personal Tao in harmony with the universal principles of life – the great Tao. To be able to execute those decisions and choices one makes as a sovereign being. And to do this with elegance and panache. To be truly successful and enjoy the life of your choosing: to live the dream without causing injury or harm to any other living being or to life itself; the ability to turn your goals into reality and manifest your innermost desires.

Finally, *BeComing One* puts it all together in a harmonious symphony of life, light and laughter. To be one with the creative forces of life; to be one with yourself – body, mind and spirit. To be one with the Earth and all the myriad forms of life that dwell upon it. To be one with the cosmos. To be congruent and whole. To be at peace and to thoroughly enjoy the eternal journey of your being.

Ideally, the reader should proceed sequentially in the above order for the temple to make sense. After all, we cannot construct a large building or edifice by just throwing stones together: they must be placed carefully according to the architect's design and the engineer's specifications if the building is to survive the test of time and be a pleasing work of art.

We need to redefine our understanding of what it means to be human. We need to evolve into the eighth species of homo and reach beyond the limited understanding and faulty belief systems of homo sapiens. After all, the genus homo has been around for approximately 2 million years; homo sapiens a mere 200,000 and modern man a trifling 2,000!

Evolutionary shifts often come quickly – the dinosaurs supposedly disappeared in an afternoon. Life is forever moving on and survival depends upon intelligent adaptation. Are we, as a species and as individuals, ready for this next shift? How do we know when it will come? More to the point how do we know it is not immanent?

Either way, *The Temple of Understanding* will both prepare you for the coming shift and enable you to live a more fulfilling, enjoyable and healthy life. What could be more important than that?

To be who you want to be – to exercise conscious dominion of your life. To live a truly successful life expressing your inner truth. To free yourself from the dictates of mass consciousness and the conniving of the ruling elite. To be a noble soul inhabiting a healthy body. To be one of the intrepid explorers and adventurers on this grand and glorious cosmic journey. To be a spiritual warrior and way shower lighting the path for others to follow.

To be an early adopter of the evolutionary thrust and become the new human who lives peacefully on planet Earth, communing with Gaia and participating in the brotherhood of man. To be happy and free. To be noble and pure. To have the wisdom to live the life we were meant to live: consciously aware and joyous.

INTRODUCTION

Freedom! Such an evocative word – pregnant with meaning and a challenge to all of us. Surely, freedom can be described as the number one inalienable right of the individual. Indeed, we could say that freedom and being human are two sides of the one coin: for without freedom what is life? A human being with no freedom at all is nothing more than a slave, a robot or a clone.

Freedom means liberty, the absolute ability to live one's life as one pleases – free from the forces of oppression, fear and tyranny, and free to express one's innate individuality and creativity. It means being free to openly and honestly express oneself. The joy of self-expression!

Yet, how many of us truly embody this? Are we really free to be ourselves? How many of us know who we are, have contact with this inner source of creativity and experience this joy? It seems there are so many external and internal inhibiting factors that rob us as individuals of this freedom and this joy. It takes a special courage, a certain bravado, to speak your truth quietly, clearly and succinctly. It takes dedication and commitment to honour the self and to be true to who you really are. It seems that everyone wants to tell us what to do, what to think, and who to be.

The history of humanity is the story of greater and greater external or overt freedom to the individual – a freeing from the oppression of the few over the many. Yet, as we enter this modern age of technological interconnectivity where we are all connected at the speed of light and with the flick of a mouse, the world wide web weaves its covert hold on our psyches with an ever-tightening grip. Mass media and social media now subtly seduce us into a conformity of thought and being that has never existed previously and transcends all national and geographic borders and barriers.

We are truly becoming one race. Our challenge is this: will we become a proud race of strong individuals who know themselves and who are true to their inner spirits or will we become a feeble race of weak automatons who meekly do what they are told by the collective forces of conformity, tradition, and established wisdom? Will we create a bold and glorious future or stay stuck in the past, in the safe and secure status quo? Will we honour and acknowledge who we really are – a divine spirit inhabiting a human body, or will we become a pale shadow of imitation and emptiness?

Humanity stands at the cross-roads and needs to urgently address these important questions and determine its future destiny, for it is undoubtedly clear that we cannot continue on our current trajectory. We are at war with ourselves, each other and the planet on which we dwell – our only home. It is apparent that if we do not fundamentally, at our core, change, we are an extinct species. The only question is: will we take the planet, the earth and all that lives upon it with us?

One of the most significant outcomes of space exploration was the spiritual awakening and realisation of many astronauts as they looked back at Earth from their vantage point in space. This viewpoint, never seen before, gave rise to a profound understanding and appreciation of the Earth as 'home'. No longer was 'home' a street, a suburb, a village, a city or even a country. No, 'home' was the Earth and the Earth was our only home.

Astronauts Edgar Mitchell, Russell Schweickart and others experienced deep inner spiritual transformations where they knew intrinsically and intuitively that they were an integral part of life on Earth: one with its ecosystem, and with its other inhabitants, both human and non-human. And thus was born a global or planetary consciousness. Overnight, we became planetary citizens sharing one blue planet, one tiny orb spinning in this vast magnitude of space. It was not only a cathartic moment for those individual astronauts but also for any of us with the intelligence to be aware of this shift.

This is one of those psychic shifts, changes in paradigm or game-changers that alter everything. Once upon a time, humanity believed that the world was flat and that the sun revolved around the earth. This quantum shift in consciousness and perspective is at least, if not more radical than the realisation in the sixteenth century that the earth was not, the centre of the universe and that the earth revolved around the sun.

We all now know, deeply, inwardly, that we have gone too far. No matter what the sceptics say or what the entrenched forces of the scientific-economic establishment argue, our exploitative mode of consciousness, the voracious greed of our collective negative ego and our conspicuous consumption is eating up the planet's finite resources. We are polluting the planet's life systems. The great forests – the lungs of the Earth – have been felled and ravaged; the seas and oceans – the lifeblood of the Earth – have been so severely denuded and polluted and are becoming so acidic that plankton, which is the beginning of the food chain in the ocean, is no longer able to breed.

Without the forests to counterbalance the dioxins produced by the burning of fossil fuels, the holes in the stratosphere are growing exponentially. These dioxins are eating away at the substances that create oxygen. Because of these holes and the resultant global warming, the great icecaps are melting, and raising the sea levels. To anyone objectively observing, nature is changing dramatically and rapidly and this is due to human greed and disrespect for nature.

Thus, humanity and nature are on a collision course. But humanity refuses to listen. It is not so much a case of global warming but one of global warning. The Earth, like any living being, is now in survival mode and has started to kick back, as it must to survive. Down through the ages, humanity has lived in harmony with the greater life cycles and rhythms of nature. But no longer. In the last 50 years, in one generation, we have become an aberrant species – a scourge and cancer upon the earth.

As a matter of urgency, we need to find our way back to this harmony, to this state of oneness with the Earth and with the forces of nature. The Earth existed very nicely without humanity for over 4,000 million years and if need be, will do so again. Modern man is eating its way indiscriminately across the surface of the planet destroying everything in its path. Within the last 100 years, we have voraciously consumed and destroyed what has taken billions of years to create.

In 2015 alone, humans produced enough concrete (50 billion tonnes) to pave the entire surface of the planet; displaced 57 billion tonnes of earth in mining; and produced enough plastic wrap to totally wrap the entire planet. More than half the world's land surface has been transformed for human use and carbon dioxide is being emitted 100 times faster than at any time in the last 800,000 years. CO2 emission is now recognised as the most damaging human activity.

This is all the beginning of a new epoch in the evolution of the Earth called the Anthropocene Age, which is characterised by human activity and influence upon the planet. Such changes require a massive transformation in our conscious awareness of who we are and the impact of our behaviour on our own survival and that of the planet on which we live. This transformation begins with the taking of personal responsibility.

Personal sovereignty is the journey to this self-awareness, to this responsibility and to this freedom. For without responsibility there can be no freedom. With no planet to live on, there will be no life and thus no freedom. If humanity is forced to evacuate planet Earth because of its foolish, selfish and reckless behaviour, our freedom will be severely curtailed. Many of these philosophical discussions will give way to the necessities of survival in space.

I offer this book, *Personal Sovereignty*, as a roadmap to finding our way back to harmony, to peace and to a prosperity that is aligned with the principles of life, and not in conflict with the natural order of the universe. It is only one such path. This is a journey of inner exploration to discover the truths of the necessary debate we need as a species and as a matter of dire urgency to have if we are to survive.

I firmly believe that if we do not have this conversation and if we do not take this journey seriously, we will soon be extinct. Personal sovereignty is all about our collective and personal relationship with free will choice that began in the mythical Garden of Eden. Each and every one of us needs to make a personal choice, and time is running out.

The Earth is a part of nature and nature is aligned with the whole of the universe and with the whole of the evolutionary process throughout time. Humanity is now out of that alignment. There are definite and precise evolutionary and universal principles of life: there is a universal law of life. If we continue to transgress and ignore this one law, we will forfeit our right to life.

Humanity's continued survival down through the ages depends upon a healthy respect for and acknowledgement of the universal principles of evolution. The Earth has reached its limit of tolerance and patience and is saying to humanity enough is enough. It is time for real and enduring change with regards to who we are, and to our planetary responsibility both collectively and individually.

This change must begin by accepting conscious, personal, and sovereign dominion and taking our rightful place in the Infinity of Being. For those brave souls willing to take this glorious journey, I offer this roadmap as a guide only to your own personal journey of self-discovery. Happy travelling!

Contents

Part I:	**The Process of Individuation**		1
One:	Sovereignty – an Historical Perspective		1
Two:	The Evolution of Consciousness		12
Three:	The Dialectic of Integration and Repression		19
Four:	The Grand Deception – the Mythological Fall		27
Five:	The Ego and the Spirit		35
Six:	The Nature of Evil and the Fear and Abuse of Human Freedom		44
Seven:	Individuation		65
Part II:	**The Conspiracy of Repression**		79
Eight:	Unnatural Childbirth		79
Nine:	The Mechanics of Repression		92
Ten:	The Search for Outside Validation		107
Eleven:	Domination, Co-dependency and the Significant Other		125
Twelve:	The Collective Negative Ego and the New World Order		146

Part III:	The New Human	**161**
Thirteen:	Roadmap to Recovery	161
Fourteen:	Personal Powah	168
Fifteen:	Inner Clarity	177
Sixteen:	Intention	188
Seventeen:	Self-mastery and functioning with Dominion	198
Eighteen:	Purity of Purpose	210
Nineteen:	Self-Love and Self-Acceptance	215
Twenty:	The Joy of Self-Expression	221

Conclusion: The Liberated Self – The New Frontier	231
Twenty-one: Sovereign Love and Real Relationships	231

Notes	**243**
About the Author	**245**

Part I: THE PROCESS OF INDIVIDUATION

One: Sovereignty - an Historical Perspective

'Sovereignty' is usually a term or quality that we ascribe to a political state or situation. We talk of a sovereign state or the sovereign of a state, for example: a monarch or a ruler. The sovereign was historically the supreme ruling authority or power in the land. A sovereign state is one that has the power and ability to rule over itself, and to make its own laws free from external control or influence.

The dictionary defines sovereignty as:
- supreme power, especially over a body politic
- freedom from external control – autonomy
- controlling influence
- an autonomous state.

Thus, the sovereign or a sovereign state denotes the ability to rule, to decide, to make laws, and to be absolute. In other words, to be sovereign is to not be accountable or beholden to any other force or power. Up until the advent of democracy or the constitutional monarchy, the monarch ruled supreme. The sovereign held undisputed power over the land and could do as he or she saw fit. Then came the days of the sovereign nation state whatever the form of political persuasion. Whether it was a western capitalist democracy or a communist totalitarian regime or a fundamentalist religious sect, each jealously guarded their inherent independence and freedom from external control and influence.

The history of humanity is basically the sad and sorry story of various sovereigns and sovereign states jostling for control and domination of, and independence and freedom from, each other. Most, if not all, wars and conflicts arise from this one question of sovereignty. Thus, we can see the significance and importance of sovereignty in the evolution of mankind. Even today, if we examine any of the geopolitical hotspots on the planet and ascertain the true cause of the conflict, it will invariably revolve around this concept of sovereignty. Whether it be a movement of people to throw off the shackles of an invading oppressor, the desire for economic or political imperialism, ethnic cleansing, or even a religious conflict, it is all ultimately a question of sovereignty. It is an attempt by people to rule themselves as they see fit, free from the control and influence of a perceived other.

Indeed, one of the most significant questions being raised internationally, is just how far the international community, through the agencies of the United Nations or NATO or the European Union, can and should interfere in the internal affairs of a sovereign nation state, for example the economic situation in Greece or the political situation in Syria. The world is not ready to forego its claim to independence for the sake of planetary peace or the new world order. However, it is obvious that there will need to be some compromises made in the foreseeable future if any real peace is to be established.

So, these are obviously important and pressing issues that need to be addressed. But before we, as a body of humanity, can intelligently and rationally deal with this sensitive question, we must be clear within ourselves about the overriding spiritual and philosophical implications for us as individual members of that body. Humanity is not a conglomerate of unfeeling, mechanical parts. Rather, it is a body made up of six billion individual cells, and each of those cells is a living, breathing, sensitive, intelligent human being.

Unfortunately, in the past, we have seen ourselves as part of a subset of that body, aligning ourselves with others in that set at the exclusion and ultimately, at the expense of the larger whole. If we use the analogy of the human body, we readily perceive that it is a whole. We do not mistake a part, whether that be an arm or an internal organ, for the whole. Nor do we perceive one part as being in conflict with that whole for this is disease, most particularly cancer.

We understand that each and every part has a specific and vital role to play in the maintenance and well-being of that whole. Each organ, each limb, and each component is a subset of the body and is essential to its overall health and functioning. An individual cell may unite with any number of other cells to form a particular organ, but it is still aware of itself as being a part of the total organism. It does not perceive itself or its grouping as being apart from the whole. We do not witness the body attacking itself except in more recent history where cancer and other auto-immune diseases have become the inner mirror and representation of this outer confusion.

To really understand this question of sovereignty we need to examine it from the point of view of an individual cell in the body of humanity – that is from the perspective of an individual person. Thus, this book is an exploration of personal sovereignty: the meaning of the term and its deeper philosophical and spiritual implications for each and every one of us.

We need to adjust our thinking, as Arthur Koestler suggests in *The Ghost in the Machine*, understanding that we are both part and whole. We are wholly human as individuals, but we are also a part of humanity and in this sense, we are not whole for we each need other human beings to complete us, to make us feel whole, and to make our lives worthwhile. No man or woman is an island. We need and depend upon each other to make life work and to give it meaning.

Koestler coined the term 'holon' to describe this state of being both part and whole and further suggests that all systems are composed of sub-systems that are organised along these lines of whole and part matrices:

> But wholes and parts in this absolute sense just do not exist anywhere, either in the domain of living organisms or of social organisations. What we find are intermediary structures on a series of levels in an ascending order of complexity: sub wholes which display, according to the way you look at them, some of the characteristics commonly attributed to wholes and some of the characteristics commonly attributed to parts.[1]

It is the thesis of this book that it is the confusion between these two dialectic opposites, and our failure on the individual level to reconcile their opposition, that has led humanity into its present state of disharmony and self-destruction. We need as a matter of urgency to understand the principle of personal sovereignty.

For if we look at the planet globally or at the overall body of humanity, we see the conflict and hostility that result from this state of confusion and misunderstanding. Economically and politically, we perceive conflict between nation states and the international community. If we look at the well-being of the planet itself and the delicate life support ecosystem upon which all life depends, we are immediately aware of a disconnect. If we look at the distribution of wealth and sustenance throughout the body of humanity, we notice gross inequality and the suffering that brings. If we look at the lives of the individual cells, particularly in the advanced industrialised nations, we see addiction, dependency and co-dependency that are pandemic.

All of these are nothing more than symptoms of the misunderstanding of the concept of personal sovereignty. So, what is personal sovereignty, and what is its significance in these all-important issues in our daily lives? I would suggest that on the personal level, sovereignty is the capacity to decide for and by oneself. Now on the surface this sounds simple and self-evident, but if we delve a little deeper and look a little more closely, is it really so? For capacity has two components: an ability plus a willingness to use or utilise that ability. For if we have an ability that we do not use, then it is merely an untapped potential. The ability is not actualised and has no effect on reality. The end result of personal sovereignty must be self-actualisation. It must be realised. An ability must be brought forth onto the plane of manifestation, into one's daily life, otherwise it merely remains a potential.

We will discover that the historical development of humanity has been an evolutionary journey of an ever-increasing ability to make decisions on three levels: sociological, political and economic.

Sociologically, this has been the emerging process of egalitarianism. Historically speaking, humankind has always existed within a social order. From the earliest cave clan there has always been a set social hierarchy and structure within which the individual had a given place and social position. This position was invariably decreed by birth and was fairly inflexible. It has only been in recent times that the concepts of social mobility and egalitarianism have allowed the freedom of movement of the individual within the social order.

Eric Fromm was a German-born American psychoanalyst and social philosopher who explored the interaction between psychology and society. Fromm wrote many books on the subject of human freedom and believed that many of the ills of the individual human were caused by imbalances in the culture within which they lived. By applying psychoanalytic principles to the remedy of these cultural ills, Fromm believed, mankind could develop a psychologically balanced sane society.

> What characterises medieval in contrast to modern society is its lack of individual freedom. Everybody in the earlier period was chained to his role in the social order. A man had little chance to move socially from one class to another; he was hardly able to move geographically from one town or one country to another. With few exceptions he had to stay where he was born. He was often not even free to dress as he pleased or to eat what he liked. The artisan had to sell at a certain price and the peasant at a certain place, the market of the town. Personal, economic and social life was dominated by certain rules and obligations from which practically no sphere of activity was exempted.[2]

It is only in fairly recent times that the individual has been free to express themselves and move socially within the existing order. One is no longer immediately cast at birth into a social role that dictates one's standing for life. Modern man is free to move socially, geographically and economically according to the dictates of his or her own will. We look on in horror at such outmoded practices as apartheid, ethnic cleansing or any rigid caste system.

In the modern western world, it is one of the inalienable rights of man that we are all created equal. The individual is no longer limited by parentage or birth but only by his or her own individual effort, will and creativity. The modern hero is no longer the royal born prince or princess but rather the individual who has risen from social poverty and lowliness to achieve greatness and personal success through dint of their own effort. We can see this same development in the political arena as well. There has been a corresponding movement towards greater and greater personal freedom. As people gained social and economic mobility they demanded political power. The process of democracy is the political arm of this evolutionary movement – it is the call for self-determination. Social media has exponentially accelerated this movement in the last decade.

Political history is the story of power to the people. In the beginning, the sovereign was absolute. He or she had absolute and total control and power. Their word was final – there was no court of appeal. Democracy gives the individual the political power of self-determination. However, it is up to the individual as to whether and how they will use that power:

> The great revolutions in England and France and the fight for American independence were the milestones marking this development. The peak in the evolution of human freedom in the political sphere was the modern democratic state based on the principle of equality of all men and the equal right of everybody to share in the government by representatives of its own choosing. Each one was supposed to be able to act according to his own interest and at the same time with a view to the common welfare of the nation.[3]

Economically, this same movement towards personal freedom can be seen in the rise of capitalism and the development of the free market economy. Once again, this was a question of mobility. The individual was no longer constrained or impeded by existing social or economic forces but was free to move within the economic system creating their own fortune or misfortune. Wealth was no longer an inherent or absolute right. Fortunes were made and lost according to the individual's ability to choose. The successful entrepreneur or capitalist was one who had both the ability and willingness to take risks, to make decisions, and to gamble on both himself and the future.

The overriding principle of the free market is the right of the individual to act. It was postulated by Adam Smith that if the individual was left free then the 'invisible hand'* would direct activity in such a way that the good of all would best be served by the profit motivation of the individual entrepreneur. Supply and demand would sort out the details. Historically speaking, this has not always been the case, but the underlying philosophical implications for personal freedom are valid nonetheless. The individual is *potentially* freer under the capitalist system than any other. However, in reality this freedom is seldom realised.

Indeed, the recent demise of communism as a viable alternative economic system can be traced directly to the lack of personal motivation and productivity that accompanies a lack of personal freedom.

For the first time in history the individual could succeed on the basis of their own effort, ability and activity. This had a profound psychological impact upon the psyche of the individual. One could no longer hide behind the excuse of birth, social standing, parentage or lineage. The individual truly had become a free agent and what became of him was directly attributable to his own self and decisions. The individual started to become self-reliant. This ability and willingness to make decisions now became the single greatest determinant of personal success or failure.

> The individual was no longer bound by a fixed social system, based on tradition and with a comparatively small margin for personal advancement beyond the traditional limits. He was allowed and expected to succeed in economic gains as far as his diligence, intelligence, courage, thrift or luck would lead him. Under the feudal system the limits of his life expansion had been laid out before he was born; but in the capitalist system the individual had a chance to succeed on the basis of his own merits and activity.

> In one word, capitalism not only freed man from traditional bonds, but it also contributed tremendously to the increase of positive freedom, to the growth of an active, critical, responsible self.[4]

---

* Adam Smith was an economist in 1776 who argued that the invisible hand was a self-regulating mechanism of the free market whereby the forces of supply and demand, if left alone by governments, would deliver the optimum outcome for all concerned.

It is not my intention to deal with these external historical developments that describe the structure and form of society, but rather to concentrate on the inner psychic development of consciousness that has paralleled this outer growth. How has humanity reacted to this exponential increase in personal freedom? Prior to these historical developments the individual was not free. He was constrained socially, politically, economically and physically. He did not possess the means nor the ability to move. His position and station in life were given and set; personal mobility was severely circumscribed. Things were even worse for women! A woman's life was even more limited than a man's. Indeed, it is only in very recent times that women in general have enjoyed any real taste of freedom and mobility, and that some women in particular have availed themselves of these opportunities.

Thus, we can see that the first component of personal sovereignty – the ability to make decisions for and by oneself – is historically speaking only a fairly recent phenomenon. Prior to the Industrial Revolution and prior to the great political revolutions, humanity *en masse*, did not possess this ability. It was reserved for the privileged few – the ruling elite. Whether an individual did or did not belong to this oligarchy was determined by birth. There was very little room for movement or personal growth.

However, modern man is at present externally free. He can go where he likes; he can work as he chooses; he can decide to live where he pleases; he can marry as his heart desires; he can drive the car he wants and so on. The modern economic marketplace is a virtual cornucopia of choice demanding never-ending decisions. We are continually being bombarded by advertisements recommending that we do this, buy that, or be like that person.

Upward economic mobility is no longer an option but an obligation. We feel obligated to do better than, to earn more than, to be more successful than our parents, our peers and our own past. It is no longer enough to keep up with the Joneses – we need to be the best.

Thus, there is no question that the ability to make personal decisions is there. We can use the analogy of modern transportation. It is not that long ago that Christopher Columbus sailed off, thinking he was in danger of falling off the edge of the earth. Or that James Cook went off in search of the 'Great South Land'. At that point in time, the individual was not physically capable of travelling the world as we can, for he did not possess the technological ability to do so. We now have the ability to travel geographically across borders and indeed across the world in a matter of hours. We also have the ability to travel to the Moon and beyond. This increase in technological ability has given us a freedom of choice that was unheard of merely 100 years ago. It is all a question of availing ourselves of the available opportunities. But we must be willing to make the trip.

So too, we must be willing to use our newfound personal freedom. And this is what personal sovereignty is all about. How many of us have grown inwardly, psychologically enough to handle this increase in availability? Do we really exercise our freedom, or do we merely pretend? How many of us are truly comfortable and confident in making our own decisions and how many of us actually enjoy the decision-making process?

Why do we feel so guilty when we express our choice, particularly if that is to say *no*? Why do we have such difficulty in knowing what it is that we truly want? Why do some people thrive on making decisions while others only seem to end up tangled in knots reaching no conclusion? Why has co-dependency (which in its purest sense is a fear of making decisions on one's own) become one of the most significant psychological problems of the present?

It is obvious there is more here than meets the eye. We need to explore this inner psychological dynamic. At first glance, it would seem obvious that inner psychic growth has not kept pace with outer social, political and economic freedom. Although we are all equal within the social system, we are obviously not equal within our own minds. This is evidenced in each of those three areas. There are those who move socially, aspire to greatness and achieve tremendous acclaim and success while others merely remain where they are. There are some who use their political rights to achieve their goals and further the emancipation of humanity while others do not even vote. There are some who very visibly move economically upwards, amassing great fortunes, while others barely survive.

Thus, we need to examine this whole concept of free will choice. For after all, is this not where the original story (for western society at least) is supposed to have begun: in the Garden of Eden with Eve and the serpent and the Tree of Knowledge? Was this not the 'original sin' – mankind's abuse of free will? Down through the ages all the mythology, all the religions, all the mystery schools have alluded to this fundamental question of free will and humanity's abuse of it. Is it just possible that we have never really understood what the parable was all about? Obviously, it is not to be interpreted literally but is intended to make us ponder and question the real meaning of free will choice.

Humanity's evolutionary journey is intricately linked with this phenomenon of choice and somehow we do not seem to be doing a very good job at choosing. Most of us do not really know what we want; most of us do not make wise choices with our lives; and globally, we are not making wise choices as a species with our home – the Earth.

So, what is the problem? We sit at the pinnacle of civilisation, at the command of the most sophisticated technology humanity has created, with the greatest opportunity for social, political and economic freedom, yet over 99 per cent of the world's wealth is owned by under one per cent of the population and we all live in the constant fear and anxiety of our technology either blowing us all up or our own pollution making us extinct.

We have the greatest ability for personal freedom ever created, yet we lack the personal integrity and power to exercise that freedom correctly. Oppression and tyranny still abound. In a word, we do not possess the second component of personal sovereignty – the willingness to make decisions by and for ourselves.

What inhibits this willingness is fear. We have a fear of freedom, a fear of taking hold of our own lives, our own destinies, and our own realities. We are afraid of making a mistake, afraid of being wrong, afraid of humiliation, afraid of what others might think of us.

Ultimately, all this is only the fear of being seen to be wrong. And so, we shrink into conformity, into mass consciousness, into consensus reality, into blind acceptance, into co-dependency and eventually, into unconsciousness. We forfeit our God-given right of free will choice and our light of awareness. We sink into mediocrity and an inner psychological bondage that is even more insidious and pernicious than that from which we emerged in the dark ages.

The outer historical journey has been the progressive removal of external oppressive structures and forces that impeded and inhibited personal freedom. We are now free from the constraints of limiting social classes, political oppression and economic exploitation. But as Eric Fromm points out in his masterful work, *The Fear of Freedom*, 'freedom from' implies 'freedom to'.

Personal sovereignty is the discovery of that newer and more positive freedom – the freedom to realise the full self; the freedom to express ourselves totally and completely as we truly are. Ultimately, this book is about personal self-expression. We must now release the self from the inner psychic forces of tyranny and suppression, just as historically we have released the individual from the outer forces of limitation. We must now do the inner work of releasing ourselves from psychological bondage, fear, inhibition and dependency.

These forces take many forms: addiction to cigarettes, drugs, sex, fame, work, endorphins, a significant other, relationships and so on which are all escapes from personal freedom. The addict of whatever form is definitely not free. It is evident from the prevalence of addiction in modern society that rather than taking up the challenge of inner personal freedom and sovereignty, modern man is retreating *en masse* into the bondage of physical, emotional or psychological dependency.

Once again, socially, politically and economically we are allowing ourselves to be dominated. We are relinquishing our personal freedom, not only to extreme and bizarre pseudo-religious fanaticism and fundamentalism but also in more insidious and subtle ways in daily reality. In so many little ways, on a daily basis, we are willing to give away our power and hard-earned personal freedom. We willingly choose to allow others to decide for us.

This is not personal sovereignty!

How many of us can say we are truly free to fully express our inner selves? How many of us even know who or what that inner self is? This book is a discussion of the principles and concepts involved in discovering and learning just who we really are and what are the forces that keep us from that knowledge. This book is a journey of self-discovery. It is a travel manual for a journey we each need to take as a matter of urgency if we are to survive as a species and if the planet is to survive as our home.

It is the only journey worth taking and that is the journey that leads you home – to the realisation of your full self.

TWO: THE EVOLUTION OF CONSCIOUSNESS

In order to more fully understand this question of personal sovereignty, we need to explore the nature of consciousness and its evolutionary journey. It is a common misconception, especially in western philosophy and religion, that the nature of God is static; that God created the world, whether that is understood to be the universe or the planet Earth, in one final act of creation, in seven days. Nothing could be further from the truth.

Neither God* nor creation are static. Rather, evolution and change are the only constants in the universe. One is reminded of that song by Talking Heads: 'heaven is a place where nothing, nothing ever happens at all'. How could this be bliss; how could eternity exist without constant change and motion?

We normally think of God as a being in heaven: an old man with a beard perhaps, who is either benevolent or autocratic according to one's personal spiritual perspective and religious upbringing. But this is merely one aspect and level of God – that of God the Father as spoken of by Christ. The concept of the Trinity is a symbol of the multiple aspects of God. God the Father represents wisdom and power, God the Son represents unconditional love without any personal, physical feelings or desires and God the Spirit represents the Life aspect.

However, the Trinity is an aspect of God that pertains to the Earth planet and that is easily understandable by humanity. It is not the end of the story, rather the beginning. It is one nature or aspect of God that we, as humble human beings, can relate to. Beyond the Trinity is Almighty God, which is another aspect of God pertaining to the universe. This being directs the evolutionary journey of all that is in existence

---

* I use the word 'God' in its widest sense of the creative principle of the universe or the divine intelligence of creation. There are absolutely no religious, spiritual or philosophical connotations implied. I am merely using the word 'God' as it is the most acceptable term to describe this universal force.

throughout the firmaments and is infinitely more expansive than the Trinity. Yet, Almighty God still exists within the boundaries of creation.

Beyond creation, without any form whatsoever, there is a far more abstract aspect of the Godhead which precedes and predates creation itself. On this plane there is only the potential before it becomes actualised in the process of manifestation. This is the aspect of God that deals with projection. Beyond this there is the plane of pure intention where intelligence begets the intention or ideation of existence. Still further out is the plane of light and power that generates the forcefield wherein which all the mechanics of creation lie.

On the purest level, the ultimate definition of God is a self-generating thought that brought itself into existence and which can sustain itself without disintegrating. That self-generating thought then manifests as creation, and creation similarly manifests itself through down-stepped levels of further self-generating thoughts. The point is that God is not a static state or being, rather it is a complex harmony and synergism of many parts that are all evolving in a dance of progressive perfection.

God is most definitely not some warped image or variation of a human being. That we believe so is the height of our myopia.

There can be no such thing as a completed state of perfection. The whole purpose of life is that God can know itself through expressing itself in creation. Creation and evolution are ongoing. They are never and will never be complete or finished; this is the meaning of eternity. Creation did not occur in seven days but is an eternal process of becoming. Evolution is the instrument by which and through which that occurs. Perfection is a state that can never be attained for as each level of perfection is achieved, there will always be greater and higher levels that come into view. Evolution must always be considered as a form of perfection which is being eternally sought after, and never finally attained.[5]

The point is that life is always seeking improvement, development, evolution and that consciousness itself, of which we are a part, is also evolving. As above, so below. Just as God begins in the unformed, unknowable state that precedes creation or manifestation, so too, consciousness begins in this primordial state. This is the beginning of higher consciousness: preformed – concept without object, the explosion of the Big Bang, infinite open potential. We could say that the unformed gave birth to itself in a gigantic explosion of consciousness, a myriad of sparks of consciousness came into being as yet with no form, no control and no manifestation.

As Lao-Tzu said so long ago:
> the way that can be spoken of is not the constant way;
> the name that can be named is not the constant name;
> the nameless was the beginning of heaven and earth;
> the name was the mother of the myriad creatures;
> hence always rid yourself of desires in order to observe its secrets but always allow yourself to have desires in order to observe its manifestation.[6]

In the physical world, the life force first moved into the unconscious plane: this was the beginning of form, of matter, of geometry, of physicality. The mineral kingdom and early plant kingdom exist within this level. This is the development of chemistry, of geometry, of crystals. This is the beginning of life on planet earth.

Next consciousness moved into the subconscious plane which is the level of instinct, biology, habitual reaction, and compulsive behaviour: the animal kingdom and lower or early human. This is the survival level, the level of Freud's Id† with its sex and death urges, the murky subconscious of psychotherapy, the land of dreams and symbols, of magic and superstition.

And now, finally, consciousness has moved into the conscious plane: the realm of free will choice and conscious decision-making where we are no longer the helpless victims of uncontrolled urges or the gravitational pull of the collective unconscious. This is the level of personal sovereignty and of modern man. We are no longer dictated to by our chemistry or our biology or our subconscious but are free to choose and decide according to the promptings of our higher minds.

---

† According to Sigmund Freud's psychoanalytic theory, the Id is that aspect of personality that is totally unconscious and includes instinctive and primitive behaviours that are driven purely by the pleasure principle.

Indeed, there is ample biological and behavioural evidence to support this theory of the division of consciousness. The embryo passes through each of these evolutionary phases in its early growth and development. At first it is very geometric and crystalline. Then it develops gills, a tail, etc. and goes through the evolution of the species. The brain also develops in concentric spheres known as neuropils. The first and inner of these regulate the organs that deal with survival. We can be quite unconscious and still the body's biology will maintain necessary life support functions. This is the visceral level. The next brain to develop is that of feelings and emotions and centres on the limbic system; it relates to the subconscious. Finally, there develops the higher or thinking brain, which is the conscious mind and relates to cognition, understanding and decision-making.

Dr Arthur Janov, in *The New Primal Scream*, equates these three distinct areas to different levels of consciousness:

> There are in fact 3 distinct principal minds. The survival, feeling and thinking minds function on three different levels of consciousness. First level: this is the visceral, sensory level which deals with sensation and mediates bodily impulses and states. This level incorporates the survival mind. Second level: this is the affective-expressive level that mediates the complex processes involved in the creation and expression of feeling and emotion. It is the level of the feeling mind. Third level: this is the familiar cognitive or thinking level. It also provides discrimination, comprehension and meaning with regard to feeling states. This is the level of the thinking mind.[7]

The planet is 4.6 billion years old. If we equate this to a person 46 years of age, then vegetation only began at the age of 42; mammals arrived only 8 months ago and apes evolved into early humans about 10 days ago. Humans have been around for 4 hours and the Industrial Revolution occurred one minute ago. The transition from subconscious mind to conscious mind is happening in the last few seconds! Thus, it is understandable that we are having a little difficulty in getting our consciousness into gear.

But if we talk of consciousness moving from the unconscious to the subconscious and finally into the conscious mind, what precisely do we mean? We are talking about the seat of power, from where we are motivated, from where we operate and have our being. We are all aware that we operate on different levels in different situations and under various circumstances. For example, certain bodily functions such as breathing, heartbeat, and digestion etc. are under the control of the autonomic nervous system and completely bypass the higher conscious mind. Indeed, were it necessary for us to consciously be aware of and direct these activities, the conscious mind would rapidly become overloaded and our very physical survival would be threatened.

In life too, as we learn motor skills we pass these onto the autonomic nervous system in order to keep the higher mind free for more important functions. When we first learn to walk, to talk, to play a sport, to drive or use a keyboard, it is usually painful and awkward. Much of the conscious mind is engaged and involved in coordinating and executing the relevant movements.

However, with proficiency synergy takes over and the dance begins. The body does a much better job at it than the conscious mind. We are no longer consciously aware of changing gears, striking the keys, how we talk or walk and so on. Elite athletes work hard at passing these movements over to the unconscious mind which does a much better job at achieving proficiency. Mastery of any activity means allowing the autonomic nervous system to just do it for us without conscious interference.

Similarly, we are all now becoming more aware of how the subconscious is another area of the mind that deals with emotions, feelings, love and affection. A feeling is not a thought. An emotion is not a part of the reflective, reasoning, logical mind. The experience of life is not merely intellectual; it is also emotional. To know something totally is not just to have an idea or a thought about it but to have a feeling as well, to experience it on a cellular level.

Real faith is not merely a belief, but a deep inner knowing and certainty. It is a feeling. Just as the unconscious is the survival mind and directs and motivates basic physiological necessities for our survival, the subconscious is the feeling mind which directs and motivates the emotions and feelings that are equally necessary for our well-being, health and survival.

The higher mind also has two separate and distinct functions that are biologically separated into two hemispheres: the left side that is concerned with thinking rationally, sequentially, and putting things in order – with causal connections; and the right side that is spatial, artistic, spontaneous, intuitive, holistic and is concerned with knowing, and understanding without reason or reflection and putting things together synchronistically. The left is the masculine side of doing and conquering while the right is the feminine side of being and nurturing.

Thus, we can begin to glimpse and appreciate the complexity of consciousness just as we began this chapter glimpsing the complexity of God. All consciousness is divine; God is within every unit of consciousness. Creation is the ever-evolving and developing of consciousness towards greater and greater heights of progressive perfection. It is a journey back to that original state of higher consciousness or oneness from which it all began with the Big Bang. It is a return to the original point of departure – the explosion of consciousness.

A healthy or balanced being is one who has fluid access to all aspects and levels of consciousness. However, this is not as easy as it would seem. For humanity is only just emerging into full consciousness. It is in only fairly recent historical times that the seat of power has come to the higher, conscious mind. This is precisely why our recent history reflects this inner development on the social, political and economic stages.

In reality, we are just emerging from the grip of the subconscious. The vast body of psychology, psychotherapy, the human potential movement, positive thinking, mind power, visualisation, affirmations and so on are all aspects of this understanding.

Humanity is just starting to shake off the shackles and domination of subconscious influences and take conscious dominion of its reality. At long last, the individual can truly say that it is master of its own destiny, ruler of its own fate; that it can be a sovereign being. For too long mankind has been at the mercy of superstition, religion, suppression, oppression, fear and other limiting forces. This is truly the age of freedom and we must all begin to arise from our subconscious slumber and greet the challenge of consciously creating our own reality as equal co-creators with cosmic forces.

Up until now there has been some excuse. We could say, in our defence, that we were not fully conscious – that we did in fact not have dominion; but no longer. It is also true that up until now there have been a number of pre-set programmes that have ensured our continued growth and development as a species, just as in the case of the individual human embryo, biological and physical growth towards a mature, adult body continues whether we consciously participate or not. We can neither hasten nor retard our physical maturation – it happens on that first visceral level of automatic consciousness.

Yet, just because we grow into a biological adult does not mean we automatically reach emotional, intellectual or spiritual maturity. We must do this part of the work ourselves. So too, humanity, as an organism has reached biological maturity. Mankind has come of age. There are no more pre-set programmes to take us into the future. We must now chart our own course and find our own way. And the rudder for that journey is personal sovereignty.

THREE: THE DIALECTIC OF INTEGRATION AND REPRESSION

The only way to rise to a higher consciousness is by descending to lower levels. This is the true dialectic of mind.

Dr Arthur Janov

If we are to truly embrace being conscious then we need to turn around and embrace both our subconscious and our unconscious. The most highly evolved yogis are able to demonstrate remarkable feats of autonomic nervous system control. They can consciously control their heartbeat, blood flow, respiration and so on. Similarly, the more whole and balanced we become, the more conscious control we have over our subconscious. The healthier we are psychically and spiritually, the less we are controlled by the murky waters of our personal subconscious or the collective unconscious.

For the sad fact is that most of us are to some extent or another controlled or influenced by forces that we are not even aware of. The subconscious stores and files every piece of information, every feeling and emotion, everything that happens to us every moment of our lives. If we repress these events and do not allow them to come to full consciousness, they will continue to clamber for attention and resolution for the rest of our lives.

It is interesting that at about the same time that the aforementioned external historical developments that enabled an increase in human freedom were occurring, parallel developments were occurring in the field of this understanding. As early as the seventeenth century, the Dutch philosopher, Baruch Spinoza was formulating the concept that unconscious forces determine our behaviour: 'Men are conscious of their own desire but ignorant of the causes whereby that desire has been determined.' Spinoza realised that to be truly free, we had to develop an increased understanding and awareness of our inner reality. Friedrich Nietzsche also alluded to the power of the subconscious and our tendency to deceive ourselves of our real motivation.

However, it was Sigmund Freud who really discovered the power of the subconscious as the overriding determinant of irrational or neurotic daily behaviour. Freud maintained that man was not free at all, but that he was: '…in fact, a marionette moved by strings behind and above him which in turn are directed by forces unknown to his consciousness.'[8]

Freud viewed the individual as being dominated and controlled by the first or visceral level of consciousness. He postulated that man was primarily motivated by biological urges, namely that of the sexual urge or the libido. This urge if unsatisfied caused pain and if released gave pleasure. Thus, this was called 'the pleasure principle', in contrast to 'the reality principle', which ensured survival in the real world. Freud viewed mental health as achieving balance or equilibrium between these two competing forces.

It is important to realise that Freud reduced man to a biological or even mechanical level. The primary motivating factor in life, as he perceived it, was this sexual appetite or instinctive urge. The Id was the sum total of man's instinctive desires. However, these baser, animalistic urges had to be sublimated so that society or civilisation could exist. Thus, Freud's Ego was that part of consciousness that controlled or repressed the Id. Most, if not all, of the Id's impulses had to be denied or repressed according to Freud's thesis.

However, if something is denied access to full consciousness, then it becomes buried in the subconscious. Freud referred to the contents of this repression as the individual unconscious. Psychoanalysis was the system whereby these repressed contents were brought back into conscious awareness, for it was these repressed events or urges which pulled the strings of the marionette.

In psychological or Freudian terms, the word unconscious came to be associated with these repressed and therefore unhealthy contents, rather than, with an actual neurological region and thus healthy level of mind as we have been using it. It is essential to keep this distinction clearly in focus as we proceed, for we will see that as we repress we 'go unconscious', we lose awareness and we lose touch with reality. This is in direct contrast to the healthy unconscious which is quite capable of spontaneously directing the most intricate biological and motor skills.

According to Freud, there is a primary layer of instinctive urges, the Id, that needs to be repressed and kept under tight control for the continuous development and safe functioning of society and civilisation: 'the more society evolves into higher forms of civilisation, the more these instinctive urges become incompatible with the existing social norms and thus the more repression must take place.'[9]

But the repression of an urge does not mean that the original motivating force or valency has been eliminated; merely, that it is not allowed to reach awareness. Repression always leads to distortion and a symbolic or symptomatic expression of that primary urge for its charge has not been discharged and maintains its potency. It merely goes underground and like a resistance movement that is denied expression, seeks to determine behaviour on an unconscious level or in disguise. We will return to this theme again and again, for we cannot assume personal sovereignty or conscious dominion of our reality while we are the hapless victims of repressed psychic urges.

It is the conflict between this unconscious reality, hidden within the deeper recesses of the mind, and the denial of that reality in the conscious mind that causes neurosis. Freud saw that the essential path to health lay in uncovering this unconscious, in bringing the dark recesses of the mind into the light of day, making the unconscious conscious.

Freud recognised that most of what is real within ourselves is not conscious, and that most of what is conscious is not real. Freud was concerned with a search for the truth, for what lay behind our conscious thoughts, for he realised that we do not tell ourselves the truth, that we all deceive ourselves to some extent or another.

After repression comes rationalisation. Because repression does not remove the force of the original impulse, desire, urge or motivation but merely blocks its innocent entry into consciousness, it must find a back route. It will return again and again, seeking access to higher consciousness and resolution. The thinking mind now steps in and creates the justification, the story, or the excuse that allows the repressed item legal entry into consciousness.

Usually this will take the exact reversal of the disallowed form. Sadism will cloak itself under the guise of duty; voyeurism under the guise of censorship; corruption under the guise of officialdom etc. The emerging truth of J. Edgar Hoover's secret homosexuality, gambling addiction and mafia associations while outwardly and vigorously denouncing these as 'depravities' is an excellent example of the hypocrisy that ensues when an individual does not recognise and honour but rather denies and suppresses their own inner nature.

Freud termed this refusal to admit the truth of one's reality 'resistance'. The strength of one's resistance is directly proportional to the strength of one's repression. Anyone, who has attempted to mirror the truth to a severely repressed person in denial, will be aware of the ferocity and violence with which such well-meaning attempts are met.

Resistance is denial of the truth and the untruth or rationalisation must be protected at all costs lest the whole cover or façade of the ego be blown. There will always be a cover up to camouflage the original impulse and to offset the repression. The end result of repression is not elimination at all but distortion and an increase in valency. The end result of rationalisation is to cloak the forbidden fruit in acceptable and noble disguise.

The study of psychology and the practice of psychotherapy have evolved considerably since those early Freudian days. As we continue on our journey we will quarrel with many of Freud's original findings but let us give credit where credit is due. We would not drive a Model T Ford on today's freeways; but if we wish to explore the simple fundamentals of the original automobile we could find no better example. So too, Freud's theories, in their essence and their simplicity, do lay bare the underlying dynamics of the workings of the various levels of consciousness.

What is even more important is that Freud correctly pointed to the subconscious as the seat of power just when we, as a race, were emerging from its grip. What may have been true historically, in the past, is no longer applicable in the present. We have emerged from the control of the subconscious and the unconscious and while Freud and many still look back to discover where we have come from and to uncover its hold, it is now time to move forward.

As Dr. Arthur Janov points out, if we wish to attain a higher consciousness, we must first be prepared to delve deeper. For the point is not to emerge from the subconscious as from a murky swamp, or a dark and dingy cellar full of forbidden vices, as Freud would have us believe, to which one never wishes to return and from which one flees in horror. To Freud, the unconscious always signified the dark side of man: the bestial, the primitive, the anti-social and the destructive; the forces that needed suppression and sublimation.

As a result, we now have an extremely negative picture of our subconscious as something not to be trusted, dark and evil, full of weird and wonderful ghosts and ghouls, a remnant of a more primitive time, like the tailbone. We view the subconscious as something illogical, irrational, superstitious, untrustworthy, too emotional and erratic. We look back at the dark ages as being the personification of the subconscious, and to a certain extent it was.

The point is, however, that all of these pictures are of the subconscious without the guiding and controlling influence of the higher conscious mind. Evolution is not a backward movement but a forward one. It is time to move into and embrace the subconscious with the conscious mind, to actively take dominion and control of the subconscious and then of the unconscious so that we can return to that state of higher consciousness, but this time, with full conscious awareness enlisting the support of both.

We need to turn around and embrace both as trustworthy and loyal friends, to view them as allies and servants rather than as an enemy to be feared. We need to work together. The fundamental flaw in Freud's scheme is the concept of the Id. The cornerstone of his whole theory is this pool of primitive sexual impulse that needs to be repressed for the sake of society. For if this is true, then the energy flow of the entire evolutionary process must eventually break down and descend into entropy. According to Freud, all culture and civilisation are nothing more than a fabrication built upon this repressed and sublimated energy.

Carl Jung was one of the first to realise Freud's obsession with sexuality and correctly view it as a form of neurosis itself. Jung agreed with the process of repression but not with the content. As Jung wrote:

> ...numerous cases of neurosis where sexuality played a subordinate part, other factors standing in the foreground –

for example, the problem of social adaptation, of oppression by tragic circumstances of life, prestige considerations, and on and on.[10]

Freud rejected any notion of the higher faculties of the human mind. He denied any spiritual reality and suspected that all forms of art or culture were aspects of repressed sexuality or psychosexuality.

Jung challenged Freud on the logical extension of this narrow-minded view, correctly pointing out that: '…culture would then appear as a mere farce, the morbid consequence of repressed sexuality. Yes, it is Freud assented, so it is and that is just a curse of fate against which we are powerless to contend.'[11]

Freud had reduced man to a biological and chemical equation replacing true spirituality with the god of sex: '…the sexual libido took over the role of a deus absconditus, a hidden or concealed god.' Freud had become the unwitting victim of his own process of rationalisation. In repressing his own spirituality, he had to conjure another principle that he could justifiably embrace as the motivating factor of human existence.

In other words, according to Jung, Freud failed to grasp the duality of reality; the dialectic principle of yin and yang. He could see one side of the coin but refused to acknowledge the existence of the other. Jung, on the other hand, began to understand this concept:

> The idea dawned on me that Eros and the power drive might be in some sense like the dissident sons of a single father, or the product of a single motivating psychic force which manifested itself empirically in opposing forms, like positive and negative electrical charges.[12]

Jung split from Freud's dogma and picture of the subconscious as a cellar full of vices and went on to develop his own formulation of the subconscious as a magical cave filled with man's original but forgotten treasures of wisdom and innate spirituality. Jung had a dream in which he saw the many levels of consciousness that we have spoken of represented in the image of a house with many floors or stories. In the dream, he descends to deeper and symbolically more primitive levels of the psyche, which led him to the realisation of what he termed the collective unconscious:

> The house represented a kind of image of the psyche, that is to say of my then state of consciousness, with hitherto unconscious additions. It obviously pointed to the foundations of cultural history; a history of successive layers of consciousness. My dream thus constituted a kind of structural diagram of the human psyche; it postulated something of an altogether impersonal nature underlying that psyche. It was my first inkling of a collective *a priori* beneath the personal psyche.[13]

It was this dream that eventually led Jung to his formulation of the concept of the archetype as a form of instinct. The importance of Jung's discoveries and disagreement with Freud's theories lies in its interpretation of the nature of the subconscious. In keeping with his view of the subconscious as being the dark side of man, Freud saw dreams as a façade behind which the real contents of the subconscious were hidden.

On the other hand, to Jung, the subconscious was a part of nature and therefore spoke plainly, directly and clearly, 'as best as it could.' It was the conscious mind that tried to deceive and wished not to understand what the subconscious was endeavouring to illustrate. The subconscious needed to use symbology to bypass this resistance. In contrast to Freud, Jung befriended the subconscious and began to learn its secrets by allowing it to communicate to him in its terms and images. This led him on a fascinating journey of self-discovery in which he uncovered his deeper emotions and feelings.

Jung realised that to evolve to a higher state of consciousness he needed to 'plummet down' into his psyche. 'I saw that there was no other way out. I had to take the chance, had to try to gain power over them; for I realised that if I did not do so, I ran the risk of their gaining power of me.'[14]

Thus, Carl Jung became the pioneer of this journey that we all need to make. We need to befriend the subconscious so that we can learn its secrets, so that it can reveal to us the depths of our being. For it is only by going within that we can go forward. It is only through knowing ourselves that we can know God. It is only through embracing our totality, through integrating all the parts of our consciousness that we can become whole, that we can go home to that original state of higher consciousness, of oneness.

In Freud's terms, the evolutionary movement was one out of the primitive swamp of the subconscious, via the tortuous route of repression and sublimation. To Jung, it was a journey to the centre of his being:

> ...the goal of psychic development is the self. There is no linear evolution; there is only a circumambulation of the self. Everything points towards the centre. One could not go beyond the centre. The centre is the goal, and everything is directed towards that centre. The self is the principle and archetype of orientation and meaning.[15]

Within this context we are reminded of the oldest spiritual admonitions: 'to know thyself; to thine own self be true!' Evolution, enlightenment, wholeness, spiritual or psychic health – call it what you will – cannot be gained through denial, repression or any other form of inner separation. It can only be achieved through integration; by embracing all the parts of ourselves, all the aspects of consciousness.

FOUR: THE GRAND DECEPTION – THE MYTHOLOGICAL FALL

...you are not a linear experience; you are an explosion of consciousness and things are always in constant motion. They will change, so just let it happen. You don't have to do anything or change anything in your outer world to find God.

Bartholomew

So, what really is in the centre? Are we to believe the story that has been handed down throughout the ages by religion and mythology, that at our core we are fundamentally bad, ugly, rotten, mean and unworthy? Is it in fact true, as Freud believed, that if we give free reign to our inner psychic beings and allow them free expression, that this will mean the unleashing of primitive, sexual urges and desires? Do we really need to keep our inner selves under constant lock and key by surveillance and repression? And is all progress and cultural development a distorted and disguised expression of this repression as espoused by Freud?

After all, this is precisely what we have been told and led to believe. From time immemorial, from the age of the Bible and other ancient texts, from both the east and the west this is the picture painted of humanity. We were expelled from the Garden of Eden because we disobeyed God's command not to eat of the forbidden fruit of the Tree of Knowledge – good and evil. Moreover, this is not just a Biblical myth. The wheel of karma, the Koran, Buddhism and so on all posit life on Earth as a necessary path of suffering to earn salvation in another life.

Most religions are built on guilt. We committed Original Sin, were cast out of the garden into the wilderness, and into the world to suffer. Life on Earth was a penance and a suffering; a punishment for our sins. Henceforth, we were to wander in the wilderness, cut off from God and the splendour of the Garden, having to work to re-earn our salvation, our return to Paradise. We are not only at odds with God, but also with nature and ourselves. Man and woman turn against each other; brother against brother, Cain against Able. We are naked and ashamed; aware of ourselves in a sexual sense. The myth emphasises the suffering resulting from this one original act.

The fundamental message is that man's nature, although originally good and made in the image of God, was corrupted for all time by the sins of Adam and Eve. The sins of the father are visited upon the son. Both the Judaic and Catholic religions stress this inherent unworthiness of mankind, and the fact that of himself he cannot attain salvation. This belief now permeates the modern western Christian world.

This philosophy teaches that the individual needs both the intermediary of the church and the intercession of the grace of God to be 'saved'. Throughout the Bible, mankind is repeatedly cast in the role of the helpless sinner and God as the authoritarian, autocratic, harsh and judgemental father figure. Man is at the mercy of God's forgiveness and grace. In and of himself, man is not deemed worthy. Moses leads the Israelites into the wilderness where they wander for 40 years before they enter the Promised Land. Moses himself is denied this privilege because of his indiscretion. Again, God is cast in a stern, unforgiving role.

God sends his only begotten son to redeem the unrepentant sinners. He dies a cruel and bitter death to amend for the sins of the world and to appease the wrath of God. Man, in his unworthiness and sinfulness crucifies Jesus, the son of God, the Prince of Peace. The message that we are unworthy is driven home again and again. In the Middle Ages, Martin Luther and John Calvin both take up this theme of the inherent evilness of humanity.

> Luther assumed the existence of an innate evilness in man's nature, which directs his will for evil and makes it impossible for any man to perform any good deed on the basis of his nature.

To Luther, man is powerless and evil. All that he can hope is for the grace of God to change his nature from evil to good. However, there is nothing man can do to earn salvation on his own; he is at the complete mercy of God to give him the faith required for this union with Christ and a return to a more noble nature. Whatever happens, man will never really be free from his evil tendencies and will never be completely virtuous in this lifetime.

The essence of this doctrine is the insignificance and powerlessness of the individual; the individual, unworthy as he was, had only one means of salvation – and that was complete and utter surrender to and humiliation before this tyrannical and authoritarian God. The individual was robbed of his significance, of his self-power, of his self-worth, self-respect, self-confidence and personal dignity.

It is important to note here that Luther's philosophy and teachings were instrumental in paving the way for the rise of fascism in the centuries to come. He broke the ground for this belief system as it were. The breaking of the will of the individual is such an important ingredient in the giving away of one's personal power to a 'fuhrer' or leader. It is significant in this regard that Luther's influence was paramount in Germany.

Calvin also stressed the insignificance of the individual. Calvin preached that man needed to abandon himself, to throw himself at the mercy of God. 'We are not our own, we are God's; to him therefore let us live and die.' Calvin maintained that we needed to humble ourselves before God and should not even strive for virtue, for to do so would bespeak a certain vanity; better to: '...repose all confidence and assurance of mind on the Lord, so much as diffidence of ourselves, and anxiety arising from a consciousness of our own misery.'[16]

Calvin also believed man was inherently bad: '...there is a world of vices concealed in the soul of man,' and that there was nothing he could do of himself to improve his situation because man was so fundamentally lacking in any form of goodness. '...no work of a pious man ever existed which, if it were examined before the strict judgement of God, did not prove to be damnable.'[17]

Calvin takes the theme of the powerlessness and helplessness of the individual before the throne of God even further. His doctrine of predestination taught that the destiny of the individual had already been decided by God before birth. Some were predestined for salvation while others were predestined for damnation. This theory took the theme of the tyrannical, authoritarian God to new heights:

> ...no doctrine could express more strongly than this the worthlessness of the human will and effort. The decisions over man's fate is taken completely out of his own hands and there is nothing man can do to change this decision. He is a powerless tool in God's hands.[18]

The obvious implication and conclusion of this dogma is the inequality of humanity. Some are born saved and some are born to damnation. There is also complete renunciation of personal responsibility here, for it makes no difference what one does in this lifetime; one is already saved or not according to whether one is chosen or not.

The doctrines of Luther and Calvin are important for a number of reasons. In their extremism, they epitomise this pervasive underlying belief in the inherent evil of humanity with its attendant implication of the insignificance and powerlessness of the individual. Their success lay in the fact that they touched a raw nerve in their historical epoch and appealed to the sentiment of the time. Both men merely expressed ideas, beliefs and feelings that were common to the masses.

Moreover, their doctrines lay the groundwork for much of what was to follow in modern history. Although we may look back with cynicism, scorn and even amusement at these outlandish ideas, there is much hidden subconscious truth in their dogmas. Collectively, as a body of humanity, and as individuals, we do hold to these beliefs more than we are prepared to consciously admit. Thus, it is necessary to examine just how great a hold they do have upon us today.

As Dr. Janov points out, many of these religious ideas of the past have been embraced and taken over by modern psychotherapy:

> ...in general, the mind is considered something to fear; every religion sees the notion of man (and therefore his unconscious) as basically evil, seeing man as compelled to battle constantly against his impulses. The notion is that we do have to keep the beast under control or we shall go crazy. Almost every current psychotherapy extends this religious idea into the realm of psychology, where mind is still considered basically evil, in the sense that we are

haunted by demons that do not have to be exorcised so much as understood and controlled.[19]

These ideas and beliefs have become a part of the status quo, the collective consciousness, and the commonly acceptable modus operandi of modern man. They are now a part of our commonly held belief system, our operating meta-paradigm.

Yet, we really need to examine this whole belief system carefully. Is the centre of man inherently evil? Are we all guilty until proven innocent? Do we need to throw ourselves at the feet of the merciful Lord? Are we as helpless, hapless and hopeless as these dogmas would have us believe? Indeed, do these theories even pass the test of common sense?

I would suggest that this is the grandest deception of all time. If creation is the spontaneous outpouring of divine love, an explosion of cosmic light and consciousness, then that universal love and eternal consciousness exist within the centre of each and every unit, each and every cell, and each and every particle of creation. If creation is God in manifestation and God is indeed omnipresent then God is all there is. This is the only definition of God that makes sense. There can be no 'other'. God is everything and everything is God! There can be nothing in creation that is not God for nothing exists beyond God. God is in everything in creation issuing out of it, energising it, giving it spirit and life, maintaining its form. There can be no other definition of God and there can be no other that is not of the spirit of God.

Man is an integral part of creation. Thus, man is a part of God. The individual human being is a personalised expression of the universal. Individual human consciousness is a spark of infinite divine consciousness. We are a piece of God! Each and every one of us is divine. This was the real teaching of Christ.

Thus, within the centre is not some dark and malevolent force but the purest of divine beings. The closer to the centre of our own being we get, the closer we become to our divinity, and the closer we get to God. Man is not inherently evil. On the contrary, he is a divine and majestic being. Man was made in the image of God; not in the image of the Devil.

> Humanity is learning a great lesson at this time. The lesson of course is to realise your godhood, your connectedness to Prime Creator and with all that exists. The lesson is to realise that everything is connected and that you are a part of it all.
>
> When you ask, 'what am I here for'? I say to become enlightened. I ask you to see this as your job.[20]

The problem is not that man is inherently evil at his core; the problem is rather that man believes the lie that he is.

This was and is the real fall from the state of grace in the Garden. For the fall, like creation, is not something static that occurred thousands upon thousands of years ago by just two people and for which we are all still paying the penalty. We have explored the dynamic nature of God, creation and consciousness and argued that everything is evolving towards progressive perfection. It is mythology that says that these past events are set in stone in time; in reality, these are ever-recurring events in the present. For, there is no time; only the eternal now of creation.

It is the *myth* of the fall that is frozen in time; somewhere in the past. It is this myth that lurks in our collective unconscious haunting us, not our own natures. It is a lie – a grand deception passed down through the ages. And it is time for humanity to wake up to the truth and take its rightful place amongst the Infinity of Being that is truly God. It is time for mankind to awaken from his subconscious slumber into the dawn of the light of full conscious awareness. This is the process of personal sovereignty.

Humanity has accepted a limiting belief in its own limitation and is thus blind to the reality of its own magnificence and grandeur. The fall must be re-enacted daily by each and every one of us, every time we deny or doubt our true selves. It is not a permanent state of affliction for a past wrong; it is an error of perception, a blindness that we all agree to share and to live our lives by. It is an illusion and a delusion.

But it is no more necessary than any other cultural norm or convention that we choose to abide by, whether that be language, clothing, morality or indeed even the rules of the road. These are all merely collective conventions or social mores and commonly accepted ways of being. They are not absolutes in their own right and do not have any universal validity apart from what we choose to give them. We all agree to drive on a particular side of the road or to speak a certain language, but these norms vary from country to country. Our morality and ethics vary from culture to culture. These are all examples of commonly accepted belief systems – that is all.

> The fall has no power or momentum of its own; it must be regenerated daily. And it is within each individualised spirit cell, within your own individualised spirit and ego, on an intimate and immediate level that you must recognise and correct this imbalance. It is vital that you recognise the fall for what it is: a lack of trust that has become habitual, culturally encoded, and passed on from one generation to the next.
>
> To doubt yourself is to doubt the wisdom and viability of the human design. To fully trust in God, you must also trust yourself. No one is created without everything required to make healthy, wholesome decisions. The fall is regenerated each time you doubt your ability to meet creatively the challenge of life.[21]

In the beginning, we defined personal sovereignty as the ability plus the willingness to decide by and for oneself. In other words, to trust oneself, and to have faith in one's own decision-making ability. We then explored the growing availability of personal freedom in the external historical world, giving the individual increased freedom from social, political and economic constraints and an increased freedom to make personal decisions. We then contrasted this with the lack of corresponding inner psychic willingness to take up this newfound freedom. Thus, personal sovereignty, which necessitates both, is still limited.

We then explored the evolution of consciousness, discovering that there were many levels or layers within our beings and it is a basic lack of open and free communication between these various levels that impedes this willingness. We discovered the process of denial and repression that resulted from a fundamental distrust of our inner natures. According to this belief system, at our core, in the centre, we are inherently evil and therefore we cannot trust our primary, initial urges and desires for these spring from the primitive, evil, sexual and basically antisocial centre. It is therefore necessary to limit, to censor, to contain and control, to deny and suppress our inner being. This is all the direct antithesis of self-trust.

Yet, it is precisely this denial, doubt, and lack of trust that is 'the fall' and not that we are intrinsically evil at our core. On the contrary, we need to embrace that inner self, to listen to its voice, to heed its suggestions and impulses, to trust its guidance as our chief navigational system to guide our way through life. For far from being the distracting and tempting voice of the serpent, of the Devil, it is the pure inner voice of our own divine nature – it is the call of God.

History, tradition, convention, society, religion, culture, our upbringing, education, mass media and social media all conspire daily to keep us from trusting ourselves but rather to look without for the answers to our problems and not to look within. This is the conspiracy of the ages; this is the lie. This is the real and tragic fall of man from self-assurance and self-confidence to self-doubt and despair.

The truth always lies within. But to hear this truth we need to be silent and go within. We need to listen to that still, small voice that is within us all but cannot compete with the noise, confusion and restlessness of the outer world.

We need to learn to trust ourselves. We need to learn to be silent, to be still, to be quiet. We need to learn to be alone with our inner selves. We need to befriend our subconscious self, like Carl Jung, to accept its inner wisdom and cease the vilification, distrust and hostility. This is what the mystics of all persuasions have encouraged and exhorted us to do. This is the voice of sanity and ecstasy.

FIVE: THE EGO AND THE SPIRIT

*...the negative ego has never once told you the truth;
the negative ego has only one objective and that is to destroy you!*

Lazaris

So where did this lie originate and why does it have such a pernicious hold on humanity down through the ages? We need to go back and examine these creation myths a little more closely, to ascertain the truth. What is the original nature of humanity and where did all this confusion and misunderstanding come from? For many of us realise deep within our beings that something happened, that something went horribly wrong, that some misunderstanding or some error occurred somewhere along the line.

It is time to give up the easy answers of being the victim and the martyr. It is interesting that in early childhood, the child will always blame itself for whatever happens in the family. If there is a death or a divorce, if there is any major or even minor upset or discord, the young child will always assume responsibility and blame. If a parent leaves, the child will take it as a personal rejection rather than seeing it correctly as a problem between the parents. This is because the young child lives in a very myopic world in which it is the centre. Everything revolves around it.

In much the same way an emerging and youthful humanity could only see itself as the centre of the universe. Did not the sun revolve around the earth; was not humanity supposedly the top species on the planet? Many of us still believe we are the only so-called intelligent life form in creation. Our dominating and exploitive attitude towards the planet and the other life forms with which we share this all too precious earth, is a pregnant example of this myopia.

We simply cannot see ourselves within the larger context of creation. So, just as the child lives in a self-centred world of its own making, choosing to blame itself for all that happens in the family, an emotionally immature humanity has also chosen to adopt this self-centred perspective making itself wrong for all that happens in the universe.

But just as the child who blames itself for the departing parent will develop into a neurotic and self-destructive adult, unable to develop or maintain real intimacy, so too, humanity has developed into a neurotic and self-destructive species unable to fulfil its spiritual purpose of dominion of the earth. The word dominion is not to be confused with domination. Rather it means to care for, to look after and to nurture. To take dominion of the Earth is to work *with* nature not against it.

It is not that man is being punished for the sins of Adam and Eve or for a fall that occurred millennia ago. We are not punished for our sins but by them. Humanity, daily, creates its own suffering as a collective body and on a personal individual level. There is no vengeful God in heaven dispensing judgement and punishment. There is no predetermination. On the contrary, man has free will. This is the greatest gift one can give or receive; but it is also a challenge and an obligation. Having given us this gift, the universe is not going to interfere in our reality for that would not really be free will.

The real challenge of free will is that we must accept the responsibility for our decisions and the consequences of our behaviour. Like the child, we have created a reality of our own choosing. We have created both the joys of our success and the suffering of our error. We do not need to look to the past, to an ancient wound or an unforgiving God; we do not need to blame our forefathers or ancestors; we do not need to take refuge in the excuse and justification of an unloving and inherently evil nature. We merely need to look to today, to what we are creating right now, at this very moment with that divine gift and that divine power that lies within.

It is precisely because we choose not to look, that we create the rationalisation, the justification, that we excuse ourselves, like Luther and Calvin, by creating reasons that we cannot change, that are beyond our control, that prove that we are not responsible for ourselves. For if we are inherently evil, then it is not really our fault, but rather a design fault within the system and therefore the responsibility of the creator and architect, not us. We are exonerated and excused from blame and the responsibility of fixing the problem. We cannot be expected to deal with a situation that is beyond our control.

Thus, at one and the same time, we move in two different directions. On the surface, it would appear that we are taking responsibility; we humiliate ourselves before God, supplicate and beg for mercy. We pray for divine intercession and grace. All fundamentalist religions still practise this immaturity – it is not a thing of the past. We expect God or Jesus or Mohammed to come down and save us.

Yet, in doing so we are abandoning the very thing we came here to demonstrate and cultivate – our free will choice. For if God was to fall for this trick, we would lose that very freedom, we would be as puppets in the hands of God; the very teachings of Luther and Calvin. We are too ready to give away our personal power and we are too unwilling to take up the challenge and responsibility of personal sovereignty. We do not really want to decide for ourselves; we do not really want to take personal responsibility for the mess we have created on the planet and in our personal individual lives. For to take real responsibility is to accept the challenge of finding a solution, and of rectifying the problem.

It is undoubtedly true that God could come down and fix everything in the twinkling of an eye and restore us all to the Garden of Eden. The fact that he, she or it does not do that is not because we are the low-life of the universe, or that we deserve to suffer, or that we are being punished. Rather, it is because of the greatest gift there is – the gift of free will.

There can be no freedom without the responsibility of one's decisions and choices.

Having been given the freedom to mess up the planet – we are now being given the opportunity to fix it up. There is plenty of assistance available, if and when we choose to do the work. But the onus of responsibility is squarely on us as a body of humanity. As any psychotherapist or healer is well aware, you can only assist a patient to heal themselves if and when they are ready to do the necessary work themselves. Similarly, anyone who has fallen victim to trying to help or save another from their self-inflicted self-destructiveness will know this same truth.

Cosmic forces stand ready, eager and willing to assist but it is humanity that must be ready to make a stand and change:

> ...we are not gods; we are brothers who hold forth their hands. We cannot come to release you from that which you have created. We stand by until the hour when through love of brother and love of the Christ within yourselves, you have altered your own vibrations to the place where there is a degree of compatibility with ours.[22]

There can be no real freedom without responsibility. The gift of free will demands that we take honest responsibility and accountability for what we have created and not seek refuge or shelter behind the cover of false rationalisation or justification. After all this is the methodology of neurosis: denial and repression create rationalisation. We have denied the truth and rationalised it with the myth of the fall of man, with the lie of the inherent evilness of humanity. We have excused ourselves completely.

The first stage of the process of responsibility is recognition; the first stage of healing is diagnosis. To solve any problem, it is first necessary to discover and correctly define what is the cause of that problem.

In order to discover precisely what did go wrong we need to return to the process of the evolution of consciousness. Consciousness entered physicality as raw energy with no specific form or sense of separation. This is the level of higher consciousness – undifferentiated form – the beginning of the Big Bang. It then adopted form, distinction and direction, becoming sub-atomic particles, which vibrate at a particular frequency and possess individuality of being. It then evolved into molecular structures to create the mineral kingdom. At this first stage of physicality movement is motivated, controlled and regulated by pure chemistry and geometry.

Consciousness then evolved further, entering the plant, animal and early ape-man kingdoms where movement is motivated and controlled by biology and instinct – by the autonomic nervous system. Up until that point, all is well. In mythological terms this *is* the Garden of Eden. Nature regulates itself perfectly. As we have said before, life on planet Earth was doing very nicely, thank you, for approximately 4,600 million years before the true human kingdom appeared and in less than 4,600 years we have created chaos.

The World Wildlife Fund estimates that we have accelerated the natural extinction rate of all species on planet earth by between 1,000 and 10,000 per cent, causing the extinction of up to 100,000 species annually. We have decimated the lungs of the planet: the forests. We have polluted the waterways and oceans, blown holes in the atmosphere, and are continually destroying each other in senseless wars. We are not particularly happy or healthy as a species or as individuals, and we run the very real and imminent risk of destroying ourselves and the planet! Somehow, we do seem to have lost the plot. Is it no wonder we seek refuge in the banal excuse that we are bad and evil, that we cannot be trusted and need extra-terrestrial help to sort out our mess?

Consciousness then evolved into the human being, who was no longer controlled by chemistry or biology. This was the advent of free will choice. Individuality could now choose and decide for itself – the raw beginnings of personal sovereignty. The self-aware, conscious individual was the goal and purpose of this evolutionary journey. Nature had completed itself in the individual.

Now just as any structure becomes more complicated as it evolves, by the time consciousness had developed into the human being, it too had created a fairly sophisticated structure. Life was no longer as simple as that of a mineral, plant or animal. The human organism with conscious awareness and free will choice represented an extremely complex and highly evolved being; it required a corresponding extremely sensitive and sophisticated operating system. We can use the analogy of the operating system and computer needed to navigate and fly an advanced spaceship or modern jet liner.

We have already examined the multifaceted nature of human consciousness. There is the autonomic nervous system, which is a function of the older unconscious mind. It operates to maintain and regulate survival bodily mechanisms without the knowledge of conscious awareness. There is the second layer of the subconscious mind, which deals with inner states of being, feeling and emotion, and stores all information. Then there is the conscious mind, neatly divided into two parts, expressing logical, rational thought and spontaneous intuitive understanding and knowing. Then there is the superconscious mind which is the beginning and end of all human development. This is the over-mind, which is often referred to as the higher self, spirit or soul.

And then there is the ego.* The ego was developed as the assistant and servant of the conscious mind. Its function was to gather information and data pertaining to life on the planet – data necessary for physical survival; information about external reality and deliver it to the conscious mind. The ego is the filter through which the five senses deliver their data to conscious awareness.

The ego was also designed to execute the decisions of that conscious mind once it had received the pertinent data, made its necessary evaluation and decided what to do. The ego was an aspect of the human earthly personality whose sole function was to act as intermediary between the external physical world and the inner psychic world. It was still up to the conscious mind to hold the seat of power, to evaluate and reflect, to exercise free will choice and make the decisions, to be the source of motivation: the controller and regulator of the whole being.

Just as the ego was to deliver the content or information concerning the external physical world, the subconscious was to deliver data from the inner personal world. The ego used the senses to report on external reality; the subconscious used dreams and feelings to report on inner states of being. The unconscious was to deliver data from the deepest recesses of the being: the primary programmes, habits and patterns that become our personalised instinctive responses.

These three units all operate independently but harmoniously to deliver a holistic framework or context for the conscious mind to make an informed and intelligent decision. The conscious mind was designed to receive these inputs, compute, decide and respond, directing and conducting the other subordinate areas of consciousness accordingly. A neat and orderly structure that was the blueprint or design for human consciousness that housed free will choice that was efficient, effective and healthy: the picture before the so-called fall.

Each of these information units gathers and delivers data concerning the content of its own world. Each of these is an assistant and subordinate to conscious awareness: an eye or doorway through which

---

* It is important to note that this definition and understanding of the term ego differs widely from commonly accepted and Freudian terms where the word ego means the conscious mind or awareness of one's own identity and existence.

the conscious mind can monitor the various levels of the structure of consciousness. It is the function of the conscious mind to process and interpret the information and then decide the appropriate response. If we use the analogy of a sophisticated modern computer system, the ego, the subconscious and the unconscious are all terminals delivering data to the main processing centre, which is the conscious mind.

However, this is what was supposed to happen. What did happen was actually quite different. Lazaris uses the analogy of the corporate structure of consciousness to explain where things went wrong. In this analogy, the ego is the delivery boy whose sole task it is to deliver the mail from outside and bring it to the chief operating officer who is the conscious mind, wait for a response and then deliver that reply to the relevant branch. It is not the job of the mail boy to open the mail or read it, to make a decision or to instruct others.

However, in terms of this analogy and in keeping with the Peter Principle, we have promoted the ego to its level of incompetence. We have instructed the ego to not only open and read the mail but also to decide on an appropriate course of action or response. Furthermore, we have put the ego in charge of the whole structure of consciousness, commanding the ego to do our job for us. We have elevated the mailroom delivery boy to become the Chairman of the Board plus CEO while we have gone AWOL!

We have given away our control and our responsibility. We have instructed the ego to make the decisions in our absence. The ego, who is our assistant, has no choice but to comply. We have not only commanded the ego to take charge of our physical reality but also to take charge of the subconscious and unconscious worlds as well. We have completely and utterly abrogated our personal sovereignty.

This is the real fall of man. We have fallen, not because of some inherent design fault, not because we are basically flawed and evil at our core, but because we have simply given away our power, given away our control, and given away our sovereignty to a relatively junior aspect of ourselves that is quite incapable of handling that level of complexity or responsibility.

For this is precisely what happened. The ego was not designed to be the CEO of the corporate structure of consciousness any more than the delivery boy is capable of taking over the reins and running a large organisation. The ego tries to do its best but is incapable of making intelligent decisions. It stutters and promises but cannot deliver. It is driven further and further into incompetence trying to cover up its mistakes and errors, only making things progressively worse.

Moreover, it is thrown into survival mode, fighting for its life, frightened, cut off and isolated because it is out of its depth in a reality it was never designed or equipped to handle. Needing to cover its incompetence, it attacks anybody and everybody who comes close, for fear of being exposed for the fraud it has become under our instructions.

The ego accepts this responsibility because it has no choice; it must obey the conscious mind, and its duty is to ensure our physical survival. It therefore does its best. But it is incapable of doing the job of the conscious mind, and so it becomes distorted, alienated, disordered and fails miserably to achieve any real results. In a word, it becomes ill, negative and destructive.

Moreover, the ego can no longer do its own job as it is preoccupied endeavouring to do that of the conscious mind. As it fails more and more, it not only tries to cover and justify its actions, but it also becomes angry, and the conscious mind becomes the enemy. It decides that if it is to take charge then it will take over everything – it becomes the megalomaniac we have all observed. It takes over the whole system causing greater and greater chaos, more and more destruction.

Ultimately, the assistant becomes the tyrant, the loyal and faithful servant becomes the autocratic master, the friend becomes the enemy. The ego becomes negative and its sole goal becomes to destroy the conscious mind for putting it in that untenable position in the first place.

This is the sorry history of humanity. This is the story of each and every individual human lifetime. This is the truth behind the mythological fall.

It is vitally important to understand and appreciate the significance of this event. Mankind is not inherently evil. We were not expelled from the Garden of Eden; we merely refused to take up the necessary responsibility when the seat of power and control shifted to the conscious plane. We were given the greatest gift in the universe – that of free will choice, the power of self-determination, the ability to co-create with the gods, capable of exercising individual freedom of choice, of making our own decisions, and the opportunity to live by our own will, effort and creativity.

But rather than taking up this challenge, we relinquished this power and commanded our assistant, servant and loyal companion, the ego, to do it for us. This is the real tragedy of man; this is the fall that must be, and is recreated daily, each and every time we doubt ourselves, relinquish our power and refuse to exercise our free will rather handing over control to the by-now negative ego.

It was a simple enough mistake in the beginning – we merely demanded too much of our ego. The ego did not set out to destroy us or be negative. It began as an assistant that was overloaded to the point of incompetence and illness. Its natural growth and function were stunted, and it became negative. We would not admit the mistake we had made, refusing to take back the power and control.

Rather, we sought to justify, to rationalise, to excuse our abuse of human freedom, explaining it away with a myth and a belief that that was the way it was supposed to be, that that was the human condition, that that was human nature.

En masse, we bought the story; individually we refused to think for ourselves. It was far easier to allow the ego to do the work for us. We did not want to accept the responsibility of conscious awareness, of spiritual maturity. It was far easier to stay asleep in our historical subconscious slumber and allow the ego to direct the play. We were too lazy to take up the challenge of individual personal consciousness; far easier to command the ego to do the work for us.

And so, we refused to grow. We refused to come of age, to admit our mistake, to forgive ourselves, and to rectify the situation by taking back our power and getting on with the glory of co-creating a beautiful life. As Buckminster Fuller says: '...to sin is to refuse to admit a mistake.'

We were not expelled from the garden; we refused to enter!

Humanity is not inherently evil by nature or by default; we have created evil by refusing to admit our error. We are not being punished for the sins of Adam and Eve, we are punishing ourselves by the sins we create daily by our constant refusal to become fully conscious, aware and alive, and taking responsibility for our own creation.

SIX: THE NATURE OF EVIL – THE FEAR AND ABUSE OF HUMAN FREEDOM

> ...*fear has owned this planet, its people and their systems for a long time. It does not wish to give up the property it has acquired because it is a parasitic life form that cannot live separated from your life form.*
>
> J Z Knight

Order depends upon the correct delegation and execution of authority. There is always a natural hierarchy or chain of command in any organic structure. The healthy functioning of that structure depends upon control and power being held by the appropriate forces and being administered properly.

As anyone who has worked within a corporate structure, a bureaucracy, a social organisation or even a family will know, disaster always follows when the right people are not put in charge. The young child should not be allowed to be the master of the house. We have all experienced or at least witnessed what happens when a child's will is given free rein and not sufficiently disciplined. Over time, it becomes more and more demanding, throwing tantrums to get its own way and eventually taking complete control of the household even if that control is a state of chaos.

> From the beginning each child must be accustomed to firmly established rules of order, before ever its will is directed to other things. If we begin too late to enforce order, when the will of the child has already been overindulged, the whims and passions, grown stronger with the years, offer resistance and give much cause for remorse.[23]

It is always important that those with the appropriate skills, talents, personal power and capability be put in charge of any situation.

Position should be a function of ability. Ideally, external authority and rank should be a reflection of inner personal worth and power. But as the Peter Principle so eloquently states this is seldom the case. '…in a hierarchy every employee tends to rise to his level of incompetence.'

Human history is invariably the story of the wrong people being in the wrong positions of authority causing chaos and confusion. This is nothing more than the external manifestation or reflection of the inner control of the negative ego. There is an ancient Chinese saying: '…if the multitude assume leadership of the army, misfortune will ensue.'

Consciousness had evolved through millions and millions of years to the point where it had developed to a stage of maturity where it was capable of exercising control of itself. Up until that point when the seat of power entered the conscious mind, there had always been the pre-set programmes of chemistry and biology to motivate and regulate the growth process. It was now time for the introduction of free will, the sovereignty of individual conscious awareness in the form of the human being. To aid in its navigation of the physical world and to better ensure its physical survival, consciousness gave birth to the offspring of the ego.

In this context, consciousness is the parent and the ego is the child. The ego does not have the inner strength, experience or the connection to the divine spark of consciousness necessary for controlling the complex structure of consciousness or for taking charge of life. The ego is an immature and naïve life form. The young child is not capable of taking charge of the household.

Like any child placed in this untenable position, the ego was driven into a state of fear. Now, fear was one of the tools of the ego to arouse the attention of its master, the conscious mind. After all, the specific task of the ego was to alert consciousness to physical danger. The conscious mind needed an assistant to warn it when there was a threatening danger of harm or impending injury to the physical body.

The conscious mind needed to be free from monitoring this sort of trivial information, so that it could be free to explore the realms of creativity that was the real purpose of its incarnation into the physical world in the first place. If the conscious mind was preoccupied with all of the data pertaining to the autonomic nervous system and the five senses' sensory input of the external conditions on planet Earth, it would very quickly become bogged down and overloaded with this mountain of information.

It was the ego's function to alert the conscious mind to danger and the alarm system was the activation of the biological current of fear. Thus, in its original and positive aspect fear was a necessary alarm system to avoid impending physical danger just as a smoke alarm or fire detector warn of impending fire.

However, because the ego was placed in this inappropriate position, the fear alarm was continually ringing making it impossible for the primary motivating current, which was love, to be heard. It would be like trying to listen to a beautiful concerto while the fire alarm is continually blaring. The ego was designed to be the servant of the conscious mind; fear was designed to be the servant of the ego. Now fear was motivating and controlling the whole show. The system was being perpetually jammed by the current of fear.

Free will necessitates a choice between alternatives or there is no real freedom to choose. Thus, this is the plane of duality. There is a positive and a negative aspect to everything that exists. Life is the process of love expressing itself through truth. But there must also be the opposite. Evil is the denial of the truth expressed as fear. The denial of the truth is the lie. The opposite of love is fear. The reversal of the word 'live' is evil.

Love and truth are the two hands of God whereby creation comes into existence. Love is the primary motivating current of life, of all there is. The original emotion is love. The word e/motion means to move, to motivate. Emotions move us to act. We discovered earlier that before creation existed there was an aspect of God seeking to express itself through creation in order to know itself. This was the original, primordial explosion of love. God is love and love is God. But this emotion needs to express itself in form. Truth is the aspect of God that gives form and structure to creation, that leads to individuality and gives rise to the evolution of consciousness and the progressive perfection of form.

If love is the inner feeling or emotion that gets the whole thing going, then truth is the external ordering process that regulates form. If love is the primary, motivating force, current or feeling then fear is its counterpart. If love is the accelerator, then fear is the brake that gives control and direction to that movement. If love is the green light of go, then fear is the red light of stop.

Like the ego, in its rightful place fear has a necessary and correct function. It is a mechanism of survival. But just as we do not attempt to drive with the hand brake permanently on, we cannot live by the dictates of the current of fear. Fear was never meant to be the primary motivating force, just as the ego was never meant to take control. So, we now have a humanity driving a high-performance vehicle with a young child at the wheel and the hand brake jammed on. Is it any wonder we are skidding wildly out of control heading for disaster?

Just as the spoilt child uses tantrums and emotional blackmail to get its own way, once its will has been overindulged, so too, the ego, in its altered negative and destructive state uses fear to get complete and total control of the corporate structure of consciousness. Down through the ages fear has become institutionalised, culturally encoded and adopted as a normal part of man's everyday life.

Fear is a real thing and has a life form that has been inflated and sustained by mankind's fearful thoughts and emotions. The force of fear is nourished by our emotional natures and the more we give into our fears of insecurity, loneliness, rejection, abandonment, humiliation, failure, and not being good enough, the greater the power or force of fear becomes on the planet. Now we have reached the stage where rather than controlling it, we are controlled by fear. Once again, the servant has become the master.

The ego gained control because of the abuse of human freedom. We were unwilling to take up the responsibility of personal sovereignty. We refused to exercise our God-given gift of free will, choosing instead to give that power away to the ego. We commanded it to take command. Similarly, the altered negative ego was able to enlist the services of fear to more completely take control because we had already laid the foundations.

The reason we gave away our power was because we were afraid of the responsibility in the first place. By doubting ourselves and our ability to choose correctly we had already given into the dictates of fear.

As we have discovered, the fall must be re-enacted daily, and the fall basically is a lack of trust in our inner divine nature. We doubt ourselves. And self-doubt is a form of fear. We gave away our power because we were afraid and doubted our ability to use it correctly. Any unwillingness to make a decision, to exercise the sovereignty of free will springs from a fear of being wrong. To doubt oneself, to lack trust in one's own inner divinity is the primary expression of fear.

Before the Grand Deception, the lie of the inherent evilness of humanity, was the original lie of fear. Fear is the first lie; the original denial of the truth: the belief in separation. All fear is a symptom of a belief that is faulty. Just as love is the original positive emotion, fear is the original negative emotion. When the primary current of love exploded into the creation of consciousness, the myriad sparks of that love became the manifested universe.

Each and every one of us is one of those sparks. And in the beginning life was a grand and glorious adventure of adopting specific frequencies and taking form and then dissolving back into the sea of primordial oneness. There was no sense of separation and there was no continuity of form or identity. It was a dance of creation – taking up the form of individuality and putting it down again, emerging from the sea of cosmic consciousness and dissolving back into it.

However, what happened was the seed of doubt, the voice of fear, the lie of separation. At first it was the fear of loss of identity and individuality if one returned to the cosmic ocean and so this fear begat a holding onto form, a clinging to external individuality. As this holding pattern cemented in, the fear changed into a fear of separation, of not being supported, and a fear of loneliness, of the sense that one had gone too far into individuality and over-identified with form, and somehow got lost from the protective love of God. This was the alarm bell ringing, warning of the impending danger of separation. This was the correct functioning of fear breaking our journey and descent into matter, warning us that we had gone too far, to turn around and find our way home.

The young child does much the same thing with its parent in new surroundings. Motivated by the positive current of curiosity and love of discovery, it wanders off to explore this new and exciting reality. It gets to a certain point, feels the secondary current of fear and runs back to mother. After a while, once fear has abated, it wanders off again to explore, this time venturing a little further, then returning, and so on. Eventually, it wanders too far, loses sight of the parent and the secondary current of fear takes over, becoming the primary motivating force, and the child feels lost, cut off, separated, lonely and fearful. Fear, panic and terror take over and the child starts screaming for Mummy.

This is precisely what happened in the early stages of the development of individuality except that just as we would not admit the mistake of giving too much power and control to the ego, we would not admit the mistake of going too far into separation. We continued to ignore the alarm bells and denied the original fear, pulling ever further away from oneness and increasing our sense of separation.

It is important to realise that this process of separation from the source and return to it is as necessary to the healthy development of individual consciousness as is the exploration of the child to the development of a healthy and robust human being. If the child is too timid and does not explore ever-increasing degrees of separation, it will become psychologically dependent upon the parent and its personal growth and development will be retarded. On the other hand, if the child is not to suffer psychological dysfunction, there needs to be no traumatic loss or loneliness. As in all things it is a delicate dialectic dance.

The child can only go so far as it feels safe and secure. Emerging individuality could only go so far as it was connected to the creative current of love that was its primary motivating and guiding force. In not listening to and heeding the initial warnings of the alarm of fear, these individual units went too far and eventually felt themselves cut off from the source of their being and adopted the belief of separation.

It is this belief that is the real source of the mythological fall from grace and exit from the Garden of Eden. Mythology and religion are the collective ego's attempt to rationalise and justify man's refusal to heed the correct warnings of fear. Just as the lost child believes it has been abandoned by its parent, so too, humanity believes it has been expelled from the Garden and abandoned by God.

Once this original fear was ignored and the correct function of fear denied, the potential fear of loneliness became an actual reality of being alone and fear became a permanent part of man's life. The force of fear grew and became the ally of the altered negative ego. Hand in hand, they have waltzed through history, creating chaos and destruction wherever they roam. And all because of the abuse of human freedom!

It is humanity that has given away its power to the ego and to fear. Both were designed to be servants of consciousness and in their correct place are necessary parts of the structure. The ego is the messenger and fear is an alarm and guidance system of that messenger. The conscious mind is the master of both and should exercise control and dominion over both. Now, however, both the ego and fear have usurped that control. We allow fear to run our lives; we are motivated out of fear rather than out of love.

The principle of free will necessitates duality. Creation is the expression of the two hands of God. In the east this dialectic is understood in terms of yin and yang: the creative and the receptive, light and dark, spirit and nature, heaven and earth, time and space, masculine and feminine, spirituality and sensuality. However, both are viewed as two sides of the one coin; both are necessary for creation. They are merely the polar extremes of a unified whole within which the process of creation operates.

In the west we have viewed good and evil as being two separate things. We have personified both in terms of God and the Devil, failing to grasp the underlying oneness of creation. We have created a belief in separation and put God out there somewhere and us in here. We have cut ourselves off from our source, from the unified field of divine consciousness from which we emerged and of which we are an integral part. We have cut ourselves off from the primary motivating current of love aligning with the secondary inhibiting current of fear.

In adopting this belief in our own separateness, we have failed to understand the principle of dualistic monism – the oneness of the Creator expressing itself in the duality of creation. For the essence of this principle is the clearly defined hierarchic relationship that exists between the two poles of creation. In and of itself, each pole is equal and just as important as the other. However, as emphasised at the beginning of this chapter, natural order demands a hierarchic delegation of authority, a specific chain of command that is a reflection and function of inner worth and power.

It is only when this inherent natural order is upset, and power is not exercised by the correct principle that disorder and evil are created. Evil is not an intrinsic quality of creation, but rather a characteristic of malfunction within the system. Individual units of consciousness create evil when they allow the yin principle to rule.

> In itself the Receptive is just as important as the Creative, but the attribute of devotion defines the place occupied by this primal power in relation to the Creative. For the Receptive must be activated and led by the Creative; then it is productive of good. Only when it abandons this position and tries to stand as an equal side by side with the Creative does it become evil. The result then is opposition to and struggle against the Creative, which is productive of evil to both.[24]

However, it must be emphasised that the yin principle can only gain power when it is willingly given over by the yang force. The yin principle cannot take control of itself. The ego did not take the power of control from the conscious mind; it was willingly given. Fear did not take the power of motivation from love; the emotion of fear was fed at the expense of the emotion of love. In both cases, power was willingly given away.

By its fear and refusal to willingly accept the responsibility of its own emerging freedom and sovereignty, humanity created a state of disorder within the hierarchic structure of consciousness. It created a situation where the yang principle abandoned its rightful position of rulership, thrusting command and control into the hands of the yin principle of following. It is this distortion which is the nature of evil.

Personal sovereignty is the positive expression of free will. There is no freedom without responsibility. The altered ego is the negative expression of the abuse of this freedom or the refusal to accept responsibility. It is too easy to blame this on a mythological 'other' or on a generalisation about the nature of humanity. Both of these are rationalisations which excuse our reluctance to take individual personal responsibility for our decisions.

We have already discovered that repression, denial and justification are three phases or aspects of neurosis. They are three manifestations of the one phenomenon. Repression is the suppression of a natural feeling or fear that is too painful to acknowledge consciously. It is therefore a denial of the truth and results in a state of separation from our real inner selves, a separation from the source of our being. It is a denial of real feelings and a substitution of these with a symbolic or neurotic acting out. The whole purpose of repression is to conceal the truth; it distorts that which is too painful to bear into a more acceptable form.

It is far easier to accept the myth of the Garden of Eden and the generalisation of the inherent evilness of the nature of humanity, than it is to acknowledge the overwhelming implication of the acceptance of our own personal responsibility in this matter. We simply do not want to face the truth of the mess we have created on the planet.

Yet each and every one of us is totally, 100 per cent, responsible for our own reality, for our own re-creation of the fall in our daily lives, and for the current situation we find ourselves in globally. We are the world. Just as each individual human body is a distinct and unique organism, recreated anew at every act of conception, so too, each individual cell of consciousness ontogenetically recreates the inner psychological state of separation and allows or invites the ego to assume control of the corporate structure of their individual consciousness.

It is now time for each of us to admit and acknowledge the abuse of human freedom that has led to this state of separation and to reclaim our personal power by taking back the responsibility for directing, motivating and controlling our individual lives.

The suppression of the original fear of loneliness is re-enacted by each individual human being, resulting in a state of inner separation and denial. Because of this state of separation, we believe in our separateness and we separate ourselves from reality. Thus, we see both the forces of creation, the yang and the yin, the good and the bad as being without – something external to and separate from us. We externalise and personalise them as God and the Devil, thus excusing us from responsibility.

This is the real function of religion and mythology. We create the human personalised version of a God in heaven and a Devil in hell.

We create God the father as the cranky old man with the beard and Satan as the serpent or the demon with a pitchfork. These are seen as separate from mankind. They are seen as external forces, rather than being viewed correctly as inner states of being. We are not separate from God; we are a piece of God, an aspect, a spark of divine consciousness, just as the spark is a part of the flame or a drop is a part of the ocean.

There is only oneness and we are a part of that oneness. To create Satan as a force in contradistinction to God is to deny the very existence of God, for it assumes that there is a part of creation that is not God, and this by definition cannot be. For God is everything and everything is God. God is all there is. Nothing else exists.

Evil is not a state external to man; it is not a pole of creation. Evil is the condition that results from the abuse of freedom, when power is not exercised correctly and the structure malfunctions. It is an internal condition of creation that we have created.

Good and evil are not abstract external conditions imposed upon the individual because of events and circumstances beyond his or her control, but inner states of being that result from the correct use or incorrect abuse of the divine gift of free will and personal sovereignty. Man has separated himself from God and then believed in the existence of an external malevolent power of evil, just as the lost child separated from its parents, feels lonely and frightened and in that state of fear imagines the existence of external threatening forces.

The creative principle denotes spiritual potential; the receptive principle denotes spatial reality. The creative begets and the receptive gives form to creation. The light principle represents life and the dark, death. But death is not evil; it is merely the opposite polar extreme to life. For an electric current to flow, there must be a potential difference created by a positive and negative pole. We do not evaluate or judge either of these to be preferential or better. We understand that both are necessary for the establishing of the current.

So too, the process of creation requires the flow of chi, or the Tao, the cosmic current that is established through the dynamic interplay of the dialectic opposites of yin and yang. Neither are preferable or better states: both are necessary for the manifestation of the phenomenal universe.

They are both the parents of creation just as both the mother and father are the equally necessary parents of the newborn. There is biological specialisation in the sexes – one cannot replace the function of the other; but one is not superior to or better than the other. Just different.

However, just as in a marriage, this union can be pleasing, ordered and harmonious or disordered, chaotic and destructive. The choice is ours. The essential point to understand is that good and evil are not external polar extremes, within which man is a helpless and powerless puppet being tossed between the two, but rather a characteristic and quality of the relationship and interaction between the two.

> Heaven and earth unite: the image of peace. Heaven has placed itself beneath the earth and so their powers unite in deep harmony. Then peace and blessing descend upon all living things.
>
> Heaven and earth are out of communion and all things are benumbed. The creative powers are not in relation. It is a time of standstill and decline. What is above has no relation to what is below and on earth confusion and disorder prevail.[25]

Eastern philosophy has a more profound understanding of this concept of dualistic monism than that of the west. It was accepted that each principle had its correct place within the workings of the universe. In the west, the negative pole was externalised, personalised and vilified; viewed as a totally destructive force. This is why in the myth, humanity, who had been seduced by the serpent in the Garden and had gone over to the dark side, was seen as inherently evil.

In western thought, the two poles are mutually exclusive and fundamentally antagonistic. In the dialect of the east, the poles are more correctly seen as extreme points within a comprehensive whole. Confucius viewed opposition as the natural prerequisite for union. Polarity is necessary for the creation of physical life: '…the opposition of heaven and earth, spirit and nature, man and woman, when reconciled, bring about the creation and reproduction of life.'[26]

Chinese social and political life was organised around this conceptual understanding that the light principle needed to occupy a position of power and sovereignty, exercising influence and control over the dark principle. If this occurred, then all was well; peace and prosperity reigned. The forces of light had to occupy the key position at the centre; the forces of darkness needed to be at the periphery in a position of submission. Evolution was seen as a continual process whereby the superior forces of light were beneficially influencing the inferior forces of darkness.

> In this way each received its due. When the good elements of society occupy a central position and are in control, the evil elements come under their influence and change for the better. When the spirit of heaven rules in man, his animal nature also comes under its influence and takes its appropriate place.[27]

Now although this sounds suspiciously like Freud's concept of sublimation there is a subtle yet real distinction. Freud postulated that man was fundamentally antisocial; that is was society's role to domesticate and tame the wild, animalistic passions of the individual; and that these suppressed urges then become transformed into the cultural superstructure of civilisation. And here lies the difference between the two systems of thought and their implication for social organisation.

In western philosophy, man's nature is inherently evil, and the level of culture is directly proportional to the level of suppression. In the eastern viewpoint, at his core mankind is intrinsically good:

> ...man has received from heaven a nature innately good, to guide him in all his movements. By devotion to this divine spirit within himself, he attains an unsullied innocence that leads him to do right with instinctive sureness and without any ulterior thought of reward or personal advantage.[28]

Thus, we can see a radical departure from the traditional western doctrine of the inherent evilness of man. Furthermore, the free market economy was based on the concept of Adam Smith's invisible hand, which stated that although the individual was fundamentally selfish, the market forces of supply and demand, would tailor the self-seeking profit motive of capitalism for the common good. On the other hand, Chinese philosophy is telling us that man's actions are guided not by a selfish, economic, invisible hand but by a benevolent, divine one.

The whole aim and thrust of ancient Chinese thought is not to suppress an unwieldy, dark and dangerous pool of inner psychic sexual urges, but rather to enhance and develop this inner divine spirit that lies within us all. Culture does not spring from suppression and denial but is the natural and spontaneous expression of mankind's inner divine nature. It is not the function, therefore, of the light force to control through sublimation or suppression of the dark force but rather to create those necessary conditions whereby this inner, natural, divine spirit can operate. '…the real nature of man is likewise originally good but becomes clouded by contact with earthly things and therefore needs purification before it can shine forth in native clarity.'[29]

In this philosophy, the core purpose and function of mankind's role on the planet is seen as creating the right conditions to enhance this evolutionary journey. Everything was aimed at awakening and developing this higher nature, not only of man, but of the ascending forces of consciousness in nature as well. This is a totally positive philosophy. Things only go wrong when mankind fails to play its part. It is man who spoils conditions through the abuse of human freedom. We will return to this concept of natural order later.

All that is necessary to grasp here is that good and evil are not external conditions imposed upon the individual from without. Rather, good is that state that comes from being in alignment with the creative forces of the universe, which has its own intrinsic harmony and beneficence. Evil is the condition that results from a system out of alignment with the creative forces and it too has its own inherent disharmony and destructiveness. Within order there is the harmonious interaction of the two creative poles: the yang and the yin, the creative and the receptive, the forces of expansion and contraction.

I would now like to return to our earlier model of the corporate structure of consciousness and see how this discussion of the polar nature of reality helps us to understand it better. I began our discussion with an examination of the composite and ever-evolving nature of God that expressed itself as the outpouring of divine love in the Big Bang of creation, causing the explosion of consciousness into billions of myriad individual sparks. This creation then seeks its way back to God via the continuous process of the evolution of consciousness and the search for progressive perfection. Perfection is a process of perpetual becoming; it is never achieved, nor is it an achievable state or condition of completion.

This is the promise of eternity.

In the physical world, consciousness enters into the unconscious realm of primary form – the subatomic, atomic and molecular particles of the mineral kingdom. It is motivated controlled and regulated by chemistry. Evolution then moves into the subconscious realm of plant, animal and early human kingdoms. Here, life is motivated, controlled and regulated by biology or instinct. As life evolves to higher and more complex animal forms instinct becomes less and less compelling. '… instinct is a diminishing if not a disappearing category in higher animal forms, especially in the human.' By the time consciousness had evolved to the point of creating the human kingdom, these subconscious forces were no longer exercising a decisive influence. This is where the gift of free will entered.

The seat of power or control was now within the conscious mind. Not fully or immediately with the first human but gradually, over time, with the course of evolution. The instinctive determination of behaviour lessened its control and the individual became more free to consciously determine its own destiny.

However, not everything became conscious. This would have resulted in unnecessary clutter in the conscious mind and the jamming and overload of the higher faculties of mind. It was deemed more appropriate to delegate specific functions to the already evolved departments within the overall structure of consciousness. The chemical and biological processes were left within the jurisdiction of the lower unconscious mind in the form of the autonomic nervous system. The subconscious mind was given the responsibility of coordinating feelings, emotions, beliefs, attitudes and states of being of the inner self. It was also to act as the database or memory of the system.

The ego was created as an aspect of the personality to be the resident expert on external, planetary, and physical conditions and entrusted with ensuring the physical survival of the organism. Survival, previously, had been ensured by instinct, biology and chemistry. As these were no longer compulsive forces there was a danger that the overriding spirit would not be aware of the necessary conditions for survival or be that concerned about physical survival *per se*. After all, it was a spirit inhabiting a human body and therefore not trained in physical survival. The ego's job was to report on external terrestrial conditions. Its role was purely informational – its function was to deliver data, not make decisions or act upon that data.

The conscious mind was divided into two distinct yet complementary functions. The ego had use of the left brain, whose function was the rational analysis of the physical sensations coming from the nervous system of the body. The software of the left brain was extremely limited and specialised as it was not intended to be the main regulative or decision-making system. This was the function of the right brain with its holistic, intuitive awareness and comprehensive understanding. Just as the left brain was the instrument of the ego, the right brain was the instrument of the residing spirit. Both ego and spirit shared the same bio-circuitry but there was a natural hierarchic relationship between the two. In fact, there was a natural hierarchic order within this beautiful sophisticated structure of consciousness.

The motivating, controlling and regulative force lay within the spirit and its seat of power was the right brain of the conscious mind – the seat of intuitive awareness. This brain did possess the necessary software to drive the sophisticated biocomputer of the evolved human structure. Moreover, the spirit had the access codes and knew how to operate the software; the ego did not!

For the primary access code was love – that understanding of the oneness of creation – an ability to comprehend the connectedness of life. Intuitive awareness sees things holistically, spontaneously, and synchronistically. On the other hand, the ego is the instrument of division and of separation. The left brain's function is to break up, to analyse, to dissect, and to view things logically, rationally and linearly. This is how it processes information. After all it is an information processing unit. Its software is designed for that function. It was not designed to interpret the data, to reach conclusions and make decisions. This is the function of the resident spirit using the more holistic software of the intuitive right brain.

Thus, we can see a very orderly and highly developed hierarchic corporate structure of consciousness. At the top is the chief executive operating through intuitive awareness. This is the seat of conscious control, connected to the source of all-being or God. This is that original spark of divine consciousness that is God, that is the innately good divine spirit of Chinese philosophy. Then there is the subconscious which is the department of feeling and emotions and connects us to our inner selves; the unconscious which controls the autonomic nervous system and the survival and maintenance of bodily mechanisms, and finally the ego which is tasked with coordinating this data and delivering it to the conscious mind.

Each of these is an assistant to the higher conscious awareness of the spirit delivering information from its area of jurisdiction. They are all subordinates, lieutenants, servants, helpers – call them what you will – of the overriding divine consciousness, and therefore have a hierarchic relationship to that spirit if order, health and harmony are to prevail.

However, as already noted, this is not what happened. As the individual sparks of consciousness left the sea of oneness and explored the domain of individuated separateness, they ignored the whispers and warnings of the servant of fear. They denied and suppressed these original positive messages and as they first entered the material world they ventured too far into separation. Like the little boy lost, this original positive fear, through suppression, denial and distortion, became an overwhelming and all pervasive negative feeling of separation, loneliness and fright.

In this isolated, cut-off state, contact was lost with the sea of oneness, the source of being and the primordial motivating current of pure love. Doubt and fear started to take over as substitute motivating currents. Remember e/motion is motivation; emotions impel us to movement. These individual units started to distrust their own perceptions and ability to adequately deal with and successfully negotiate physical reality. They thus turned away from this primary navigational system and their own decision-making ability, calling on the ego, as the earth plane resident specialist, to take control. The ego, obedient servant that it then was, had no choice but to obey and tried desperately to drive the now out-of-control vehicle of consciousness.

Moreover, under the stress of this unnatural burden, the ego's nature started to change for the worse becoming the now all too familiar destructive, alienated, paranoid and negative ego that we now know. Besides being an instrument of analysis and division, the ego in its disoriented state became even more separated, isolated and lonely, thus furthering the original dysfunction of the system. The ego lacked the comprehensive vision of the spirit and therefore created the myth of the separation from God.

Repression eventually creates rationalisation:

> …a mind that conceives of itself as fundamentally separate from all that it perceives is an instrument of division. It can do nothing but divide, analyse, compartmentalise and dissect. Everything on which it turns its attention is reduced to disconnected segments, while the spirit, the life of the whole is forgotten. With the fictitious premise that it is fundamentally distinct from both God and nature lying at the root of its thinking, it is not capable of reason, for its premise is a lie.
>
> This is why the historic egoic use of the human mind has been so destructive: it creates thoughts, images, personal identity structures, cultural institutions and ultimately entire civilisations that are based on the illusion that the individual is fundamentally distinct from the ground of being from which it and all creation have emerged.[30]

The ego was commanded to take control, to operate the sophisticated software of the brain, to assume sovereignty, to not only deliver the information from its own department but to decide what to do in its own and every other area. This the ego could not do. It became overworked, confused, disoriented, isolated – in a word, ill! The ego became smothered by its inappropriate burden of responsibility. Its nature became altered from that of a helpful servant and friend to that of a deadly and destructive enemy.

Because we did not listen to the messages of fear, we dived too far into separation too quickly becoming lost and feeling abandoned. In this cut-off state we no longer trusted our motivational system of intuitive awareness and our divine right of being. We gave away our control; we willingly surrendered our sovereignty and turned our backs on the gift of free will. The structure of consciousness was in a state of malfunction. The inferior power of the ego was now in control. This was the birth of evil which is not an inherent quality of creation but a function of being out of alignment with the evolutionary principle. As emphasised, in their correct places neither creative power is wrong or evil; both have their place. It is only when their correct functioning is disturbed that evil is created. Because of this abuse of human freedom and the giving away of control to the now negative ego, the whole balance of power in the evolution of consciousness on the planet was disturbed.

The principle of contraction or the dark power, which regulates and controls the forces of materialisation, and should in its turn be regulated and controlled by the principle of expansion, the light power, was able to gain too strong a hold and influence on the process of evolution. The creative begets and the receptive gives form. It is the principle of contraction that regulates the unconscious process of crystallisation bringing about subatomic, atomic and molecular structures. Without this force of materialisation, matter would not exist.

Below the level of conscious awareness and the gift of free will there is no personal sovereignty. Before the emergence of the individualised self, the forces of materialisation rule and control the unconscious and subconscious processes that regulate creation. This is how it should be. The yin principle implements the laws that govern physical existence and it does so with unerring accuracy.

On its own the yin principle is not evil. As the autonomic nervous system fell within the unconscious realm, it too was under the influence and control of the forces of contraction or materialisation: the yin principle. The receptive needs to be activated and led by the creative; the yin receives its instructions from the yang. The subconscious forces of materialisation are under the jurisdiction of the conscious forces of mind and spirit. Thus, the forces of materialisation are under the charge of individual human beings and must obey their every command.

As the ego and subsequently the altered negative ego assumed control of human consciousness, they also took control of the forces of darkness. The yin principle was now able to extend its influence too far up the ladder of corporate control. Humanity fell under the spell of matter; the domination of materiality. The circle of destruction was complete.

Rather than having a neat, orderly, harmonious and correct division of responsibility and function with the appropriate light-giving power exercising authority and control for the good of all, we ended up with an upside-down chain of command where the servants had become the master: the classic definition of evil. With the altered negative ego at the helm, the forces of darkness were invited to take control creating havoc, disruption and chaos.

Subconscious forces were being asked to influence conscious decision-making processes, that like the ego they were simply not equipped to handle. The more reliance the individual placed on these well-meaning but incompetent assistants, the more lost it became. As we became more and more lost, the less we trusted ourselves and the more we relied on their inappropriate and inadequate guidance. Down through the ages, the situation has only become more and more hopeless as humanity sinks deeper into its dependence and folly. The deeper we fall into the spell of matter and the more reliance we place upon the negative ego, the less we are able to hear the voice of our spirit and intuition calling us back.

It is essential to realise that in and of themselves these forces are not evil or destructive. In their rightful place they function perfectly with divine wisdom. They are the very voice of God calling matter into crystallisation; they control the physical laws of the universe. They bring creation into existence. It is our abuse of human freedom that has led to this current state of disorder and decay. And it is our rationalisation and justification that has created the myth of Satan and his evilness. We have blamed him for our own refusal to take responsibility; we have made him responsible for the mistake of our own ego:

> ...the materialising influence only becomes evil or destructive when it enters the sphere of human decision making. There

> it translates into myopic, fear centred logic that is not compatible with the more expansive awareness with which humanity is designed.
>
> While it is appropriate for materialistic values to dominate atomic and subatomic realms, they become extremely destructive when they dominate human determination.[31]

It was humanity who instructed the yin power to take control of its reality and thus put it in an untenable position. For those forces were not designed to influence or take part in human conscious processes but to regulate and control subconscious events, activities and processes. The participation by those forces in the conscious realm has resulted in confusion, interference and static that impedes the individual's ability to receive cosmic guidance that is the lifeblood of intuitive awareness and intelligent decision-making. Consequently, humanity increasingly becomes dominated by self-doubt and fear-based logic rather than the divine voice of spirit which was designed to be its primary motivating current.

Without this inner awareness and contact with the divine source of his being, mankind became filled with self-doubt, losing self-confidence and the power of self-determination. The original primary fear of loneliness had now become the artificial, secondary and negative fear of being wrong. It is because of this fear that the individual is unwilling to decide, to make its own choices, to assume personal sovereignty and take up the challenge of free will. It is in this way that we have given away our power and corrupted the natural state of order and authority in the structure of consciousness.

The gift of free will and the fact that we hold the position of power and authority over ourselves means that we can enter the domain of the ego and the subconscious forces of contraction and command them to take charge of our reality. However, the price is diminished intuitive awareness and a lack of true perception that results in a grossly distorted picture of our world, dominated by the forces of fear and separation rather than those of love and oneness.

Personal sovereignty must begin with the taking back of that power that we have so carelessly given away to those very forces we came to regulate. It is time for humanity and more particularly for the individual to take conscious control of his or her reality. We must assume the position of sovereign within our own life, exercising dominion over those forces which truly are our assistants.

By becoming the master and enlisting the creative support of those forces, assigning them to their correct duties and functions, order will be restored and peace and harmony will prevail upon the planet. This process must begin with the individual spirit returning to its rightful place at the helm, re-engaging the right brain of intuitive awareness as the correct navigational system and taking responsibility for making our decisions that determine our destiny.

We must begin with the ego. The ego must be released from its burden of responsibility and returned to its correct role of servant, gathering data and reporting to the spirit of consciousness. The objective is not to destroy the ego or make it wrong but to see that it is unwell because of its excessive burden. By removing this weight of responsibility, the ego will become well again and return to its natural role of devoted and loyal friend.

The goal is to engage the ego in a co-creative partnership that is mutually beneficial and to disengage from the present co-dependent relationship that is mutually destructive to both. However, before we can examine how to reclaim our personal sovereignty, we must first explore the process of individuation.

SEVEN: INDIVIDUATION

You create your own reality.

Seth

This statement, made by Seth in the early seventies, was in many ways the beginning of a new age of wisdom for humanity. The Seth material is a collection of writing dictated by Jane Roberts to her husband from late 1963 until her death in 1984. Roberts claimed the words were spoken by a discarnate entity named Seth and the material went on to become a cornerstone of New Age philosophy in the 20th Century heralding in a new interpretation of humanity's purpose and potential. Up until that point mankind had always believed that to some extent or another he was the victim of more powerful cosmic forces, or the victim of an impersonal mechanical universe. His life, his luck, his good fortune or misfortune, his destiny were decided by fate, by God or by chance; but never by his own creative output.

Now we were being told, categorically and unequivocally, that we and we alone created our own reality by our beliefs, thoughts, feelings, attitudes, desires and expectations, imagination, choices and decisions. What happened in our external physical world was nothing more and nothing less than a movie or play – an out-picture or projection – of inner psychic states of being. Indeed, we were being told that physical reality was the grand illusion; that the real world was this inner world of spirit.

Whether one was asleep and dreaming or awake and perceiving, there was very little difference. Both were projections of the inner mind. Consciousness created all.

Over the last four decades many have taken up this theme of personal power in many fields of human endeavour. There is now a chorus all singing the same song: we do indeed create our own reality.

The power of positive thinking, visualisation techniques, programming for successful outcomes, and affirmations are not just the prerogative of the New Age alternative fringe. They have also become the norm in many fields of successful human endeavour, from elite athletes to high business achievers and cutting edge psychological studies. The power of the conscious mind to create whatever it focuses its attention upon must be the greatest scientific discovery of all time.

Even in the sceptical corridors of science, it is becoming well known that there is no such thing as an external, objective reality. This is especially pertinent in the realm of quantum physics, where sub-atomic particles behave according to the expectations of the scientist conducting the experiment. The outcome is no longer viewed as an *a priori* fact of the observed, but rather as a manifestation of the observer. The double-blind experiment has become the normal operating procedure in many scientific fields to avoid this interrelationship between mind and matter.

New Age literature and modern psychological texts are rife with this idea of co-creativity. The basic premise is that man is not the helpless, insignificant, powerless victim that mythology, religion, tradition and convention have handed down throughout the ages. Rather, he is an all-powerful creator of his own world: a co-creator with God. What we think and believe and what we focus our attention upon will become in time our external physical reality. The external is a reflection of the internal. The inner comes first and projects itself upon the outer screen of daily life, just as the movie exists first within the roll of film and projects itself upon the screen of the theatre.

Life is a process of projection in order to learn what we do actually believe. The physical reflects the psychic to teach us what our inner mind holds. It displays before us, in a linear fashion, the multitudinous and multidimensional aspects of our inner consciousness. This is why we became physical in the first place.

The point is that we do create our own reality. We either choose to do this consciously, knowingly and wisely or unconsciously, unknowingly and foolishly. We either exercise personal sovereignty, using the gift of free will to consciously create a life that is full of joy, success, fun, love, peace and harmony or we decide to remain the willing victim of unconscious and subconscious programmes, forces, influences, fears, habits and patterns that are negative and destructive. The choice is ours and ours alone.

This is the real meaning of the gift of free will. Once free will is granted it is binding. This means that henceforth the individual could not be stopped from self-destructive behaviour by any well-meaning cosmic force or being; not even God can interfere in the execution of free will, once granted.

Once the seat of power entered the conscious mind, the individual was no longer compelled by the subconscious forces of chemistry, biology or instinct. One could be guided by what was right but not impelled. One was now free to consciously decide and determine one's own destiny. With the gift of free will came the advent of the consciously aware individualised self, the pinnacle of creation on planet Earth. Man had become a god – a co-creator with God, with the power to help or hinder the process of evolution on the planet. His task was to work with the creative forces as the representative of the light power on the planet, assuming sovereignty and dominion over the lower subconscious and unconscious forces.

The whole purpose and thrust of the evolutionary movement up until that point had been the development of the consciously aware individual. Nature completes itself in the sovereign being; this is called the process of individuation. The history of humanity has been the story of the emergence of the mature individual from a state of oneness with nature and his fellow man, in early prehistoric times, to the awareness of his separation from his environment with its attendant fears and feelings of powerlessness and loneliness in the historical process, to the now- dawning awareness of self-realised individuality, not separated from God but as a co-creator with God.

> In order to understand the meaning of individuality you must understand the purpose of individual existence. Life is creation, including the creator and the created and nature conceals life in itself. When that life in nature develops and becomes focused in the individual then nature has fulfilled itself. The whole destiny and function

of nature is to create the individual who is self-conscious, who knows the pairs of opposites, who knows that he is an entity in himself, conscious and separate.

So life in nature, through its development becomes self-conscious in the awakened concentrated individual. Nature's goal is man's individuality. The individual is a separate being who is self-conscious, who knows that he is different from another, in whom there is the separation of you and I. But individuality is imperfection; it is not an end in itself.[32]

Individuality is the goal of nature but not that of man. Man's problem arises from the fears and loneliness that come with the awareness of separateness that accompanies the beginning of individuality. Eric Fromm, in his masterful work, *The Fear of Freedom*, points out this dialectic nature of the process of growing individuation. On both an ontogenetic and phylogenetic level, man's development is characterised by the growth of the opposing forces of the emergence of individual strength and a sense of self on the one hand, and that of personal loneliness and separation on the other.

Fromm correctly argues that if these opposing forces are kept in balance as the individual develops, then the process of individuation culminates in the healthy, emotionally mature adult capable of handling the responsibility that comes with personal sovereignty. If this growth of the sense of self is hampered and lags behind the evolutionary and thus automatic growth in the sense of separation, then this results in: 'an unbearable feeling of isolation and powerlessness.' This produces psychologically disturbed individuals, unable and unwilling to take up the challenge of free will and who seek psychic mechanisms of escape from that unbearable burden of responsibility.

Fromm points out that in an evolutionary sense:

> ...human existence begins when the lack of fixation of action by instinct exceeds a certain point; when adaptation to nature loses its coercive character; when the way to act is no longer fixed by hereditarily given mechanisms. In

other words, human existence and freedom are from the beginning inseparable.[33]

Fromm interprets the myth of man's expulsion from the Garden of Eden as the point of the beginning of human history. It is the first human choice; the first act of free will. In the Garden there is no separation from nature but there is also no choice, no freedom and no thinking. Eating of the forbidden fruit is symbolic of the knowledge of the duality of good and evil, which is a prerequisite for the ability to choose and decide for oneself; to know right from wrong.

He reinterprets man's disobedience as the beginning of human freedom, the first human act: '...acting against God's orders means freeing himself from the coercion, emerging from the unconscious existence of prehuman life to the level of man.' For reasons that we have already mentioned, religion has emphasised the sinfulness of this act and the suffering supposedly resulting from it, rather than the positive aspect of personal power, freedom and emerging individuality. The negative pole of the dialectic of the process of individuation, namely that of the feelings of aloneness, separation, loneliness and powerlessness are given emphasis over the positive pole of individual strength, creativity and freedom.

'The newly won freedom appears as a curse.'[34]

However, this is not a fixed and definitive point in history. It is rather a slow and gradual evolutionary journey that humanity is just now completing. We are in phase one. We are just beginning to take up the challenge of our freedom. As Fromm emphasises, freedom has a dialectic nature: there is the negative pole of freedom *from*: constraint, coercion, instinct etc. and the positive pole of freedom *to*: choose, decide, act, create and so on.

Freedom *from* does not necessarily guarantee that one will take up freedom *to*. When man emerged from the Garden, he did not immediately become a fully realised or actualised, self-conscious, self-aware, emotionally mature adult. This was merely the beginning of the evolutionary journey of individuation, not its completion.

Mankind, itself, now equipped with the gift of free will and the power of self-determination had to find his own way balancing these dialectic forces of increasing personal strength, power and self-mastery on the one hand, and increasing fear, loneliness and separation on the other. For ultimately, this is the journey. This is the whole meaning and purpose behind the gift of free will; the point of being human.

Freedom necessitates choice and choice necessitates duality. This is the essence of dialectics or dualistic monism. Everything on this plane has positive and negative characteristics. The choice is always between the two, hence the symbology of the Tree of Knowledge of good and evil.

In early man's consciousness, the seat of power was still very much in the subconscious mind. Man was still very connected to the earth, to nature, to the cosmos and to his clan. He did not view himself as a totally separate and distinct individual but rather as a part of a group. He was still very influenced, though not controlled, by subconscious motivation, superstition, instinctive behavioural patterns and identification with primary blood ties.

Because of this sense of connectedness and solidarity, there was security, belonging and a feeling of being a part of, but also a limitation on his development as a self-determining individual. During the ensuing history of humanity, these original primary bonds were progressively weakened and severed. However, even at the time of the Middle Ages, the individual was still very much a part of his social structure; he did not really enjoy meaningful personal freedom. Life was still dominated by customs, rules, obligations and the social mores of the time. The individual still belonged.

> Medieval society did not deprive the individual of his freedom because the individual did not yet exist; man was still related to the world by primary ties. He did not yet conceive of himself as an individual.[35]

As already mentioned, it was not until recent times, beginning with the Renaissance, that the process of individuation reached its climax. We began our discussion with an examination of the sociological, political and economic developments of recent history that have given the individual human freedom from external constraints necessary for the ability to make his or her own decisions. The evolutionary process of individuation automatically propels the individual in the direction of increased freedom from external constraint. It is up to each individual to create the corresponding growth in inner strength and personal power.

As I have outlined, this has not been the case. Because of the suppression of the original fear of loneliness, the individual ventured too far into the belief of his own separation from the source of his being. This resulted in a pool of denied and repressed fear and anxiety. With every increase in historical freedom from constraint, this primary pool was activated.

The individuation process did not follow a balanced and harmonious path: ever-increasing freedom from external constraints was not matched by an increased willingness to explore our inner beings. Rather, as the primary bonds were severed, man felt increasingly alone, isolated, insecure and frightened. Freedom became an unbearable burden that the individual tried to escape from, rather than becoming valued as the precious divine gift that it really was. By the time the individual was beginning to taste real freedom and becoming fully aware of himself as a separate conscious entity, the deep-seated feelings of fear and insecurity were starting to take their toll. Just as the seat of power was moving into the conscious mind, these subconscious forces were assuming ever-greater influence and control.

The most destructive of these influences was the breeding of anxiety and self-doubt. It was to this doubt that the ideologies of Luther and Calvin appealed. These doctrines fed on the feelings of fear, increased the element of doubt and suggested the basic unworthiness, insignificance and powerlessness of man. The only escape from the deep-seated insecurity and anxiety reflected in these doctrines was to take refuge in an unfounded, irrational and compulsive certainty. Far better to have the certainty of man's inherent evilness and separation from God and beg for mercy, than the uncertainty and doubt associated with self-determination.

Rather than taking up the challenge of free will that the process of individuation was offering, and developing the inner personal strength required, humanity moved in the opposite direction. It externalised and personalised the poles of good and evil, aligning itself with the dark forces, throwing away individuality and totally surrendering before a tyrannical, authoritarian image of God that it had created. The way to salvation lay not through the personal effort of self-determination but via a warped and humiliating concept of predestination, in which the individual was totally powerless before an all-powerful God. Man had not only separated himself from God and the divine source of his being, he was now also separating himself from the source of his power.

The overriding belief here is that in the life of man evil is powerful and good is weak. There is the creation of a separate idealised good – God – that is far removed from the practical ever-pervading state of corruption and evil that exists on the planet and in man's heart. Because man believes he is inherently evil at his core he must suppress his inner natural urges. He is taught through these doctrines more than ever before not to trust his inner impulses.

Yet, it is these very inner promptings which give the individual his power. It is these impulses that are the creative urges of the being towards action that help develop natural physical and mental power. The motivating power of the universe within each and every cell of consciousness, from sub-atomic particles up to people, expresses itself through natural spontaneous urges and impulses. This is the divine current or Tao of creation.

Humanity was now being taught by the collective wisdom of society not to trust these spontaneous promptings and thus became divided, separated even from himself. These natural impulses were dammed up, repressed, and denied. While the natural expression of consciousness leans towards growth and fulfilment, these doctrines considered the inner voice to be chaotic, selfish, and destructive, carrying messages from a dark and nefarious subconscious.

The very self came to be suspect and distrusted. Mankind denied the very power of its own will. For decisions are the results of listening to and weighing the consequences of feeling these impulses. Personal impulses are the guidelines for our decisions. Once we become afraid to trust our inner, natural, spontaneous impulses we lose our power to make decisions. We have no rudder; no navigational system. We are disassociated from the source of our own personal power, and we become unable to act!

The natural expression of consciousness is growth towards progressive perfection. Once the thrust of this growth is interfered with, it turns in on itself in a self-destructive and devolutionary process. Nature exhibits this natural tendency towards growth, harmony and development. The unconscious and subconscious realms effortlessly and unerringly express the divine will of creation. The culmination of nature is the self-aware, fully conscious being who can willingly join in this evolutionary journey, consciously aiding and abetting the positive forces of creation. However, conscious cooperation and co-creation necessitate free will, the option of choosing between the forces of light and dark.

But there is no middle ground. There are no grey areas in this choice. We either choose to operate in harmony with the natural order of the universe as motivated by our inner spontaneous impulses or we choose to deny and repress these divine urges, mistaking them for the call of the wild beast that supposedly dwells within. We either trust our inner being or we do not.

We either align ourselves with forces of light, accepting the responsibility of our position of authority and power at the head of the structure of consciousness, taking dominion of life on earth, or we throw away our power and become the unconscious puppets of the forces of fear, anxiety and negativity. We either embrace our divinity or believe in our inherent evilness. We either graciously accept the gift of freedom, making decisions with courage and self-confidence or we give into the debilitating force of self-doubt, commanding the ego to do our job for us because we are too afraid to choose.

We either join with the universe in a holy alliance and joyous dance of co-creativity and oneness or we join forces with our negative ego in an unholy alliance and death march of humiliating and arrogant co-dependency.

We either choose to be motivated out of love or fear.

I originally defined personal sovereignty as the capacity to decide by and for oneself: to rule oneself. We then said that any capacity depends upon both an ability plus a willingness to use that ability. Like so many of these concepts there is a dialectic: the ability is the female pole of potential; it is receptive, spatial, the yin principle. The willingness is the male pole of action; it is the creative, the temporal, the yang. For freedom to give birth to power both poles must unite.

Power is the ability to act. Free will is the exercise of choice; to choose is to make a decision and once a decision has been made it is necessary to act. Decision without action is stillborn and leads to the debilitating force of doubt.

Reflection, deliberation, decision, action! This is the process of personal sovereignty. This is the function of the power of will. For it is will that is the ruling principle; it is will that is the function of character. We have spoken at great length of the hierarchic order that must exist within any structure for peace and harmony to prevail. We have also defined evil as that state of dysfunction that inevitably comes about when control and authority are not exercised by the light principle. The dark principle cannot be the ruling one. We have further explained how the ego, which is of the dark principle came to hold power because of our unwillingness to take control.

It is the power of will that needs to be the ruler in the corporate structure of consciousness. The power of will is not to be confused with the more common term 'willpower'. 'Willpower' is what we use when we wish to repress, suppress or deny our inner urges and impulses. This is a negative and destructive force. On the other hand, will is the power of motivation. It is that ability to decide and then execute that decision through necessary action. Strong will means strong character – weak will indicates a weak character. Character is the antithesis of the negative ego!

If intuitive awareness is the correct navigational system for the fully conscious individual and love is the correct emotive current, then will is the correct seat of power. For it is with our wills that we create our reality. A person of strong will, of strong character holds to their values and does what is right and what the situation demands. A person of weak character will always find opportunity to excuse and justify the easy option or just not choose at all. The power of positive thinking, visualisation, affirmation programming and any other manifestation technique require concentration, focus and a strong will.

A self-reliant individual, capable of making their own decisions and then carrying them out, has a strong will. A weak-willed individual is easily led and influenced and has great difficulty in choosing by and for themselves. They will always need another to bolster their decision-making – to tell them what to do. In our discussion of the multi-dimensions of God, we discovered that before and beyond the manifested universe there was ideation, or intention. The creation of reality begins with intention. Before the physical comes the potential: the idea, the thought and the blueprint. Everything starts as a plan and then finds its way into actuality. But before the potential comes the inspiration, the intention, the explosion of love, and the desire for expression.

It is this intention that is will. The primary motivating force in the universe is the original explosion of divine love seeking expression in creation. Before all else this was. This is the intention of the supreme and infinite being that is beyond all of creation but expresses itself in creation as the divine will, which is the Way, the Tao.

So too, we as mirrors of God, as mini sparks of divine consciousness, as co-creators of our own reality begin with the intention of what we want. This original motivating force then expresses itself as our will. A strong intention begets a strong will and manifests a strong creation in personal life. A weak intention and will result in a mediocre existence.

Where there is a will, there is a way!

Will is the power of creation. A successful person has strong intentions and a strong will. This is why the whole intention of nature is to create the conscious individual so that it can be given this immense gift of free will. The whole thrust of the evolution of consciousness is the development of will. Every spark of consciousness in the lower unconscious and subconscious realms is seeking to become human so that it too will have the conscious ability and will to create its own reality, and to determine its own destiny. For it is through making decisions and choices, holding beliefs and attitudes, and registering the thoughts and feelings of our natural, spontaneous impulses that we consciously create our own reality.

Willingness is the function of will.

We are learning to become gods. We are learning to consciously create success. The reason there is now this chorus singing the praises of man's inherent power and potential for creativity is that he has now come of age. The process of individuation may have begun with the mythological representation of the eating of the forbidden fruit, but it certainly did not stop there. We have been trying to get it right ever since.

We have been balancing the dialectic forces of an increasing sense of self-power and self-worth as opposed to an increasing feeling of fear and self-doubt, down through the ages. There have been many failures but there have also been many glorious successes. We did run from the fear of freedom; we did feel isolated, vulnerable, insignificant and powerless; we did not trust ourselves, consequently giving into doubt, and we did give away our power to the ego.

But we have also arrived at the point of spiritual maturity where we are ready to take that power back. Maybe not as a species, but definitely as rare and courageous individuals. There are those fully realised, aware human beings who are waking up to and exercising their personal sovereignty, who are willing to take back their power from their egos and exercise conscious dominion of the earth and their personal lives.

The way is always spearheaded by the adventurous few. Throughout history, significant change has always been the result of those few with the vision and the intention, the courage and the will to bring the new into existence. There have always been the way-showers, the map-makers, the visionaries, and the prophets; the radical few who have dared to go beyond the conventional wisdom and limited beliefs of mass consciousness.

It was not that long ago that man believed the earth was flat, that it was the centre of the universe, that the sun revolved around the earth and that man was the only intelligent being in that universe. We now look at those childish beliefs in disbelief. Yet are we now not captivated by the same limited folly? It is always up to the courageous individual to take that first necessary step. It is through the decisions of a few that development is made.

> Decisions are not made by races, cultures or nations, unless they are first made by individuals. The most destructive decision that an individual can make is to give away his or her decision-making authority. The decision that lies at the source of human history is the decision through which you have given away your power to the very force you came here to regulate.
>
> Human history has been the process of increasing decision-making responsibility on the part of the individual. It is the story of declining aristocracies and the diminishing

power of elites. As far back as your records go, they document the steady growth of individual rights and individual responsibility.[36]

Pre-set programmes ensure that the union of sperm and ovum develop into an embryo, that the infant develops into the, at least, biologically mature adult human being. These miracles of creation occur because of the unconscious and subconscious impulses that motivate growth. These forces are not evil; they are obedient to the will of God.

So too, certain pre-set programmes have brought us this far in the evolutionary journey of individuation. We may not have been willing to cooperate with this movement to the best of our ability, but we have also been unable to impede its inevitable outcome. The child may wish to stay young forever, like Peter Pan, and might even instruct the body not to grow up, but the forces of biology take no notice.

Similarly, humanity can run from the responsibility of free will, and can refuse to grow to spiritual maturity, but the process of individuation continues regardless, for those courageous few who are willing to answer the call.

In the end it is only we who suffer. We have the personal choice of cooperation, of being in harmony with the divine order of the universe. We can choose to enjoy the exhilaration of exercising the power of our will, of consciously creating success, and of having the help and friendship of a positive ego. We can choose a healthy subconscious mind and an attuned autonomic nervous system. We can align ourselves with the divine will, feeling a part of all that is, being motivated by the current of divine love and having a thoroughly good time creating our own personal version of heaven on earth. We can return to the Garden!

Or we can resist the process, turning control over to the negative ego which becomes myopic, destructive, self-centred and evil creating only chaos in our lives. We can choose to be separated and thus live in fear, isolation and paranoia watching our personal world fall increasingly apart, making our life a hell on earth. The choice is ours. The choice is individual. The choice is personal.

The ultimate beauty of the gift of free will is precisely just that. We do all create our own reality. Everybody's life is as different as our faces and personalities. No two people are alike. Every face, every physical body, every life, every heart, every mind, and every soul is unique. This is why if ten people impart a report about an event they will all be different. We each funnel our perceptions of reality through the filtering system of our own inner selves. And these filters are not just psychological. Neurologically, we perceive reality differently according to the inner mental states we have created over time according to our background and upbringing.

Ultimately, there is no such thing as external objective reality. It is a totally personal construct. It is the outer projection of inner states of being. What you are, you experience. Being precedes doing. Your life is a reflection of what you believe to be true. It is that simple. It is the gift of free will.

The gift means we are free to create whatever we choose. Far better to choose that which is fun, productive and enjoyable, joining with the all-powerful forces of creation, than to go it alone.

Part II: THE CONSPIRACY OF REPRESSION

Eight: Unnatural Childbirth

> *... he has moved from a soft, warm, dark, quiet and totally nourishing place to a harsh sensory overload. He is physically abused, violated in a wide variety of ways, subjected to specific physical pain and insult, all of which could still be overcome, but he is then isolated from his mother.*
>
> Janov

In Part I we examined the predicament of man from a cosmological and phylogenetic point of view, that is we looked at it from the perspective of humanity as a whole and the evolution of consciousness in general. It is too easy to excuse ourselves as individuals and abrogate our own personal responsibility, through adhering to stories handed down by mythology and religion, or by simply believing that human nature is inherently evil. We emphasised that this was merely a part of the neurotic collective process of denial and rationalisation.

Moreover, we discovered that the process of creation is continuous, that life is forever evolving towards progressive perfection and that eternity guarantees that this is a state towards which we constantly aspire but never attain.

Creation *is*. The fall must be re-enacted daily by each cell of human consciousness. It is not an event or a specific act that occurred in prehistory, in the past. We are not being punished by a vengeful God for something that our forebears did once upon a time.

No, the fall is a characteristic of disorder within the system that we create on a daily basis. It has become encoded within our traditions, our culture, our commonly held beliefs, our education, our technology and just about every aspect of our daily lives. It has become a part of us. It is passed on from generation to generation, from individual to individual, from father to son and from mother to daughter.

In Part II, we will examine the ways and means by which this error and disorder is transmitted ontogenetically, that is from the individual point of view. How is it that we all, as individual units or cells of human consciousness, make the same mistake or fall for the same lie? How is this disease transmitted and what makes us as individuals susceptible and vulnerable to its attacks? For just as the beginning of a return to health is correctly diagnosing the disease, and the beginning of finding a solution is the correct definition of the problem, so too, we must correctly ascertain the mechanics by which this error is perpetuated if we would wish to eradicate its pernicious hold on our psyche.

We will discover that there are very exact and precise ways in which this lie has been handed down and protected throughout the ages by an all-pervasive conspiracy that suppresses the truth of the divinity of our natural being. I have called this the conspiracy of repression. There are many conspiracies and many conspiracy theories that abound, and there is much truth and much hysteria in all of them. However, beyond the specifics of any of these individual theories, lies a fundamental and deep-seated truth in humanity's history and that is an overarching repression of all that would lead us to the discovery of our inherent divinity and the power within. For we are easier to control, and it is easier to maintain an orderly society (or so the mainstream story goes), if individuality is suppressed.

Generally speaking, we fear that which is too different. We all want to be 'normal', whatever that means. If anyone is too outrageous or exhibits too strong individual idiosyncrasies or thinks too radically, then that person's sanity is immediately suspect. We are extremely intolerant of change, of the unusual, of the new (until it becomes fashionable), or of anything we do not understand. What we do not understand we fear; and what we fear we attack! Fear, repression, suppression, conformity, normalcy, and the *status quo* – these are the forces that rule our lives and inhibit our individuality.

Everything tells us to be normal and to fit in. Parents, teachers, the education system, peer pressure, society, the bureaucracy, the government, religion, mythology, psychology, and the negative ego – all conspire to make us afraid of humiliation, of being different, of not being accepted or loved, of being wrong, of being rejected. All play on that original and fundamental fear of being alone, and of being abandoned.

To be different incurs the immediate danger of being ostracised, of being excluded, and of being the outsider: a fear that most of us are not prepared to risk in the journey of self-discovery and self-expression. We would rather be accepted than to find out who we really are. We would rather fit in than risk the humiliation of raising our inner true voice.

Because we do not trust ourselves and because we have no faith in our own inner navigational system, because we have turned away from that inner voice, and because we have no self-confidence, we turn for reassurance and guidance from without. We place more credence in what others say; we place more emphasis on what others think than what we ourselves feel within. We have traded individual truth for conformity. We have abandoned our power of self-determination and allowed the influence of others to become the dominant force in our lives.

Each time we doubt ourselves, we turn to another for outside validation and whether that other be another person, an ideology, a tradition, a religion, a belief system or any other culturally encoded convention, it ultimately robs the individual of his or her own ability and willingness to decide by and for oneself. Listening to an external source of influence blocks the perception and reception of the divine intelligence within that should be the only necessary guidance for making correct decisions.

Probably more than anything else, we are taught from a very early age not to think independently, not to think for ourselves, and not to think originally. On the contrary, we are taught to learn, to repeat, to mimic, and to do what we are told. Society attempts to control a supposed anti-social and disruptive humanity, and so it does not encourage individual self-expression. Society has as its goal the suppression of individuality, not the enhancement of personal power and growth.

Thus, we will explore each of these areas of suppression and discover just how the conspiracy of repression is culturally encoded into the very fabric of our lives. We will see how this is passed down from one generation to the next and how it is now reaching its final climax.

For as this is the plane of duality and as everything has a positive and a negative pole to enable the creative current to flow, the dialectic process of individuation is reaching its climax in both its aspects. The yang principle is expanding into the peak of the evolution of individual consciousness on this planet with the awakening of the fully conscious self-aware individual. The yin principle is contracting into the development of some of the most barbaric and repressive terrorist regimes the world has ever seen. It is the interplay between these two opposing, yet dialectically unified forces that will make the ensuing years both fascinating and dangerous for both humanity and the planet.

For as always, those who would ride the cosmic wave into the new age of the third millennium must pay particular attention to these two competing forces and by reclaiming their personal sovereignty, decide which one they will align with. For these fear-centred forces that have perpetuated this conspiracy down through the ages must now stand aside and allow the light of truth to shine on man's innate divinity and primal spirit.

All of the recent scientific, ecological, sociological, political, economic and spiritual discoveries lead us to the one conclusion: our oneness with our fellow man and our oneness with the earth. We are also realising that time is running out for our wayward ways and that we must immediately take our rightful place as the head of this all-too precious planet we call home and exercise our dominion, rather than our domination over it.

Historically speaking, the interplay between these two opposing forces of the quest for individual freedom on the one hand and the need to fit into society on the other occurs most in early childhood. It is here that the real damage is done. It is here that the foundations are laid for the grand deception: the lie that is to rule our lives. It is here that the original corruption takes place and the primal divine spirit of love is replaced by the negative ego of fear, anxiety and separatism.

Just as we discovered a natural structure of consciousness, so there is also a natural structure of knowledge that the infant builds as it develops. The neonate is driven through its inner impulses to interact with the outer world and form an inner picture of that world that makes sense to it.

Jean Piaget, a Swiss philosopher and psychologist who developed a comprehensive theory of human intelligence, discovered that this structure evolves through clearly distinct stages, not unlike the aforementioned stages of consciousness. Each stage is characterised by different ways of processing information, with new neurological brain growth corresponding to outer physiological development. This is activated by pre-determined genetic programmes at specific times. Piaget argued that intelligence in the child is not a given, fixed at birth, but develops with biological maturation and specific interaction with the child's outer environment.

Joseph Chilton-Pearce, an American author who wrote about human development but more particularly child development, concluded that this is all a part of nature's genetic coding, or a biological plan for the natural and harmonious growth of intelligence in the human infant. Chilton-Pearce further argues that this genetic coding is: 'ignored, damaged and even destroyed' by the conspiracy of repression. The child naturally tries to construct a picture or structure of knowledge of the external world as it actually is, but the forces of fear 'inflict an anxiety-conditioned view of the world. Childhood is a battleground between the biological plan's intent, which drives the child from within and our anxious intentions pressing the child from without.'[37]

Just as the physical development of the body is motivated by pre-set programmes and follows a predetermined path, motivated and monitored by the autonomic nervous system, likewise this biological plan is regulated and controlled by certain pre-set programmes that are beyond conscious control. To ensure the successful development of the infant we must acknowledge and cooperate with that biological plan. It is our refusal to work with this plan that is the cause of the problem. As Chilton-Pearce points out, nature has been working on this plan for over three billion years in genetic code experimentation. Each and every human neonate has the advantage of this three billion-year-old experiment encoded into its brain. Through the old reptilian and mammalian brains we inherit all the gains of the past. In the new brain, or neocortex, we are given all the challenges of the future.

In Part I we discovered that mankind's problems with sovereignty and free will sprang from the misunderstanding of being a 'holon' in the overall web of life on planet earth. Chilton-Pearce concludes that man's disruption of the biological plan similarly springs from a misunderstanding of the holographic nature of the brain. 'Every single cell of the brain reflects or encompasses the workings of the total brain. The brain itself may be a hologram of the entire planet earth.'[38]

To activate the hologram of the brain, the brain must be exposed to interaction with the larger hologram of the earth. Each specific species has certain holographic pre-set programmes that are activated at birth and which allow it to function successfully on the planet. The larger the holographic representation within the individual brain, the longer the process of activation. This explains the slow maturation process for the human infant as it has the most complex holographic insert of any species. Thus, the human infant is more helpless for a longer period of time than any other species and is correspondingly more dependent upon its parents.

The idea of the conspiracy of repression argues that this period of prolonged helplessness is necessary in order to eradicate the primary, primitive urges and successfully replace them with the secondary, acceptable social ones. To the contrary, what actually happens is that the old brain's holographic content is activated not by pre-set programmes as in the case of the lower animals, but rather by the neocortex. The new brain is not pre-programed but is the seat of the programmer: the conscious mind that is able to deal with new situations, compute, make decisions and create the future. The old brain is the seat of the subconscious and unconscious instinctive behaviour, while the new brain allows for individual creativity and the development of personality.

What is essential to realise is that this activation of the hologram requires interaction with the world. In the case of lower animals, this interaction results in the activation of instinctive pre-set patterns that determine behaviour. In the case of the human with a neocortex, this results in the building of the structure of knowledge about how the world works which does not dictate but allows and facilitates creativity and choice.

The individual develops conscious control and volition over the most appropriate behavioural response. This structure of knowledge must be activated by muscular body movements through interaction with the outside world. The child is impelled to move and explore by its inner natural impulses, interacting with whatever it can get its hands on. Limiting this native curiosity and sense of exploration and adventure inhibits the natural growth of intelligence.

We return to the concept of intention. The child is motivated by intention long before it executes an action. It is this intent that carries the inner impulse to outer action. Intent is not instinct, but a conscious will to perform. Intent is that willingness that comes before an ability is mastered. Intent is the force that ensures eventual mastery, for the child will repeat an action over and over until it gets it right. A young child never gives up or gives in.

This force of intent that propels the impulse of the infant to interact with the world is a part of the three billion-year-old biological plan for the growth of intelligence. For without that interaction there can be no real intelligence. The greater and more extensive this interaction with the outside world, the vaster the body of knowledge the infant builds on the inside. 'Development is the interaction of the intent within and the content without.'[39]

Consciousness has developed a masterful biological plan over billions of years to ensure the maximum survival and safety of the newborn in the myriad species including man. In an individual animal species this results in a specific set of behavioural patterns that are most suited to the survival of that particular species: it results in a closed, definite and limited body of knowledge and instinctive behavioural patterns that motivate, regulate and control that animal. In a human being, this results in an open, indefinite and unlimited structure of knowledge that must be activated and harnessed by the higher conscious mind to facilitate the most appropriate choice as to behaviour and response in any given situation.

This is the neurology of free will. We have at our disposal all of the infinite body of knowledge gathered by evolving consciousness on the planet over billions of years encoded into the old brain, combined with the extremely fast and sophisticated computing and problem-solving software of the new brain, or higher conscious mind. In computer parlance, an animal has a specific software application that is automatically activated at conception. It must operate according to that particular software application. The human infant, on the other hand, has all of these potential applications loaded into the memory banks of the old brain, plus the new operating system of the neocortex. It is from this infinite potential that freedom of choice arises.

> The computer-brain system develops volitional control over the knowledge structured, develops the ability to decide freely between alternatives for interaction, develops the ability to interact creatively with the world through the structure of knowledge built up about that world.[40]

Thus, just as we discovered a neat and orderly hierarchic structure of consciousness, there is also a neat and orderly pattern or blueprint for the structuring of knowledge in the infant to ensure maximum survival and the operation of free will. Intent creates impulses that impel the infant into muscular interaction with the external environment. This activates the pre-set programmes of the old brain or subconscious mind and brings into play the new computing ability of the neocortex to record data concerning external reality. Physical contact results in learning and the building of the structure of knowledge about how the world works, or more specifically, about how life on planet earth works. In this way the individual mind-brain of the infant as a hologram of life on earth is activated.

However, this hologram is not all activated at once, for this would lead to overload and confusion. The neonate's consciousness is definitely not ready nor capable of creating an intelligent, mature picture of life on earth. It must first ensure its own personal survival and growth to maturity before it can direct its attention to other things. The larger and more comprehensive the eventual holographic picture, the longer the activation process. Obviously, the more sophisticated the software the longer it takes to write the programme. Most animal offspring are autonomous and physically independent almost immediately after birth. Their hologram is instantly ready for imaging reality and regulating physical survival as opposed to the human infant who is totally helpless and dependent upon parental support for quite some time.

Here too, we find that consciousness, through this biological plan, has developed a neat and orderly method for the gradual and secure unfolding of this activation process. Chilton-Pearce demonstrates that intelligence grows naturally and gradually, progressing from the simple to the complex, from the concrete to the abstract, from the specific to the general. As Piaget discovered, this growth occurs in four discrete, clearly defined, neurological stages. The child's brain actually goes through specific neurological transitions that allow it to process information or data in increasingly more sophisticated ways. These neurological shifts are unconsciously activated by the pre-set programming of the genetic structure in an orderly sequence and at specific times that correlate to external physical development.

In other words, as the infant's external world expands, and as the child interacts with a broader cross-section of the world at large, its inner processing ability also expands. The child's computational abilities increase. The mind-brain grows biologically and neurologically to facilitate increased learning and to structure a larger, more complete picture of the world. Recent discoveries in neuroplasticity verify this process.

Chilton-Pearce takes this a step further, illustrating how nature also cares for the emotional development of the infant by ensuring a gradual process of growth from one safe haven to another. He calls these safety zones a 'matrix'. Life is a gradual progression from specific to ever more expansive matrices: from the female egg, to the womb, to the mother, to the family, to the earth, to nature, to the self, to God. Within each matrix there is the source of life, the possibility for growth, and the necessary nutrients and challenges for safe exploration and growth to take place. As noted, life is a dialectic balancing act between the expansive force of love or curiosity, adventure, fun, exploration and self-expression and the contracting force of fear, safety and security. We all perform this delicate dance daily.

Life is the expression of love reaching out to know itself more fully through the evolutionary process of creation. Intelligence is always moving from the safety of the known to the uncertainly of the unknown.

Within each of these matrices or safe havens the infant goes through this dialectic of growth. First is the process of knowing, exploring, conquering and then becoming familiar with stimuli. Then follows the feeling of safety and security that comes from forming bonds with the known. However, the onward thrust and divine intent of creation operate through the individual to create the personal intent or impulse to move on. The third stage is the leaving of the current matrix of the nest, the womb, the known to explore the next matrix of the unknown and a new, higher octave of learning.

All organic, natural, evolutionary development goes through this cyclic process to create an upward spiral of growth. It is important to realise that movement into the new or unknown is only made with the security and safety net of the old familiar matrix underneath one. The impulses of nature never propel an individual beyond that which is a potentially safe and thoroughly prepared transition.

The first safe haven is obviously the womb and the second is the mother. This transition from first to second matrix is the most significant event in the life of any individual human being. It is the birth process, the beginning of life on earth as a separate, distinct conscious being. Although the neonate is not completely autonomous, it is biologically independent. From the moment the umbilical cord is cut, the two life forms are biologically separate, the infant is on its own, even though the infant is still closely psychically connected to the mother for an extended period now being called the fourth trimester.

We will also contend that this is also probably the most destructive event in the life of the individual human, for humanity has managed to subvert nearly all of the safeguards that nature has created over billions of years to ensure maximum well-being, safety and survival in this essential transition. For it is at the moment of birth, more than any other, that we culturally encode the fall by disregarding the biological encoding for the birth process that nature has handed down.

Both mother and infant are genetically equipped and prepared for the successful birth of the child. When the neonate decides it is ready to leave the safety of the womb, it triggers hormones that activate the contractions for the birth process. Experiments with monkeys given the benefits of modern hospital birthing techniques produce similar results to that found in human infants. The newborn chimps could not get their breath, had to be artificially resuscitated and were totally helpless after birth. They could not cling to their mothers, had no agility and suffered impaired motor skills and coordination compared to normal, naturally born chimps.

Moreover, the mothers were also dazed by the drugs. Their labour was longer and they were less able to assist and nurture their offspring. Autopsies performed on the young chimps found brain lesions typical of oxygen deficiency. Similar autopsies performed on human infants that had died following severe birth trauma also exhibited these same lesions even if the death occurred several years later. The brain damage was permanent.

Although, many of the following procedures, thankfully, no longer apply, over the last 50 to 100 years, much damage has been done by classical hospital birth processes. We have now arrived at a balance between modern medicine and traditional midwifery that avoids much of the psychic damage but protects the physical safety of mother and child. Many of these procedures are also culturally specific with many non-western and ethnic societies having more natural births. While the following represents the extreme example, it is important to understand the implications for child development caused by an unnatural birth.

At every step of the birthing process, modern man interferes with the natural biological plan for an easy, effortless, joyous celebration of life, turning it into a severely traumatic experience for both mother and child. Starting from the very beginning, the mother is filled with anxiety and dread from a tender age. The traditional view of childbirth in this society is anything but easy and joyous. The woman is made to feel helpless and inferior, dependent upon the doctor and modern medicine. She is rendered incapable from the moment of conception. As the birth approaches, it is complicated by the fact that once labour begins she has to rush to the hospital. This immediately creates stress, panic, fear and anxiety lest she does not make it on time.

The natural birth rhythm is delayed while the mother gets herself to hospital and then waits for the appropriate time and place to go into labour. In the meantime, the neonate is on hold, producing excessive adrenal steroids to compensate for the interruption, fear and panic that is being generated around it. The mother may then be given some form of premedication which also immediately interferes with the rhythmic natural movements of the uterus, minimising the contractions and prolonging delivery. The drugs also find their way into the infant through the placenta causing further complications.

The mother is forced to lie down on the operating table, which inhibits muscular coordination and psychologically renders her helpless. The doctor can now take charge, using various gadgets to deliver the by-now stalled birth. An epidural will sedate both mother and child so that forceps will be required to deliver the child. The mother may even need to be cut to allow the passage of the child which eventually is dragged into the world, drugged, dazed, stressed and exhausted by this unnatural childbirth.

The child now enters the world via a noisy, brilliantly lit, sterile, clinical operating theatre where it meets the white-masked inhabitants of this planet Earth, its new home. The umbilical cord is next cut prematurely and the baby is taken away from its mother, who would have been its point of reference in its new matrix.

Lest it believe that at the end of this extraordinary ordeal it is to be reunited with the safe haven of its mother, it is now bundled off to the nursery to allow its mother some rest. The final and most damaging blow of all is this separation from the safety and security of its second matrix. Is it any wonder that the child sinks into a catatonic state from which it does not emerge for the next eight to ten weeks? If the truth be known, it never really emerges. The emotional, psychological, neurological and spiritual damage remain for life. In this way, more than any other, the emotional plague of the belief in man's separateness from God and life is recreated with every unnatural birth.

Through being separated from its mother, which is its entire world, the baby is separated from security, from safety, and from the known; it has no point of reference to activate the growth of intelligence. To make matters worse it is deprived of both physical touch and movement, which constitute the sensory stimulation required to activate the hologram. The sensory touch and recognition of the mother are required to activate the bonding process to matrix two. Rather than being the safe, positive, learning experience intended, entry into the world becomes a negative, fearful, and painful experience that results in confusion and anxiety.

The biological plan for natural childbirth has been aborted and the intended intellectual growth and development of the structure of knowledge severely retarded. The child is left alone, feeling bewildered, confused, anxious, abandoned, isolated, powerless and insignificant. The seeds of self-doubt and self-denial have been sown.

The biological plan calls for a neat and timely unfolding and activation of definite pre-set programmes at specific times. This timed unfolding moves along with or without the conscious participation of the infant. Modern birthing practices result in inevitable deficiencies in the growth of intelligence and in the onset of psychological dysfunction. The system is forever caught in the past, trying to catch and make up for these initial deficiencies. Part of the mind is locked back there trying to set things right while another part must deal with present reality. The system gets further and further behind as it progresses. With each transition to a new matrix, the gap between the intent of the biological plan and the actual content of intelligence widens. We become increasingly more dysfunctional.

NINE: THE MECHANICS OF REPRESSION

> *...repression effectively produces two selves at war with each other: the real self, loaded with needs and pain, and the unreal self, the self out of touch with the other self that was still able to deal with the outside world. The function of the unreal self is to keep the real self from showing its face.*
>
> Janov

The human brain is the most sophisticated computer that we could possibly imagine. If we tried to duplicate its computing ability, it would take building upon building of the most advanced computers we have developed and still we could not come close. The brain contains upwards of ten billion neurons, each composed of twenty million complex molecules. Each of these individual cells reaches out and is connected along pathways to up to half a million other cells. In terms of an information exchange system, the possibilities are infinite and open-ended. It is estimated that we use between ten and fifteen per cent of our brain's computing ability.

The cells do not connect directly but meet at junction points called synapses. These synapses have the function of directing the flow of data so that only appropriate information is channelled to the correct neuron. Different parts of the brain specialise in processing different types of information. In our earlier analogy of the corporate structure of consciousness, we likened the ego to the messenger boy whose task it was to gather data concerning the outside world via the use of the senses and deliver that data to the chief executive officer of conscious awareness. All of this sensory information passes through the reticular formation, which is a small area in the midbrain, and directs it to that area of the brain that specialises in that information. The reticular formation is also a general on/off switch for consciousness including the function of sleep.

The growth of intelligence or learning is a system of information patterning. As sensory data comes in, millions upon millions of neurons are continuously processing and firing between each other, filing the information according to already existing patterns. There must be points of similarity between the newly incoming data and previously held information for learning to occur. If there are no points of reference or similarity, the reticular formation does not know where to channel the information to and the synapses will not allow it to pass onto the neuron. In other words, there must be enough similarity for recognition to occur and thus enable processing.

Intelligence is the transformation of percept to concept. The senses perceive the outer world; the ego delivers that perception to the reticular formation which passes it onto the higher mind. The conscious mind then processes the data of that perception creating an inner mental picture or understanding of the information. It creates a concept. All new incoming information is interpreted against the backdrop of existing concepts.

Obviously, the larger the individual brain's repertoire of concepts the greater the potential for learning and the growth of intelligence. As we grow we expand our ability to conceptualise and to think. The brain is constantly communicating between its internal departments, scanning for points of similarity to existing concepts, whenever new or strange information comes in. This is how the brain works and develops: it is a process of continually adding the unknown to the known.

To kick-start the whole process of learning, certain pre-set programmes are already in existence through the genetic informational units of the DNA/RNA structure. This is why in the animal kingdom, the newborn knows instinctively and immediately what to do. Similarly, the neonate knows to suck when the nipple is placed in its mouth. It is a preprogramed biological response.

In healthy learning, pathways are established between neurons processing similar information. As these pathways are used repeatedly tracks are formed – the connections become stronger, more durable, smoother and faster. Patterns of connection are established in the brain and information exchange is facilitated. The first time the infant tries to do something it is awkward and usually fails. Intent precedes ability.

However, with repetition, the synaptic pathways are formed and learning becomes more fluid, proficient and successful. Eventually, the dance of synergy takes over and mastery is achieved. Intelligence is the ability to interact successfully with one's environment in the present. The growth of intelligence is the ability to process more and more sensory information producing ever clearer and more expanded concepts of how the world works and to successfully integrate into that world.

This growth of intelligence depends upon two essential prerequisites, either of which, if lacking, will retard growth and development. The first are the points of similarity and the second is a feeling of safety and security. If there is any perceived threat to survival, then that information or danger must take precedence. Anxiety cripples learning. The organism will naturally seek to deal with fear before it can concentrate on processing less urgent data.

Unnatural childbirth disturbs both of these necessary preconditions. In the biological plan, the neonate should move directly from the womb to the mother's belly and breast with no interruption. It still exists within the same energy field – there is no sense of separation, no insecurity and no perceived danger.

Moreover, there are numerous points of reference: the mother's smell, taste, voice, touch and now the new and added sense of sight. The eyes of the newborn are locked on the mother's face and eyes while it processes this new incoming data. The mother massages the vernix caseosa (a waxy or cheese-like white substance coating the newborn's skin) into the skin which nourishes the baby's body, activates the reticular formation and creates the necessary feeling of bonding and security.

It is essential to grasp the significance of this point. For all subsequent learning on the planet will be influenced by this moment of birth. The first hour of life on the outside is the single greatest determinant of the quality of life of the individual for the rest of that life on earth. Natural childbirth is not some sentimental alternative fantasy. The neonate neurologically needs these points of reference and this bonded security if intelligence is to be correctly activated. This is precisely why extreme hospital birthing techniques deliver babies that do not activate for two to three months after birth and have severe learning difficulties and adjustment dysfunction for life.

There must be a balance between the known and the unknown otherwise sensory overload sets in, causing confusion and neurological breakdown. If the child enters a hostile, bewildering, brightly lit world, is immediately separated from mother, spanked, bathed by strange hands, clothed and taken off to a nursery, it is not only alone, isolated, afraid, and anxious, it also has no points of reference with which to process incoming data. The reticular formation has not been activated correctly and it is thrown into survival not learning.

Rather than enjoying a pleasurable entry into the world so that its initial learning experience is fun and rewarding, it is taught from the moment of birth that life on the outside is cruel, harsh and painful. This is the world it is born into on the outside and this will be the worldview it creates on the inside: the world is a scary place.

In the biological plan, breastfeeding releases specific hormones that ease any stress caused by the birth and cement the emotional bonding between mother and child. Only at this stage is the placenta cut, after there has been sufficient time for the neonate to successfully start breathing of its own accord. There is no asphyxiation with no resultant brain damage. The birth process is complete, with the infant moving successfully from the security of the womb, through the stress of birth, into the insecurity of the unknown, and then onto the comfort and reassurance provided by its mother, and finally to a state of relaxation and enjoyment in the security of matrix two.

A pattern of learning, growth and development has been established on a neurological level that is successful, rewarding and fun. The inner informational patterning creates templates or concepts that will affect all future learning. This pattern is reinforced in the following months. Mother and child stay together during the day and sleep together at night. Physical contact and bonding are continuous and unbroken. The child is given a lot of tactile sensation to activate the reticular formation, is exposed to constant motor stimulation to activate muscular movement and control, and feeds on demand setting its own pattern according to its own inner impulses.

The mother responds psychically to the inner intent of the child anticipating and responding prior to its outward manifestation. In other words, the two exist within a continuum of being, of harmony, of synergy and of love. The child is empowered, for it perceives the mother and the world 'out there' as an extension of itself. As the child moves out to touch the world, the world responds.

There is no sense of separation.

On the other hand, unnatural childbirth does everything possible to interfere with the wisdom of nature, resulting in impaired learning ability and defective and dysfunctional growth of intelligence. From the very beginning, the brain development of the embryo and eventual learning ability of the infant are affected by the environment of the mother and her psychological state of being. The mother's state of happiness and wellbeing is reflected in her energy levels, hormonal activity and immune system. All of these then directly affect the foetus even though it may not become apparent until much later on in life. There is now irrefutable evidence linking the consumption of alcohol and drugs (even prescription ones) during pregnancy to later learning difficulties of the child.

Stress hormones in the mother may even trigger the onset of the birth process before the child is ready. Anaesthetics render the mother incapable of helping the foetus through the canal with the result that the birth is often long, hard and painful. The anaesthetic also drugs the foetus making it excessively lethargic, passive and sluggish just when it needs total awareness, attention and concentration. The ensuing forced delivery is painful for the foetus as are all subsequent aspects of the hospital birth. The infant is born crying in a highly agitated, stressed and anxious condition which is not relieved by proximity to its mother but is reinforced by its continued state of separation over the following months. The crying is not natural as has heretofore been believed, but is the inevitable consequence of an abnormal, unnatural birthing process that results in trauma and pain. The stress is never discharged but rather continues to gain momentum as the fear of abandonment becomes a permanent reality.

The infant is left abandoned for long periods of time in the crib, is only held occasionally, has to sleep alone, and is fed according to an artificial and academic, externally imposed schedule that has nothing to do with its innate natural impulses. Its every natural biological impulse is met with denial and frustration. The reticular formation is not adequately activated because of the lack of tactile stimulation, sensory motor skills are not activated because the infant is left to lie still in the crib for extended periods of time, often tightly clothed so it cannot move, and emotional bonding definitely cannot be completed. The neonate goes into a deep state of shock and semi-unconsciousness.

Even when it finally recovers from this birth trauma and regains full consciousness two to three months later, it still suffers from the lack of sensory stimulation. The brain quickly processes the incoming data, yet finds insufficient points of reference to adequately facilitate optimum growth of intelligence. Because of insufficient stimulation and information, the processing ability of the brain idles and stagnates. Synaptic pathways are not developed.

A template or prototype of learning is put into place in the emerging neurological structure of knowledge. The birth trauma creates certain neural pathways that are later reinforced by repeated experiences of emotional deprivation. The birth event is mirrored inwardly by the corresponding concept that then dictates a pattern of all subsequent learning.

A pattern of behaviour or personality type is born out of the birth trauma. The neonate learns how life works and how to respond. Certain beliefs and concepts are put into place and these become the determinant of future character. The nature of the birth creates a behavioural response pattern that is the basis for the development of personality.

For example, if one has been drugged at birth and unable to muster the necessary force of will to move through the canal on one's own momentum, one will probably develop a general passivity and sense of resignation to life in general. One will be unable to adequately deal with difficulty and problems in later life but will be prone to defeatism, despair and despondency. There may be a general lack of energy, vitality, enthusiasm and spirit or *joie de vivre*.

If the canal seized up because of fear or drugs, causing it to be particularly hard and unyielding, then this may be the model one adopts for life. One may feel that life is hard, that one never gets any help, or that one's mother is incapable of giving love, support and nurturing. If one suffered oxygen deprivation during or immediately after birth, one may later respond to trauma in life with respiratory problems: asthma, shortness of breath, bronchitis, etc. One may develop a pattern of shallow breathing that never gives one enough oxygen.

If one's mother was excessively fearful of the birth process, this fear may be communicated to the foetus who will later develop an inordinate fear of life, becoming timid, afraid of change and new situations. If the foetus is artificially held back for some reason, say awaiting the arrival of the doctor, then the child may develop a sense of futility and pointlessness in life because its initial attempts to exert its will were frustrated and futile.

These are not simply Freudian or psychosomatic disorders but are actual neurological imprints, patterns and templates laid down at birth. These imprints are actual electrical impulses that do not just reside in the brain but also exist on a cellular level. Each and every cell in the body has genetic memory. Early pain and fear are imprinted on this cellular memory and affect biological functioning. In other words, excessive birth trauma is stored in and alters the very genetic material of our being. This pain is waiting to be released and causes certain behavioural patterns in order to secure that release. The initial imprint and impulse is not in the brain but exists on a cellular level. It is only later that it affects behaviour.

To more fully understand how these patterns affect us for the rest of our lives, it is necessary to understand the mechanics of repression. The biological plan does not anticipate the wholesale physical and emotional onslaught of pain associated with unnatural childbirth. The delicate neurological system of the newly born is not yet equipped to deal with the electrical overload caused by this pain. It is not just the physiological pain but also the emotional pain of separation, isolation and abandonment. The young system is simply not geared to deal with the intensity of this current. It does the only thing possible, which is to repress or disconnect the incoming message.

The function of pain is to mobilise the body to move. It activates the sympathetic nervous system, which gets everything going, creating drive and momentum in order to get away from the situation of danger. Movement (hopefully) means survival! Pain is an electrochemical impulse that travels along the synaptic pathways. Fortunately, nature in her benign wisdom has created a safety valve or fuse mechanism to deal with any overload. This is why the body will simply go unconscious when subjected to intense physical pain.

Just as in an electrical circuit, a fuse will blow if there is an overload of current, so too, if there is an overload of pain the circuit breaker comes in automatically in the nervous system. If pain rises above a certain threshold point this mechanism of repression is automatically triggered, so that the intense current does not reach the higher conscious mind, causing irreparable damage.

Once again it is the synapses that are the key. The synapses secrete chemicals or hormones that either facilitate or repress neurotransmission. If pain reaches this vital threshold, hormones called endorphins, which are similar to morphine, are secreted and inhibit the transmission of the electrical impulse. Pain is anaesthetised.

However, the process of repression does not remove the pain; it merely denies it access to the higher conscious mind. The content still exists in cellular memory and the reaches of the lower mind. The mechanism of repression is a blocking of an electrical circuit, an interruption of a message; it does nothing to the original valency of that message. The pain is now locked within the body system waiting for the appropriate time for reconnection.

The problem is that the structure of consciousness now becomes divided from itself. As a direct result of this repression (which is called the gating of pain) the system is split into two. This is the personal recreation of the fall. The pain is now locked into lower neural circuits and denied access to higher consciousness. But this disconnection works in both directions. Higher consciousness is also cut off from the lower mind/body continuum. For if we repress the pain, we also repress the content of the cause of that pain – the feeling, the memory of the event and so on. This is why we cannot remember our birth and early childhood. The price of the gating mechanism is that we do in fact lose conscious awareness. We are no longer aware of those incidents in our lives that caused the pain. What is even more important, we no longer have access to those memories unless we are willing, as a structure of consciousness, to re-allow access to the pain.

The levels of consciousness lose their ability to communicate freely and the whole structure fractures. Thoughts become disassociated from feelings and feelings become disassociated from thought. We lose touch with our real and inner selves; consciousness becomes fragmented. This process of repression begins in the womb and to a certain extent it is a necessary and healthy part of the evolutionary journey. However, it would seem that at a certain critical point, when the load of pain or current reaches a particular threshold, the gating mechanism takes over.

There are two points to realise here. One is that the load of pain is cumulative, that it can reach that threshold over time as pain is added to pain. The second is that in a naturally fluid system this threshold would rarely be reached. The system is designed in such a way that when the time is propitious, when the organism feels safe enough, the pain, memory and event will automatically surface to the higher conscious mind and be discharged. The problem being that the infant never feels secure enough to release the birth trauma, which on the contrary is added to daily as the state of separation from mother continues.

At a certain time in youth, which can be at any time from birth to as late as adolescence, the psychic split of consciousness becomes permanent. It is at this point that control is given over to the ego. The newborn system was not designed to function in a hostile environment; the spirit does not know how to handle the overload of pain and turns for help to the ego who is supposed to be the earth plane resident expert. After all, it is the negative egos of others who have caused the excess pain in the first place, so it is only fair to assume that one's own ego will know how to deal with the problem. This of course only makes the situation worse for one is not born with a mature ego but one that needs to grow and develop as the human being matures.

What happens is that as we repress the pain, we also repress those feelings that are associated with that event. As we get closer to our critical threshold, it becomes necessary to repress more and more pain and hence more and more feeling. Eventually, we become disconnected from our feeling self, and from our feelings altogether. A major component of the mechanism of repression is denial.

We end up in a state of self-denial. We began with the overload of pain caused by the physical birth trauma, which was then compounded by the emotional scarring of separation from mother, with associated feelings of abandonment and loss of love. The initial pain is the pain of separation and we end up being separated from ourselves, disconnected from the inner truth of our being.

In this state of inner separation, it is impossible to act correctly. We have become dysfunctional, for we are disconnected from our feelings, which are our source of guidance. For the structure of consciousness to work correctly there must be a free flow of communication between the various levels of the mind: the unconscious (which houses the primary patterning of the structure of knowledge and our habitual behavioural responses), the subconscious (which houses the feelings), the cognitive thinking mind (which houses the ego), and the intuitive mind (which houses the spirit).

The gating mechanism of repression saves the delicate conscious mind of the infant from unbearable overloads of current but also functionally separates these diverse aspects. To stop the overload of the electrical current reaching the higher mind, the synaptic pathways, which are the communication links, compartmentalise the areas of consciousness.

To be fully conscious is not just a brain phenomenon or a mental exercise. It is rather a state of whole being. Just as each and every cell has genetic memory, so too, consciousness resides within every cell. The biological plan calls for brain and body, mind and soul, to work together as a continuum in harmony and cooperation. This is why it is so essential for this blueprint or pattern of learning to be laid down at birth between mother and child as the correct template of knowledge for the growth of intelligence.

At no time should there be a sense of separation or abandonment. No section of the brain or the body, and no area of consciousness should be cut off from the rest. To operate as a fully conscious, aware, and intelligent individual means that one has free and fluid access to all parts of the self – to one's thoughts, feelings, intuitions, attitudes, beliefs and so on. It is only when the individual has this access that it can assume sovereignty; that it can effectively take conscious control.

To be really aware of something, to be able to make an intelligent conscious choice, means that one knows what one thinks, how one feels, and what is one's intuition. When the brain becomes compartmentalised, one area is unaware what another is doing. Feelings can be processed on lower levels without conscious awareness. Moreover, they can be denied and distorted so they are no longer real. We can even be aware of a feeling without actually feeling the content of that feeling.

Repression fragments consciousness. Self-denial and self-deception are the inevitable consequence. The conscious mind can tell itself that it is feeling one thing, when in reality it is feeling something totally different. The price of repression is not only a loss of consciousness but also a loss of integrity and honesty.

Repression is not limited to birth trauma. The infant has specific genetically programmed needs that are pre-set and activated by the biological plan according to a definite timeline, just as external physical growth follows certain patterns. These needs fall into several categories, which unfold chronologically as the child develops. Any deprival of these primary basic needs will interfere with the orderly unfolding of the healthy growth and development of intelligence.

The first and most primary need is that of security. Security is not just physical; it is not the mere provision of food and shelter. Security is that feeling of safety that comes from being secure within a matrix. The paradox of growth is that the greater the security within the given matrix, the greater the autonomy and freedom once one leaves that matrix. Growth is the orderly progression from limited to more expansive matrices, affording ever-greater freedom and personal sovereignty.

In the womb the foetus is totally safe and secure to concentrate on building its human body. It is not distracted by considerations of danger, survival, fear or threat. Everything is taken care of and provided by the matrix of the womb. The more secure and pure this environment, the healthier the embryo. Any foreign intrusion such as alcohol, tobacco, drugs, stress, fear or hormonal imbalance will interfere with the full growth and development of the foetus. These substances detract from the security of the womb.

When the neonate enters the world, the second need of sensuality is added to that of security. The newborn needs to be touched, held, stroked, and massaged. Spontaneous natural affection is the next most important biological need after security. In the womb the foetus is coated with the fatty mucous of the vernix caseosa, which protects the skin from its long immersion in fluid. The sensory system of the skin is in a dormant state at birth and needs to be activated by the appropriate stimuli of touch.

This stimulation also activates the reticular formation, which is the central exchange for the channelling of sensory data. In nature all mothers spend a good deal of time licking their young at birth to activate the sensory nervous system. Experiments have shown that if a particular area of a newborn kitten is prevented from being licked by the mother, the kitten will grow to become permanently dysfunctional. In normal circumstances, the mother will concentrate on this particular area of the kitten's belly.

Moreover, this activation process is stage-specific, which means it must occur soon after birth or sensory deprivation sets in. It is interesting that statistical studies have shown a direct correlation between violence in later life and tactile or touch deprivation in early childhood. In other words, the less we are touched as an infant, the more likely we will reach out in violence to be touched later in life.

If one has not learnt a correct patterning of affection, one does not know how to reach out in love and instead, does so in violence. The infant's strongest need after security is to be picked up and held, and to be touched with love and affection. It is also interesting that this is the basic impulse of everyone who comes in contact with a newborn: to cuddle that baby! Indeed, this is the way it gets its security – its feeling of safety – through the bonding process that can only occur through touch. Deprival of this need will therefore also cause deprival of the primary need for security.

If we follow the biological plan, the natural birth process is indeed the natural fulfilment of this secondary need. The first need of security has been fulfilled in the womb, but there is no sense of touch. In natural childbirth the neonate leaves the security of the womb for the security of mother's belly and breast. There is no fear of abandonment, no sense of separation and no threat to security.

What is added, however, is the natural spontaneous response of the mother to nurture her young with continual gentle body massage, to hold the infant to her own naked body in a continuum of being. The feeling of security is now complemented by the enjoyment of sensuality. Without the feeling of safety that nurturing brings there can be no sense of bonding, of love. Thus, love is a quality that is necessary for the fulfilment of needs lest the satisfaction be perfunctory and mechanical. There is not just a need to be held but to be held with love.

In fact, the satisfaction of needs is the tangible demonstration of love. It is love in action. They are two sides of the one coin – the yin and yang of the dialectic of growth. It is love which creates security, provides safety, is nurturing, and is the glue of bonding and the essence of the affectionate touch. It is love that generates acceptance and allows the child to be him or herself.

One of the most important emotional needs of the infant is to be allowed to express its own emotions and feelings unconditionally. That is to know that it is loved whatever its natural spontaneous expression. Love and acceptance cannot be conditional upon the appropriate behaviour of the child; that is not love but conditioning.

The fourth level of needs is intellectual: the need to know, to understand, and to explore reality freely. The need for the intellectual freedom to create one's own inner picture of the world, to form one's own opinions and world view, and to build one's own set of values. The child's greatest gift is its natural insatiable curiosity and willingness to interact with the world – its desire to learn! The young child needs to be free from the imposed value system of the parent.

At first, the infant is purely on an information gathering exercise. It wants to form an inner picture, a concept of how life works, a structure of knowledge of the outer world exactly as it is, not through the lens or focus of the parent. Intelligence is the ability to interact with one's environment. In the first years of life, this interaction must be free and unfettered if that intelligence is to grow to the point where the child can form its own evaluations and make its own authentic decisions.

The child's desire for learning needs to be open-ended and free from cultural conditioning and bias, free from the utilitarian considerations of meaning and purpose. The child simply needs to experience life in all its glory and majesty without an externally imposed value and judgement system. It is for this reason that the child's survival is taken care of and provided for by the parents, so that it is free from the concerns of survival and thus free to explore the world, formulating its own personal and unique picture of reality.

Any perceived threat to survival or security will inhibit this necessary tendency to interact freely and spontaneously for the child will be forced to evaluate experience before interaction takes place.

Thus, we can see the way these needs build upon each other to facilitate harmonious growth, learning, joy, love and, ultimately, personal sovereignty. Security is first created in the womb and is augmented at birth with sensuality: the sensory interaction with a mother motivated by love. The child is then ready to develop its feeling nature: to be emotionally nurtured and to freely express its own feelings; to be both loved and to love in return. After this comes the need to explore the world, building its own structure of knowledge and understanding of how reality works, so that it too can eventually graduate to complete autonomy, self-reliance and the ability to make its own decisions and to create its own reality!

However, this is rarely what does happen. Just as modern birthing practices do not follow the biological plan, so too, the needs of the infant are seldom met in this stage-specific way at the appointed time. It is vitally important to understand that these needs are stage-specific according to a biological clock. If they are not met at that specific time, then need deprivation occurs and is set within the cellular memory of the system.

There is a timetable of needs that must be adhered to. When needs are not met they register as pain. Whether that is the pain of hunger for food or love the end result is the same. The function of pain is to mobilise the system and to alert it to the fact that needs are not being met, for any unmet need is a potential threat to survival. The intensity of the pain will be in direct proportion to the importance of the unmet need. Just as love is the overriding quality that pervades and motivates the fulfilment and satisfaction of needs, so too, the lack of love is the primary cause of pain.

The pain may arise from physical trauma at birth. It may be caused by not being held and embraced in the hours immediately after birth or for that matter in the months and years after that. It may come from not being allowed to express one's feelings freely or because one is not emotionally acknowledged. It may be caused by indifference, harshness, or an enforced, artificially imposed regime of growth that is fundamentally at odds with the biological plan or one's own inner timetable of development. One may be ignored and be expected to become an adult prematurely.

It may come about simply because one is never held and told: 'I love you!'

It may come about because one is not allowed to explore freely, to formulate one's own ideas, or to create one's own inner picture of how the world works. One may be forced to adopt a parent's picture of the world.

Whatever the specific configuration, the point is that the child feels unloved and eventually realises that he or she is not and will not be loved for himself or herself alone, the way that he or she is. It is this realisation that causes the overload of pain and implements the gating of pain and mechanism of repression. The system does not distinguish between physical or emotional pain. In electrochemical terms both are identical and will automatically trigger the gating mechanism in the event of overload.

Hence, there are three distinct layers of repression: the pain, the feeling and the need. First comes the need, as a natural spontaneous biological urge that is activated according to time specific pre-set programmes. This need gives rise to a feeling in the infant. If this need remains unfulfilled, it then manifests as pain in order to activate the necessary response.

If the system perceives there is no way for the need to be met, the alarm bell of pain is turned off. The electrical message of the pain, the feeling and the unmet need are all turned off, repressed and sent into cellular memory, locked within the body and lower mind. The native urges of the being are denied access to consciousness and for all extent in purpose are denied reality. The system cannot operate with excessive circuits of pain flooding the higher mind indefinitely.

However, as already noted, repression is not elimination. The pain, the feeling, the events and unresolved needs are all still there on a deeply buried level of cellular disconnected circuitry going around and around seeking resolution, waiting for the gating mechanism to allow entry to higher consciousness.

TEN: THE SEARCH FOR OUTSIDE VALIDATION

> *'...everyone, through tradition, through habit of thought, through custom, has established for himself a background, and from that background he tries to assimilate and judge new experiences.*
>
> Krishnamurti

The long-term intent of the biological plan is to create the self-aware, fully conscious, autonomous, self-reliant, sovereign human being. This is true human adulthood. The gift of free will means that we are able and willing to create our own reality by taking conscious dominion of our lives exercising our freedom of choice in a real and responsible way. Nature fulfils itself with the birth of every human infant. Nature's goal is man's individuality.

The human infant is the most helpless of all precisely because the human adult is potentially the most sovereign of all. This is the dialectic of growth. The human being grows from matrix to matrix in ever widening circles of freedom, autonomy and self-regulation. The more secure the individual feels within any given matrix the more fully will he or she be able to leave it and move onto the next phase of growth. The more stage-specific needs go unfulfilled at any point, the more it will be stuck back there at that stage of development trying to achieve their satisfaction and the more dysfunctional it will be in the present.

The first matrix of the totally enclosed womb gives way to the matrix of mother, which gradually opens to wider fields of exploration. At first, the neonate is physically connected to its mother by the umbilical cord. Then it is psychically connected via the continuum of being. Over the next several months it gradually separates functionally from mother and learns to move of its own volition.

However, mother is still very much the safe place: the refuge or haven to which the crawling, exploring infant returns at the slightest perceived danger or threat. Mother is still the matrix. The child then learns to walk and talk – to interact with the world at large in greater degrees of autonomy. This degree of autonomy is directly related to the degree of security felt by the child within its relationship to mother. The more love and nurturing, the more freedom to explore and develop personal individuality.

Movement is twofold: there is growth in the external sensory motor ability to interact physically with the world and there is inner neurological growth in intelligence. The child builds its inner picture of how the world works through its interaction with that world. The actual cellular growth of the brain and its neurological ability to process information is determined by the extent of this interaction. The patterning of the synaptic pathways becomes the structure of knowledge. Repeated sensory stimulation or motor coordination causes neurons to communicate and link along highly specific synaptic pathways that become established and determine future behavioural responses.

The purpose of this is not a purely information gathering exercise as in the loading of a computer with data. The intention is not the storing of knowledge as information *per se*. Rather it is the development or growth of intelligence, which is a functional ability to interact. It is not a process of filling the brain with data from the past, but one of preparing the brain for the capability of actively creating the future. With security and love come the potential for creative action. With the deprival of the fulfilment of needs comes the neurosis of reaction.

In a loving, supportive environment, the evolutionary intent impels the child through the search for the fulfilment of inner present needs to interact with the content of the external world, forming the synaptic pathways which become the inner process of conceptualisation. This process also develops in ever widening circles from the concrete and specific to the abstract and general.

The ultimate goal is pure thought – from where the whole process of creation began in the mind of God! The infant is preoccupied with fundamental daily reality: the taste, smell, touch, visual and auditory perception of the nuts and bolts of planet Earth. Perception transforms itself into concept. Highly developed intelligence concerns itself with the meaning of life, the search for truth, and an understanding of the universe. The growth of intelligence is the ever-expanding process of conceptualisation from the mundane to the divine.

In an anxious, fearful environment, this intent is thwarted through the non-fulfilment or deprival of these pre-set needs that causes retardation of the growth of intelligence. Consciousness becomes fixated with survival and cannot expand its view to wider vistas. It is stuck in the past, trying to find a way to have unmet needs fulfilled.

The ability to interact with the present falls behind and the system goes into reactive mode in a behavioural pattern functionally determined by the past. Because needs are stage-specific, when they are unmet, a part of consciousness remains behind at that stage awaiting the opportunity of fulfilment. A part of intelligence is devoted to solving that problem. However, biological growth carries on regardless, and with each developing stage the system falls further behind with ever-greater areas of the mind being monopolised by the past.

That past then begins to act as a filter through which the present is viewed. Perception becomes distorted. The past interacts with the present. The whole thrust of the biological plan is to force interaction in the present. It calls for the satisfaction of needs in order to activate the evolution of consciousness. They are rooted not only in the biological being of the child but also in the very fabric of life. They are natural, spontaneous impulses of the life-force that dwell within. When these impulses are denied a number of distorted processes are activated instead.

Once again, there is this phenomenon of something that is potentially wholesome and creative becoming evil and destructive through the abuse of human freedom and the creation of disorder. The term 'evil' is being used here merely to describe a process that is inherently destructive to the forces of life and is free from all religious, moral or metaphysical connotations.

When a primary, natural, biological need goes unfulfilled, a secondary, derived and symbolic need is created as a substitute. The deprived need registers as an electrochemical impulse of pain, which is automatically gated and locked within genetic cellular memory. The pain, the feeling and the need are all denied access to the higher conscious mind. However, their electrical force or valency, their need for expression and satisfaction are not diminished. The need is denied access in its original form, so it adopts a disguise, and seeks access through the back door. It is rerouted and surfaces as a neurotic or symptomatic need. The deprived natural need becomes the derived neurotic one.

If the child is not given enough attention, it might become the loud extrovert constantly seeking to be the centre of attention as an adult. If it is not recognised, it might develop the need to become famous. If it is not given enough love, it might grow up with the need for constant reassurance regardless of how much it is loved in the present. If it is overly dominated it will have a need to depend later in life. If there is a lack of acceptance or constant criticism, then there will be a feeling of being unattractive or not good enough.

For every individual, the exact format of deprival is different and therefore the exact picture of the neurosis is unique. What is common is that just as love is the quality that motivates the fulfilment of needs, the feeling of not being loved or loveable is the inevitable consequence of the lack of that fulfilment.

The child realises at some stage that it is not loved for itself alone, the way that it naturally is. In order to be accepted and loved it seeks to change its original nature to that of what is expected or demanded. It can no longer be its natural spontaneous self! The child adopts artificial and superficial behaviour in order to satisfy the secondary derived needs imposed by the environment. The child becomes estranged from itself. It is no longer motivated by the natural, spontaneous, biological impulses that arise from within, but rather by parental demands that come from without.

With the automatic gating mechanism of repression, feelings and needs are denied along with the pain. The child increasingly loses access to its feeling nature as feelings are denied access to higher consciousness. Emotions become suppressed and emotional disconnection follows. There is a general inability to feel, and an emotional numbness sets in. Feelings are still there but are now locked within the lower cellular system away from the higher conscious mind.

It is essential to grasp this fragmentation of consciousness in terms of our original analogy of the corporate structure of consciousness. Consciousness is not limited to the cognitive thinking mind as we so often assume. Consciousness is indeed this complex corporate structure that pervades every cell of our being. It is also true that consciousness does not just exist within either the mind or the body but that we exist within a sea of consciousness. Consciousness is a continuum with many parts working synergistically together to create the self-aware, sovereign being. Once we fragment that whole we destroy its integrity and its efficiency.

We now have a chief executive officer sitting alone in an office, isolated, cut off from the rest of the structure, with the lines of communication blocked by the repressive agents of the endorphins. The only one who can gain access to and leave the office is the messenger boy, the ego. Is it any wonder that it is promoted to a level where it is incompetent?

The conscious mind no longer has access to the services of the subconscious and the unconscious. The subconscious is the feeling, limbic, ancient brain. The unconscious is the autonomic nervous system and the genetic cellular level of DNA/RNA genome.

As in any structure, in order to work efficiently all areas must be functionally connected. There must be fluid and free access particularly to the decision-making control centre if it is to choose wisely. The head of any organisation must be aware of what is happening in all of its departments if it is to lead correctly. It need not be aware of every detail but is must have direct, intelligent communication.

Although the gating mechanism is a necessary part of the nervous system, it was not designed to deal with such an onslaught of pain that accompanies massive deprival of fundamental needs and lack of love and acceptance. Its initial benevolence becomes destructive as it causes the inner separation and compartmentalisation of consciousness. The decision-making process is not purely a rational one. It involves feelings, cellular body chemistry and intuition as well. All must operate as a cohesive whole for health and happiness and an accurate decision-making process.

Without this cohesive structure to support it, and without access to the input of the other realms of consciousness to inform it, is it any wonder that the conscious mind has gone, AWOL turning control over to the ego and demanding that it take charge?

The whole evolutionary thrust is to facilitate the growth of intelligence in the sense of the ability to interact with, to act upon, and to create. As each matrix gives way to the next, the child is given more sovereignty – the ability and willingness to make its own decisions. If the child is secure within the warmth and love of its parents and hence free from the constraints of survival, it is free to develop a strong sense of self. This sense of self is the goal; the purpose and the meaning behind the plan. But this sense of self can only be developed if the child is allowed to spontaneously respond to its innate biological impulses and to enter into a free and spontaneous relationship with the outer world. If either of these are inhibited, then the growth of that self will be retarded. Personal sovereignty will never be realised.

A true sense of self is built through developing one's own set of values, through being able to decide for oneself what is right and what is wrong. The loved, accepted and secure child can interact freely with the world, forming its own opinions, making its own evaluations, and experiencing its own discernments free from the influence, conditioning and control of another.

To develop conscious choice, the individual must be given the option of making that choice. The sad fact of the matter is that God gave us the greatest gift of the potential of free will and nature gave us the means to activate that potential through the biological plan, but mankind has aborted that potential through its abuse of that very freedom!

The child needs to be left free to build its own character and its own personality. The dialectic of growth demands that we begin as a continuum of being with our mother, but that we end as a sovereign, free, independent individual. We do this by graduating from more constrained and secure matrices to freer and more self-determined ones. Ultimately, the sovereign individual becomes its own matrix.

Character is built by determining for oneself what one's boundaries are. In this way a true sense of self is established. These boundaries are the ideals, the principles, and the values that are the end result of the process of conceptualisation that begins with the mapping of the structure of knowledge at the moment of birth. This is precisely why the initial hours of the neonate's life on earth are so vitally important, for they will eventually determine the ultimate strength of character of the individual. A strong sense of self means a strong character and clearly defined boundaries and principles. Retarded intelligence, denied needs and inhibited or frustrated interaction will weaken one's ability to conceptualise, to form principles and hence boundaries, eventually culminating in weak character.

If one's sense of self is not self-determined by one's own principles, it will be imposed from without by the blockages created by the secondary, derived symbolic needs. If we do not act according to our own inner impulses, then we will perform according to the demands of others. When the child realises it is not loved for itself alone the way that it is, it will symbolically act out in a way that is designed to gain approval. The self splits into two: the inner real self that is the natural being and the outer unreal self that is the performing fool! The unreal self is always the fool for it is constantly doing what someone else wants rather than being true to itself. One is reminded of the fool in Shakespeare, who was in truth the foil or imparter of words of wisdom!

When the deprival of need exceeds the threshold of the gating mechanism and repression sets in, consciousness is automatically split into two. For there is now an area of consciousness with its pain, unmet needs and memories that is cut-off and denied access and integration. This forms a current of bio-electrical energy carrying the denied message that is locked into the unconscious level of circuitry. The pain remains unconscious in the cells; the feelings remain in the warehouse of the subconscious. This may surface as symptomatic pain: the chronic back ache, headache, indigestion, asthma, or any other form of dis-ease or ill-health.

The force of the unmet need and its attendant pain are still trying to get out. The disconnected pain that is denied expression still has force and that force is rerouted to gain expression in a derived and symbolic manner. The headache, etc., is a symptom of the disconnected pain and the sequestered self. When consciousness is reintegrated the headaches, or other symptoms, disappear.

Moreover, this pool of pain registers as chronic anxiety. There is that perpetual feeling that something is wrong, but we do not know what it is. Quite often, when people feel this anxiety, they look around to find what is wrong in their lives, feeling better once they have localised a reason, believing this to be the cause. Indeed, it is often this anxiety that makes things go wrong in the first place. Like the headache, it is a symptom of inner disorder, but in turn it becomes the cause of further disorder. Our lives descend into deepening chaos as neurosis takes over.

The significance of this separation of consciousness is that the child becomes divorced from reality and cut-off from the present. Perception is no longer direct but is filtered through the screen of past unmet needs. This past clouds and distorts the present. For the past takes precedence. Present action is also motivated and channelled through this past, always seeking ways and means of fulfilling that unmet need. Hope lingers on eternal and current daily reality is manipulated and distorted to try and satisfy the real need via the neurotic behaviour. This, of course, is impossible because needs are stage-specific and once that time has elapsed no amount of substitutes in the present will suffice. This is the root of all addictive behaviour!

The essence of the biological plan is to create the spontaneous, free-flowing, natural and innocent child, centred in the present and interacting with the now. Secondary, derived needs cause neurotic, symbolic behaviour that is defensive, contrived, compulsive, repetitive, excessive, addictive and maladaptive. This is because there is no substitute for the real thing. No amount of praise, recognition, approval, performance, money, wealth, fame, food or sex will compensate for the original deprived need. The individual is now caught in a merry-go-round, constantly seeking outside validation because in repressing and denying its real feelings and needs it inadvertently invalidates itself.

A true sense of self either comes from self-love, self-acceptance, self-awareness and self-realisation which was the intent of evolution, and is a process of the validation of the self when that self is given love and acceptance by a nurturing supportive environment or it does not come at all.

With no real sense of self, the child must seek validation from without. If the individual does not feel loved, valued, honoured for its own sake, it will seek approval, recognition, and validation elsewhere. As the past interferes with the present, the system is less able to be sensitive and responsive to the present here and now. There is a decrease in the sense of self, the ability to interact, direct perception, and eventually the ability and the willingness to navigate one's own path.

The child, through this conditioning process of invalidation, learns to distrust its own initial perceptions. Self-doubt is born! The child doubts itself, its own perspectives and its own validity. The primary navigational system is thrown into chaos, for its whole basis is the implicit trust in one's own self. Mistrusting oneself, one loses self-confidence and self-reliance and thus increasingly turns to others and external influences to interpret reality. The meaning of life now depends upon the indirect messages of others rather than the direct perceptions of the self.

External influences, particularly what other people think, are assigned greater credibility and validity than those which spontaneously arise from within. Here, once again, we see the mechanism whereby consciousness becomes separated from itself. The individual becomes functionally disconnected from the divine source within itself. The overall thrust of evolution, which is the process of individuation, is supplanted by the conditioning of conformity. The primary motivating force of love is usurped by the secondary and symptomatic force of fear.

Through the insidious force of self-doubt, the whole wisdom and intelligence of the biological plan and the inherent divinity of creation is also doubted. Basic, primary, biological impulses are now suspect and viewed with suspicion. One no longer trusts oneself; one no longer trusts nature.

Intelligence is not the mere accumulation of data – it is the ability and willingness to meet the present creatively and deal with the challenges of life, and to actively create the future. To doubt the self is to be unable to be genuinely creative, to be unable to act in the present, but rather to react from the past. It is this lack of trust in the self, this search for outside validation, which is the re-creation on a daily basis and in every individual of the fall of man.

We separate ourselves from our source on a biological, neurological, emotional and spiritual level. This process is then handed down from one generation to the next and is habitually, culturally encoded. Tradition, convention, conformity, culture, social customs and mores, education, peer pressure, mass media and social media all conspire to keep us from ourselves.

Basically, the problem is a compliance with an externally imposed pattern of behaviour rather than a spontaneous expression of who we really are. The natural spontaneity of the child is rejected because it does not fit in with the norm. The child very quickly learns that to express its inner divinity causes rejection, ridicule and pain. The natural biological impulses are repressed and denied and the child begins to perform according to the societally implanted expectations of its particular culture and the neurotic dysfunctions of its parents. Life becomes a cultivated and contrived performance that aims to satisfy the secondary substitute needs, rather than a natural and spontaneous expression of primary biological ones. The child becomes artificial, superficial and unreal, and functionally disconnected from itself. The child learns that it is not safe to be itself or to express its true nature and denies the inner being's messages.

The historical conditioning process takes over from the inherent wisdom of the divine biological plan. The suppressive forces of fear and reason overcome the natural light-force of the human spirit. The servant of the ego with its attendant fear become master. They no longer serve the individual within the structure of consciousness but assume complete and total control. The unconscious mind, which is the domain of the genetic blueprint, is distrusted. The subconscious mind, which is the repository of feeling, has been repressed and denied through the gating mechanism. The intuition is also discredited as being too irrational and irresponsible. The child is taught not to daydream, fantasise or visualise, not to stare into space, not to relate to the other world or the inner world. Imagination, imaginary friends, inner voices and any other unusual activities or occurrences are vigorously denied and suspect. The child quickly learns to deny these inner psychic experiences, along with its inner needs and emotions.

Parents, teachers, religion, society, peers and the media all reinforce the conditioning process of conformity. Any tendency to be different or unique is immediately labelled as suspicious, and increased pressures of conformity are unleashed by society to iron out any of these idiosyncrasies. The child is not encouraged to relate to its inner self or to its inner world, nor to be alone developing its own unique worldview. Rather, the commonly accepted world picture is forced upon it at every available opportunity. The need to conform, to fit in, and to not be different becomes the single overriding determinant of the young child's life, for it learns that to be different, and that to express itself honestly and naturally incurs the opprobrium of blame and the curtailment of love and acceptance.

With the unconscious, subconscious, intuition and inner spirit all being denied by the conditioning process, the scene is set for the rational, logical, linear mind of the ego to take over. But even the healthy ego does not possess the intelligence nor the software to drive the sophisticated bio-computer of the human mind. All the ego can do is to become obsessed with outside validation. It does not know how to drive the bus, so it seeks help from without. It makes the outside world its source of being, rather than its inner divinity. Because the ego knows it is not enough, it becomes obsessed with trying to satisfy this feeling of lack through one of several ways depending on precisely when the primal split took place.

If this occurred in early childhood, the negative ego will be stuck in the infantile stage of 'am I getting enough?' This is the type of person motivated by quantity of possessions, wealth, attention, money, etc. that they can acquire. Needs are stage-specific, so any unfulfilled need will leave the ego a prisoner at that specific stage of development. For the young infant the amount of milk, food, warmth, and comfort is essential to survival. If these primary needs were not adequately met, then the ego will be locked into perpetual pursuit of secondary substitutes. But for the acquisitive personality, more is never enough.

If the split occurred later, when the child needs unconditional acceptance, the ego will be caught in an image-based concern of 'am I good enough?' This type of person is motivated by the quality of their possessions, approval, recognition, fame etc. relative to others; how they appear in the eyes of the world, taking their cue for performance from this perceived perception. They do not exist within their own right, but only in the image they create. Their satisfaction does not come from their own enjoyment of life but from others perceiving their success. The need to post every personal act online is a symptom of this type. While the infantile ego is caught in acquisition, the image-based ego is caught in performance, always trying to obtain that acceptance that was denied as a youth.

If the split occurs in the third stage of maturity, then the ego will be caught in 'am I learning/achieving enough?' This is the type of person who is neurotically concerned with career, change, and growth: always moving, restless, and never stopping long enough to enjoy what they have accomplished or where they are at. They cannot accept themselves for who or what they are but are always striving to be something more. This is the jack-of-all-trades and master of none or the over qualified specialist who simply does not fit in.

These are the three stages of growth and deprival at any stage will lock the ego in that specific time-frame, struggling to compensate for unfulfilled needs. The common theme is that activity is outwardly directed and motivated by a quest for outside validation and approval. The primary motivating force here is the fear of lack which occurred in childhood. Obviously, no amount of satiation of neurotic, derived, substitute needs in the present will compensate the unmet need of the past. The negative ego is locked in a futile and self-defeating exercise that eventually leads to some form of self-destruction. The ego becomes more and more preoccupied with the projections of its own imagination and a prisoner of its own compulsive behaviour. It becomes more lost, confused, frustrated and destructive as it chases its own tail losing focus on the real purpose, meaning and joy of life.

It is important to understand the connection between the feeling of lack or not enough and the denial of feeling in general. Personal sovereignty is gained through the development of a mature and responsible sense of self that is a combination of several distinct yet related factors. The aim is to allow the emerging human to interact freely with the world so that it can construct its own set of values, and its own picture of reality. It must be quite free from the threat of survival and that of outside interference if it is to be free to construct its own value system. It is this construct that gives value or validation to the self in the form of self-worth and self-respect. However, in order to establish this feeling of value it must be able to honour its emotional nature. It must be allowed to feel, to acknowledge and appreciate all of its emotions and feelings.

The historical process of conformity acts in such a way that it necessitates the denial of the primary needs and feelings of the child. The gating mechanism of pain is the innocent biological instrument of this inner repression. Feelings are repressed rather than expressed!

The child learns that expression of feeling leads to criticism, rejection, ridicule and pain. Rather than express what is happening within, the child performs according to whatever is expected and demanded from without. The emotional nature is certainly not honoured and the process of developing self-worth and self-respect is retarded. With a diminished sense of self within and the need to perform without, the child is left no option but to seek outside validation.

As in all these cases the forces of fear, conformity, tradition, convention, reason and so on are valid and constructive in their correct place of being the servant. However, when they become too strong and assume a dominant position they become extremely destructive to the spirit and psyche of the individual. As an organising principle in society, conformity does have its place, but in the expression and development of individuality it is a counterproductive force.

The essence of personal sovereignty and the thrust of the evolutionary process is the fully aware, awake, realised individual, not the collective mass. The individual is the focus of creation. Tradition and conformity produce the type. Life manifests itself in diversity; tradition manifests itself in conformity. We are just beginning to appreciate biodiversity as a necessary prerequisite for a healthy biosphere. The process of outside validation results in imitation and stagnation, not the spontaneous expression of creation.

Imitation is born from fear. With the loss of self-confidence and diminished self-worth comes the fear of being wrong, of being different, of being rejected and the increasing need to turn towards the safe road of conformity and external validation. Being separated from the self and being separated from the God within, the ego cannot stand the thought of being separated from mass consciousness. It seeks to belong, and to be accepted. It creates for itself a prison from which it can never escape. This prison is the historical process of conformity and tradition that recreates in every individual human consciousness this same sense of separation from its source. This prison is the fall of the individual recreated on a daily basis. This historical conditioning is how the collective negative ego passes on its dysfunction to each and every individual consciousness gaining more and more control through the agents of fear, tradition, conformity, convention and imitation.

The child is not allowed to be spontaneously itself. It is not allowed to naturally express its emotions. These emotions are not allowed to move naturally. The result is pain and dysfunction and the subsequent repression of that need, impulse, feeling, pain and the consequent repression of the real spiritual self. What is born is the unreal self which is the imitation of the known; an acting out symbolically, a striving to get approval, or trying to be what somebody else wants, a seeking of outside validation, or a conforming to the forces of tradition.

It is important to realise that the forces of conformity and the liberation of the fully-realised individual self are not always harmonious goals if that society is built upon the misconception of the inherent evilness of mankind. With this fundamental assumption at its base, society will organise itself to suppress the individual rather than to encourage its expression. The neurotic person might fit into the social structure more easily than the spontaneous individual and therefore be viewed as being more normal! Hence, it is essential to clearly define this concept of health and normality.

In social terms, the more able we are to adapt to the prevailing cultural conditioning the more normal and valuable we are to that social structure. However, this may mean that that person has merely given up all individuality and spontaneous expression. They may be valuable in society's terms but have no sense of value and self-worth to themselves.

On the other hand, someone who has not completely given up their personal sovereignty might find it much more difficult to play the required social games and thus not fit into society at all. This person may be considered more neurotic because they have difficulty adapting, yet, in reality they might be healthier because they are still endeavouring to express their inherent individuality. One is reminded of Don McClean's tribute to Van Gough in 'Starry Starry Night':

> How you suffered for your sanity
> How you tried to set them free
> They would not listen; They're not listening still.
> Perhaps they never will.
> But I could have told you, Vincent

This world was never meant for one as beautiful as you.

Many great poets, artists and authors have suffered for their sanity precisely because they did not fit in and viewed the world through a different lens. It is also interesting that, although while alive, these people were often persecuted, their works and heritage after death are seen as an inspiration and lens on the truth. Society should be structured in such a way that the aims of the individual personality and the aims of the collective mass coincide to facilitate and encourage each other's growth rather than being in conflict.

The so-called 'normal' or 'healthy' individual within this society adapts to the historical conditioning process by surrendering his or her inner self and ceding to the mould or type that cultural patterning dictates. The fear of separateness and aloneness is overcome by overcoming one's innate individuality and conforming to the stereotype of the mass. This assimilation is very similar to that of camouflage in nature. The animal becomes indistinguishable from its surrounding environment and thus feels protected, less vulnerable. So too, the individual who becomes indistinguishable from the social mass no longer feels vulnerable, exposed and isolated, but is also no longer an individual. He is no longer acting according to his primary biological impulses, but according to implanted societal conditioning.

It is important to realise here that much of what we believe is the result of our own thinking and perception is really the direct result of implanted input especially at a very early and vulnerable age which we no longer consciously remember. Many of our cherished ideas, beliefs, concepts and thoughts are not our own but are rather those learned and adopted from our parents, teachers, peers, media and other socialising influences. This is especially true today with the prevalence of mass-media and social media and the advertising industry all telling us how we should live our lives if we want to fit in and be popular. We all have authority figures in our lives, whose opinions we so totally accept that their views become statements of truth and fact regardless of their objective validity. Because we sacrifice the purity of original thought and the forming of our own unique world-view, we settle for that picture given to us from without.

The ultimate objective of the biological plan is the growth of intelligence and this intelligence is not the mere accumulation of data or the storage of knowledge but the ability to interact with the present to create the future through the faculty of critical thought. Life is always new. Spontaneous creative thought is always original. Conformity and tradition are learned and repeated responses. They are not new. They are not the present reaching for the future. They are not life. They are the past, the rationalisation and justification interfering with our ability to be totally in the present.

With the automatic gating and repression of pain comes denial and rationalisation. The cognitive brain of the ego, cut off from the feeling subconscious, the genetic unconscious and the intuitive spirit, seeks to justify its own illogical behaviour. The function of repression is to deceive and to cover up the truth. The function of intelligence is to perceive and to uncover the truth! Thus, intelligence and repression are dialectic opposites. Repression separates and compartmentalises consciousness while intelligence unifies and makes whole.

When we do not allow the denied need access to consciousness and it reroutes itself into the derived or secondary need, we fall into neurotic acting-out, and explain our irrational behaviour with the process of rationalisation. This process is the antithesis of intelligence. It is a process of thought, but it is not an intelligent one. It is, rather a dysfunction of the negative ego.

Rationalisation does not attempt to discover the truth or to understand reality. It is designed to keep the painful truth away from the conscious mind and to justify one's neurotic behaviour and secondary needs in such a way that the original primary unmet needs are not exposed. The justification is always a lie and never leads to an increased ability to interact with the present but to further maladaptive behaviour. The collective negative ego uses the historical conditioning process to validate the rationalisation of the individual ego. This is the conspiracy of repression, the tradition of denial, and the conformity to the lie.

The forces of conformity first create the circumstances of the denial of need in the infant which result in the pain, the repression and the rationalisation. They then support the denial of the truth and the justification of the neurosis by promoting it as the accepted way of being. Thus, first there is the invalidation of the natural spontaneous self which is the original cause of pain, and then there is the validation of the unreal self in its conformity to the historical process. The course completes itself and ensures its own survival. The negative ego reigns victorious on both the individual level and that of mass consciousness.

So too, with feelings. As we become functionally disconnected from our feeling nature, we are more susceptible to artificially imposed feelings from without. We learn to express and even to feel the 'socially correct' emotion. Many of our emotions are not our own at all but those we have been conditioned to accept as our own during the maturation process. We feel guilty or sad, mad or annoyed, happy or joyous, not according to our response to external events, but according to the implanted social conditioning. Quite often, we use artificial emotions or moods to mask how we really feel for to acknowledge the reality of those inner feelings would take us too close to the hidden and repressed truth. Gaiety is often a mask for inner sadness. The loud and 'happy' extrovert at the party is often deeply unhappy within. Anger is often a cover for unfelt feelings of hurt and betrayal.

Artificial feelings of socially implanted guilt become a dangerous substitute for the real function of conscience. The individual can no longer make decisions according to its own navigational system but is being swayed and influenced by religious and moral beliefs that come from without. There is a clear distinction between the positive feeling of remorse which leads us to make amends and the negative feeling of guilt which merely paralyses.

It is indeed questionable whether in this society we do make any decisions of our own any longer. We are so continually bombarded from the earliest age by parental commands, educational injunctions, religious beliefs, moral considerations, peer pressure, government regulations, media advertisements, subliminal suggestions and the incessant noise of our negative ego. We are surrounded by influences, expectations, fears and persuasions. We fall into the moulds society places before us and we enter the prisons of our own minds.

Every act of repression is both the denial of a real feeling and the supplanting of it with another artificial one. By the time we reach adolescence we are no longer acting from primary biological impulses but from imposed pressures and influences to conform to expected behaviour. Moreover, the expected behavioural patterns laid out before us dovetail neatly with those arising from the secondary substitute need. The simplest thing is to comply and give up any vestige of lingering individuality. The real self is lost, and a pseudo self becomes a puppet to the manipulations of the negative ego acting through the agencies of historical conditioning.

However, this leaves the individual in an acute state of anxiety for it is functionally disconnected from itself, adrift in the sea of life with no compass and no rudder. It has abandoned its natural navigational system and has become the hapless victim of nagging self-doubt and lack of self-confidence.

The individual has no sense of self and no inherent value system that it can call its own and is cut off from its biology and its real feelings. The natural patterning of the structure of knowledge and the growth of intelligence have been interrupted with one part of consciousness stuck in the past trying to satisfy unmet primary needs and the other caught in the process of rationalisation trying to justify the irrational pursuit of symbolic secondary ones.

The insecure ego tries desperately to shore up its identity by conforming to outside influences and by continually seeking approval and recognition. It is constantly attempting to alleviate its inherent feelings of lack and inadequacy through the vainglorious search for outside validation.

ELEVEN: DOMINATION, CO-DEPENDENCY AND THE SIGNIFICANT OTHER

To live a creative life we must overcome our fear of being wrong.
                                                            Chilton-Pearce

With separation comes the attempt to dominate. With the loss of the sense of a real self and the search for outside validation comes the necessity of ensuring the continuity of supply of that validation. When the child is not allowed to develop a full realisation of the divinity of the self, an overbearing sense of loneliness and separation sets in. This is that sense of powerlessness, insignificance and helplessness that both Calvin and Luther manipulated. The individual is not only disconnected from its natural navigational system but also from the source of power of its being which is the real and true self. Inevitably, as the adolescent becomes the adult and must move away from the protective and supportive matrix of the family into the larger matrix of the world and assume true sovereignty for itself, it is not equipped to do so.

The retarded neurological patterning of the structure of knowledge and the inability to build a personalised picture of how the world works, free from societal interference, results in an impaired growth of intelligence. The individual has grown up biologically but is not an emotionally mature human adult willing and able to make its own way in the world. It has not developed the functional capacity to interact with its environment with intelligence and to create its own reality.

Remember that the biological plan carries on regardless of whether stage-specific needs are met or not. The body continues to grow while consciousness slips further and further behind, attempting to solve the unresolved pain of the past. Less and less intelligence is left to deal with present reality and to actively create the future. The individual does indeed become more and more powerless to determine its own destiny, creating its life path by default rather than by intelligent conscious choice. We live in mediocrity.

Decisions determine destiny. The thesis of personal sovereignty is that it is our decisions with which we create our lives. These decisions are either the spontaneous expression of the inner real self on its spiritual journey of fulfilment, or the contrived manipulations of the pseudo self or negative ego on its merry dance of destruction. Our decisions are either our own or the result of historical conditioning. If they are not our own, we begin to feel more and more powerless, for we know on some deep level that we are no longer really in charge but the victim of external influences.

To allay this feeling of uncertainly and insecurity we turn to domination in an attempt to control those influences which we intuitively feel are controlling us. Feeling manipulated and controlled ourselves, we reach for these very same tools to recreate some vestige of power.

However, it is vitally important here to differentiate between the real power of dominion and the artificial power of domination. Real power can be defined as the ability to act or do. It is a taking of responsibility for one's reality and claiming complete ownership and authority in one's own life. Real power has very little to do with anyone else. It is accepting absolute accountability for the impact of our decisions and behaviour on others and the world. It is one's own ability to act for oneself; it is not power over another.

Dominion is a form of potency, a potential, an ability to actualise or realise these potentialities in the world. Dominion is the goal of the biological plan – the ability to express one's individuality by consciously creating one's personal future as one chooses it to be. It is that ability to make the potential real; to bring the future into the present. Dominion depends upon the realisation of the full self.

If one lacks this real power, if one is impotent, then one will turn to domination. Domination is actually an expression of powerlessness, not true personal power. Domination means to rule, to control, to make oneself superior to, to take a position of better than, to exercise power over another. Domination has very little to do with the self. Domination is a running away from and an escape from the burden of self-responsibility.

PERSONAL SOVEREIGNTY

If one feels powerless to act from within the self, then one will attempt to dominate another. The whole purpose of domination is to get another to act for the self. Yet domination is a double bind. Every attempt to dominate results in being dominated oneself by the very person or thing we attempted to dominate in the first place. We imprison ourselves within a prison of our own design. The bully is just as much a victim of his or her attempt to dominate as the coward. In the end all bullies are cowards. Both are functionally tied to each other and neither is free to express their inner real selves.

Domination is always a symbiotic relationship whereby both parties escape the burden of self-responsibility by making another responsible for one's life. When the individual is not allowed to mature to full sovereignty, accepting dominion of its world, it is unable to leave the matrix of dependency and enter the ultimate matrix of personal freedom. If the individual cannot relate to the world through a spontaneous expression of the real self, it will seek to recreate the security of past matrices by joining in a co-dependent relationship with a significant other.

In this co-dependency the individual seeks to ally itself with another in order to allay the feeling of aloneness, separation and powerlessness. Co-dependency is basically a situation where a biological grown-up recreates a symbolic representation of its childhood in an attempt to satisfy the unfulfilled needs of the child. The individual is still functionally caught in an earlier matrix and cannot exist in the present world of the mature and fully responsible adult.

Domination and dependency are never one way. It is always a symbiotic relationship between two dysfunctional people in that each satisfies the neurosis of the other. The aspects of domination and submission are merely mirror images of each other. Both fulfil the same function, which is the escape from the burden of personal freedom and the necessity to make one's own decisions. Both arise from a lack of real power, combined with a feeling of inferiority, powerlessness and individual insignificance. Both have the need to symbiotically join with another in order to overcome this feeling of separateness and aloneness.

It is always a sadomasochistic relationship and even though there will be a dominant partner, both seek to dominate the other.

It is just that different techniques are used to achieve this end. Both characteristics are invariably found in both partners.

The sadistic tendency to dominate is obviously easier to see. The sadistic personality seeks to make the other person completely dependent upon it, to have absolute and total control and power over the submissive partner. It is important to emphasise that sadism need not involve sexual or physical abuse or violence but may on the contrary be ostensibly quite loving. The sadistic tendency is often covered up by the appearance of benevolence and self-sacrifice. The overly concerned and overly solicitous mother is a good example of domination and manipulation by kindness. The significant other is smothered in 'love' and cannot escape the overbearing 'goodness' to be free to create its own reality. The child reared in this environment will most definitely grow up dysfunctionally dependent upon another.

The process of rationalisation steps in to justify the domination. The dominant party believing and declaring that it knows what is best or that it only has the other's best interest at heart. Alternatively, the justification may take the form of a belief in some form of superiority, which gives it the 'divine right' of rulership. Another argument follows the reasoning: 'look at what I have done for you.' Whatever the rationalisation, its purpose is to mask the domination from the self and to manipulate the other into submission.

What is very often overlooked is that the sadist is just as dependent upon the other and the relationship as the submissive partner. This is why, in so many marriages of a sadomasochistic type where the male is in the dominant position and the female eventually gets the strength to leave, it is the male who completely falls apart and comes begging for the wife to return, promising better behaviour. Unfortunately, all too often, the submissive partner returns, to their continued and escalating peril.

The sadist appears so strong and domineering that it is easy to overlook the fact that this pseudo-strength is actually a mask for deep insecurity and that the source of that strength lies within the relationship and not within the self. As long as the source of one's power is without, one is doomed to dependency. The sadist needs the person over whom he rules in order to boost and allay his own feeling of inadequacy. With the source of that power gone, the bully becomes the coward.

The sadist invariably believes that he is dominating others precisely because he loves them so much. In actual fact, he 'loves' them because he can dominate them. This is also shown in the incidence of violence that occurs when the submissive partner eventually tries to break free. The so-called love and concern very quickly turn to outright hatred, violence and overt manipulation. Both the begging and the violence uncover the true dependency of the bully. Quite often, the dominant partner needs the significant other in order to make decisions which cannot be made alone.

On the other side the story is much the same. Where it is easy to see the domination in the sadist, yet harder to see the dependency, so too, in the masochist it is easy to see the dependency but harder to see the domination. The masochist strives for submission, to dissolve within the relationship, to have another take charge and rule, to allow the significant other to lead. The masochist personality has a tendency to belittle themselves, to make themselves weak and powerless, to put themselves down, to fail to achieve. Quite often the masochist does not believe it has the right to determine its own destiny because of feelings of unworthiness.

Once again, the rationalisation process steps in to justify the weakness in terms of humility, false modesty, loyalty, devotion, love and so on. Religious rationalisations are prevalent in explaining one's submission before an avenging God. The masochist often feels helpless and powerless before the forces of fate which determine one's destiny rather than seeing that the power is within.

The masochist is afraid of their own power and would therefore prefer to give it away to the sadist. The sadist does not feel it has sufficient power on its own and therefore seeks to supplement it with that of the other. This transfer of power is the essence of the symbiotic relationship. The masochist eliminates the problem of self-responsibility by losing the self in another person or authority figure, which is seen as stronger than the self and therefore more capable and deserving of exercising control. The masochist buries the burden of freedom by totally denying their own individuality and assuming a self-demeaning role within an external relationship or structure. It has overcome the challenge of self-expression by refusing to express itself at all.

The masochist dominates through its covert manipulation of the sadist. Often, it is the weak submissive partner who really holds control! Through the voluntary giving away of their power to the other, they have the ultimate manipulative tool and threat of withdrawing that power and thus inflicting their will upon the other.

At one and the same time both parties are bully and coward locked in a deadly power struggle to maintain a hold on the significant other. Both parties' source of power and being lies without in the relationship and are therefore desperately afraid of the other leaving and the whole structure collapsing. All sadomasochistic relationships are a perpetual see-saw of manipulation to ensure the survival of the relationship and to make sure the significant other is still functionally dependent upon the situation. Love has very little to do with it.

While the sadist manipulates and dominates through overtly taking charge and ruling the roost, the masochist manipulates and dominates covertly by subtly threatening the withdrawal of support and allegiance through silence, sulking or even the threat of leaving, which is rarely carried out.

The important point is that these are just two sides of the one coin, two poles on one continuum, and two paths to the same destination. And that destination is the escape from the burden of self-responsibility that arises when the development of the self does not keep pace with the biological plan, when the structure of consciousness fractures through the gating mechanism of the repression of pain. Both are attempts to relieve the overwhelming feeling of loneliness and powerlessness that occur when the biological grown up is thrust into the matrix of the world but is functionally still caught in a past matrix of childhood dependency.

Co-dependency is an attempt to merge with another precisely because one was not allowed to merge with mother at birth! As has been emphasised repeatedly, the more complete the bonding, the more secure one is within any given matrix, the more one is able to successfully leave that matrix and move on. On the other hand, the less secure one is within any matrix, the less one's stage-specific needs are met at any point in the maturation process, the more of one's consciousness is left back there struggling to compensate for that lack, the more one is functionally stuck in the past.

Both polar extremes are futile attempts to recreate a past matrix. Both are a regressive return to childhood where the individual is not expected to operate with autonomy and independence. Co-dependency is the stubborn refusal to become the fully aware, self-conscious, autonomous responsible individual.

Which path the individual will take is a matter of biology and upbringing – the old nature and nurture combination. The birth trauma is registered on a cellular level in the genetic memory. The extent and the intensity of pain affects the neurology of the brain, the strength of the synaptic pathways and the autonomic nervous system. When the pain is denied access to higher consciousness it remains locked in the genetic structure of the unconscious. The body holds a template or pattern of response according to the type of pain experienced at birth and this template forms a predisposition to react to life in predetermined ways. These patterns are then reinforced through repeated childhood experiences and a formula or pattern is set in motion. The type of birth one experiences will predispose the infant to either dominant or submissive tendencies.

The autonomic nervous system, which is the cellular genetic level of the unconscious, has two modes or phases which control and regulate all biological processes of life. The sympathetic system activates the body to deal with life and to interact with the external world. It generally increases things like heart rate, blood pressure, metabolism, temperature, secretion of hormones, muscle tension and so on. It is the system that turns us on, gets us going, makes us active and leads us into life. The parasympathetic system turns things off. It decreases activity and leads us to rest, relax, recuperate. In a healthy organism neither system predominates: both exist in harmony to produce the even rhythm of activity and rest like all the cyclic phenomena of nature.

The birth trauma can upset this balance so that either one or the other phase of the cycle gains predominance. One system becomes overly activated at the expense of the other and this affects the neurological patterning of knowledge and the development of personality. The picture one constructs of the world is filtered through this particular bias, and the personality creates a worldview that reinforces this perspective. At each transition from one matrix to the next, this bias is increased until the biological grown-up has a personality bias to be dominant or submissive, for these are the two expressions of the two phases.

If, for example, the mother is drugged and the birth is sluggish, the neonate may be born passive and lethargic. If the infant is being strangled by the cord it may have no choice but to give in and keep still. Both of these types of birth will activate the parasympathetic system causing a predisposition towards an introverted, repressed, timid, fearful, anxious and reclusive type of personality. This person will be easily dominated for it learnt at birth that to struggle against oppression was dangerous and life threatening. This person will be given to despair and despondency and will generally be a defeatist in later life. This person has too little fire, not enough will or determination and will therefore be a submissive type seeking someone else who has a more activated sympathetic nervous system to balance their excess parasympathetic one.

If, on the other hand, the mother is sexually frigid or frightened at birth and cannot push enough to help the baby through the canal, the sympathetic phase will be excessively activated as the child has to fight for its life. It may develop a personality that is permanently turned on: the excessive, agitated extrovert who is overly ambitious, determined, addictive and does not know how to relax. This will produce a personality type that is dominating and 'pushy', just as the neonate had to push to get out of the womb.

These personality types are not the result of the birth trauma alone. The type of birth activates the autonomic unconscious in a particular direction. This then acts as a filter through which the child interprets reality and the initial bias is strengthened. Future early childhood events will either compound this bias forming into a personality type or will counterbalance the bias back to harmony.

However, most dysfunction falls within one or other category with most people being either hyper- or hypo-active. If the sympathetic predominates the personality will be outward looking, optimistic, aggressive, hardworking, energetic, success-oriented and driven to perform. The danger for this person is that they cannot stop, relax, let go, rest, or turn off and thus are a prime target for a heart attack. Not being able to go within, they feel disconnected from themselves. They can only focus without on the world and can never come to terms with their own inner essence. They will seek someone to dominate whose introspection will balance their excessive activity and give their life meaning.

If the parasympathetic predominates the personality will be cautious, anxious, non-adaptive, fearful, rigid and predictable, following routine and tradition rather than take risks encountering the new. This type is afraid of encountering life and making decisions. They have no sense of direction, no sense of purpose, no outer drive. They will often feel stuck, discouraged, hopeless, pessimistic, given to envy and look for someone more outward going to tie themselves to. This personality type will have low blood pressure, a slow pulse rate, low body temperature, low thyroid and a slow metabolism. They will fear joy and suppress emotions. They will be a typical candidate for cancer and immune deficiency diseases.

It is significant that these three diseases: heart attack, cancer and immune deficiency, are the main killers in the western world today!

Whereas the parasympath is afraid of change, the sympath is afraid of no change. Both are stuck in the past, unable to relate to the present. Everything is coloured, filtered through the bias of perception of the autonomic unconscious. Perception dictates concept. Both form a conceptualisation or paradigm of the world that is wrong and thus leads them into further experiences that reinforce and validate the original bias.

The sympath believes he must dominate the world. The parasympath believes he must submit. Beliefs are a part of the unconscious mind and are one of the most important building blocks of our reality. Belief precedes experience. Experience validates belief. What we believe comes true in our lives and reinforces those beliefs. It is through the belief system that is constructed within the unconscious mind that the original autonomic bias becomes out-pictured in daily reality.

The original event is a series of electrical impulses that have too great an amplitude or valency for the underdeveloped nervous system. The cerebral cortex or higher conscious mind of the neonate is not developed enough to accommodate the intense current and so it is rerouted back to the lower levels of the unconscious. This autonomic system, like all systems in nature, exists within a continuum of being with yin and yang polar extremes. Balance, harmony and health exist when there is a free flow of energy along the continuum. The yang pole is the sympathetic node of action and creativity; the yin pole is the parasympathetic node of rest and receptivity. One is active; the other passive. There is no right or wrong, better or worse; both poles are necessary phases of life.

However, with the cellular storage of excess unresolved pain, the system becomes permanently activated in one or either mode. The biology is constantly being given messages and signals to operate either actively or passively. Both are wrong for both are not appropriate responses to current daily reality but to a past and stored stimulus. Like any switch, its only value is in its ability to be turned on and off. Being either permanently on or permanently off is dysfunction.

The system becomes either too yin: closed, fearful, timid and passive, or too yang: open, adventurous and active. This unconscious, cellular, biological bias then colours and filters perception of the external world and a worldview or paradigm is formed that is skew-if. The structure of knowledge and the growth of intelligence follow this bias, creating a personality type that reacts to events through the model created. The original dysfunction becomes lodged deeper in the conscious mind as the neocortex develops and tries to make sense of the unresolved pain. An ideology or belief system is established that rationalises the dysfunction: 'that's the way the world is!' 'That's the way you have to behave in order to survive, to get what you want.' This is an ordering process whereby the brain seeks to make sense of the world. Belief precedes reality, so situations are set up which reinforce the original bias – the primal paradox is established.

The primal paradox is the fact that we are constantly recreating the past in the vain hope that we will resolve the repressed pain, that we will release the biological cellular tension. However, all we succeed in doing is making the original wound worse. We somehow believe that if we recreate the same situation, then we just might be able to create a happier outcome and resolve our unfulfilled needs. What actually happens is that the same outcome occurs, and the belief is reinforced. That is why in later life we repeatedly choose the same types of partners and jobs, and end up in the same situations. It is the same play with the same script and merely different actors. The conclusion is always the same.

The only way to change the outcome is to rewrite the story by understanding and adjusting the original bias in the unconscious mind and creating a new personality type and paradigm.

It is not just that portions of consciousness are functionally stuck in the past in our minds; we are also actively recreating the past in our present. The real purpose of life is to bring the future into the present through the process of actively and consciously creating our own reality. This is the ultimate aim of the biological plan and the evolutionary purpose. With an overload of pain stuck in the system, the objective becomes distorted. We try to bring the past into the present so that it can be resolved and released.

If the child is suppressed as an infant, it will attract a dominating partner as an adult in the hope that it will finally be heard and loved for who it is. Invariably, what happens is that the individual becomes more and more supressed and more and more dominated. Eventually, cancer or an immune deficiency disease will be the outcome of a life of repression.

Similarly, the restless, agitated individual that is driven to perform believes that if they just achieve that next goal they will be validated and recognised and be able to relax. But as soon as it is achieved the same restlessness occurs and drives them on to further domination and exploitation because no amount of external success in the present compensates for the unfulfilled lack of recognition as an infant. Eventually, a heart attack or mere exhaustion will silence the compulsive behaviour.

The reason unresolved pain results in the primal paradox is that activity is not consciously motivated by free choice to achieve a desired result but rather is unconsciously motivated by compulsion to relieve or escape from an unbearable inner tension. Addictive behaviour is never the result of desire for pleasure but the desire to escape from pain. The paradox is that compulsive behaviour always results in the opposite of its intended outcome. Rather than diminishing or releasing pain, it is increased. Neurotic behaviour leads further into dysfunction rather than a return to health!

Co-dependency is not love. A sadomasochistic relationship does not result in increased feelings of belonging and kinship but in increased insecurity and paranoia. Both parties are perpetually dominating and manipulating each other in a power struggle that leaves both feeling more powerless and insecure as individuality and personal freedom are sacrificed.

Love can only exist with equality and freedom where both parties are there to inspire each other to greater heights of spontaneous personal growth and expression. It is a truth that you can only love another and that you can only be loved to the degree that you love yourself. Co-dependency is a tacit agreement between two people to stay locked in neurotic, unconscious patterns of behaviour of control and approval. It is the ultimate search for outside validation. The significant other becomes the one who gives validity to the self. Without that person life becomes meaningless, purposeless and futile. This is why a classic co-dependent break-up will often lead to attempted suicide.

Co-dependency lies within us all. We all have sadistic and masochistic traits to some degree or another. Every relationship is a balancing act between the forces of personal sovereignty and those of co-dependency. For sovereignty does not imply solitude. It merely means the ability and the willingness to make one's own decisions within the framework of a loving and supportive relationship within which one is free from coercion and manipulation and free to express one's own innate individuality.

The co-dependent's source of power and strength lies not within the self but outside in the relationship. Therefore, he or she is constantly thrown between joy and sorrow according to the state of harmony and accord or disharmony and conflict between the two parties. This is the cause of the insecurity. Even the dominant partner's source of strength lies not within but without and is thus vulnerable and fraught with danger.

Personal sovereignty implies that one's source lies within the self and that one can willingly and consciously share that self with another emotionally mature human being in a co-committed intimate relationship. A co-committed relationship is the outcome of a personal preference made in the present and not the result of unconscious, compulsive behavioural patterns that are rooted in the past.

It is essential to grasp that a sadomasochistic relationship does not necessitate nor imply any weird and wonderful sexual preferences or other acts of external violence. Co-dependency does not necessitate excessive emotional attachment or reliance. We are talking about inner states of being and qualities of love. Once again, we are talking about a continuum of relating which operates between two polar extremes. The one pole is the ability and willingness to make one's own decisions, to be free, to express one's own inner divinity, to be oneself; the other pole is to need another to be there in one form or another to feel supported so that one can relate to life. Within the relationship is one free to make one's own decisions and be oneself free from disapproval and injunction? The essential point is one's attitude to life, not one's relationship with the other.

If one has personal sovereignty, then one will exhibit that in every area of one's life: in all relationships, in one's career, in one's family, with one's friends and in one's intimacy. One can be co-dependent with no intimate relationships in one's life! Similarly, if one is co-dependent then that quality will also invade every area of one's life. Moreover, it is not a simple black and white case of either or. Nothing is absolutely yin or yang. Everything exists on the continuum and is a mixture or combination of the two, and everything is in a continual state of change along that continuum in time.

Day is always becoming night and vice versa. The seasons are forever changing. Nothing in the universe is constant but exists within a constant state of flux. So too, the free flow of self-expression and the tendency to rely and depend upon another are always two sides of the one coin. This is the dance of intimacy! It is a matter of keeping both in balance and harmony.

No man is an island. To be is to be related and to relate and be involved in life demands some form of reliance, some form of interdependency. We are all related and need each other! Personal sovereignty does not imply or excuse solitude or arrogance – it is rather the ability to know what is right for the self and honour that knowing with willingness to express that inner truth and intention without fear or inhibition. There must be negotiation; there needs to be compromise. But there must also be equality and mutual respect for each other's and the self's point of view. It is OK to agree to disagree – this is the hallmark of a healthy relationship.

The whole issue of personal sovereignty within intimacy and within relationships is the cornerstone of building a successful and happy life. We shall return to this point in section three. For now, it is enough to grasp the dialectic nature of love and to see its significance in our journey of exploration.

Every relationship bears within itself the temptation to overly rely and depend, to give in for the sake of peace, to avoid conflict and confrontation, to let the other have their way, particularly when we love. This is the danger and trap of co-dependency. The way we come into life affects the way we relate to life. The birth trauma imprints on a cellular level affecting the autonomic unconscious which is then reinforced in early infancy, creating a personality bias or type in the subconscious mind in the construct of an ideology or conceptualised world picture or template that justifies and rationalises one's behaviour.

Left to itself, the child perceives, then conceives and finally achieves. If it is given the freedom to interpret the world for itself, it will create a strong and valid value system with a strong sense of self to bring to a relationship. It will know itself, first and not seek to find itself via or through another.

With excessive parental and societal interference, perception is distorted and incorrect or erroneous conception or deception takes place. The value system and the inherent sense of self are defective and deficient. The self does not mature; its intelligence is not ripe. This is the inevitable consequence of the process of repression, for reality is denied access to higher consciousness and the correct patterning of the structure of knowledge cannot occur. The growth of intelligence is impaired and the individual is left with a diminished sense of self and capacity to creatively and intelligently interact with the present. It therefore needs an ally.

It never emerges from the matrix of mother where it does not have to relate to the world on its own. Because it is functionally stuck in the past, it is incapable of adequately dealing with the present. It seeks to excessively rely and depend upon another as a mother-substitute. It seeks an ally to allay the fear of aloneness, and the sense of powerlessness that comes from an interrupted development that is the result of unfulfilled needs. This is the problem of a psychologically young child existing within a biologically grown up body trying to relate to the world as an adult. It simply does not work.

The individual then enters into a symbiotic relationship to bolster its own feeling of inadequacy and to enable it to deal with a frightening and hostile world. It is essential to understand that domination, submission, co-dependency, and over-reliance are all direct results of not being sufficiently nurtured and made to feel secure within the first matrix of life.

A belief pattern is established deep within the psyche that the world is a scary place that one needs to defend against. In later life one seeks out a partner or companion that one can join forces with in this battle against life. Life is seen as the enemy. All attempts at domination of whatever nature are motivated out of this fear of life. Domination arises naturally out of this feeling of separation that is the individualised recreation of the fall. All forms of manipulation, finding fault, blame, having power over, criticism, belittling and so on are attempts to dominate and lead away from the pole of love and towards the pole of co-dependency.

For ultimately, any desire to control or manipulate another springs from a lack of belief in the self and one's own ability to create. This is the purpose and gift of the biological plan. When this plan is interfered with, the individual does not mature with the requisite ability to interact with the world. It does not believe it has the power to create its own reality and so it seeks to have power over someone else.

Real power is the capacity to act, to realise one's potential. Domination is pseudo power: it is power masking weakness. The bully is really the coward and the coward is the bully. When one doubts oneself, one seeks another to validate that diminished sense of self, and to bolster one's own feeling of weakness. Domination is always a desire for power that one knows one really does not possess. It is a secondary substitute need for the primary real need of self-empowerment that comes from the correct loving, nurturing support one receives within a secure matrix in early life.

With a traumatic birth and physical separation from mother immediately after birth, the neonate never fully enters the security of the mother-matrix. Remember, needs are time-specific and are difficult to meet at a later time. The world becomes a scary place. The autonomic nervous system is skewed towards either polar extreme and the infant learns to deal with that threat in one of two ways: domination or submission, whichever worked in the birth process.

It then recreates that attitude to life as its way of dealing with a frightening world. It learns to play better than because it feels less than; it learns to control because it feels controlled; it learns to manipulate because it does not feel that it deserves; it learns to cheat because it is lied to; it learns to take advantage of because it feels inadequate. All forms of domination are the direct result of the feeling of not being loved as a child. 'Because I am not loved, because I am not good enough, because I do not deserve – I get to do whatever I want or need to do to get my own way!' And so, the negative ego is born.

Domination is an attempt to take by force what life would willingly give if we felt loved and lived with dominion. In the final analysis, domination or love are choices in the way we relate to ourselves. If I have been loved and nurtured as an infant, then I will develop a real and healthy sense of self and self-love. With that comes a healthy sense of self-worth, self-esteem, self-respect and a healthy relationship with life. Life is seen as being benevolent; the world is wonderful! I do not have to dominate, control or manipulate for life gives abundantly. This is the goal of the biological plan. This is why there is no domination in nature but a symphonic harmony of co-existence.

However, with the deprival of primary need and the lack of love comes the feeling of being unloved, of being unlovable, of not being worthy, of not being good enough, and of not deserving. Life is viewed as being harsh, hard, a scary place of lack where needs go unfulfilled unless I do something about it. What I do depends upon the predisposition of my autonomic unconscious but either way I have to manipulate and struggle either covertly or overtly to get what I want.

Co-dependency is the game of choice of the altered negative ego! It is the ultimate belief in the separation of the self from life, seeking refuge from that overwhelming burden of aloneness in a symbiotic relationship with a significant other. That symbiotic relationship begins with the relationship between the self and the negative ego. The beginning of co-dependency always exists within the self, first! When one hands over control to the ego and demands that it takes charge this is the first act of domination, of co-dependency. For we are making another take responsibility for our reality. We are abandoning our conscious personal sovereignty. Every time we make a decision, every time we act, we are doing one or the other. We are either exercising the gift of free will choice and strengthening that sense of self or we are abrogating responsibility to the ego and thus weakening that sense. The choice is always ours.

It is always a choice between claiming total responsibility, taking complete ownership, and being the supreme authority in our own lives – which is sovereign dominion – or refusing to accept the gift of free will and passing control to the ego. Because the ego does not possess the power, the ability, the intelligence, the codes or the understanding to effectively take charge, it quite naturally feels powerless, and inadequate, out of its depth and out of control. The only way it can solve this problem is via domination. It puts itself in an impregnable position of arrogance and superiority where it is free to rule and control however it sees fit.

It is the negative ego that is locked in separation, that views the world as a scary place, that is always looking for someone else to blame, that rationalises and justifies, excusing its own inability to perform and deliver. But it is important to remember that it is we who have asked the ego to do a job for which it was never designed. It is we who have promoted it to the point of incompetence. It is we who have placed it in this dominant position.

It is our refusal to accept the gift of free will, the responsibility of conscious sovereign dominion by our refusal to think for ourselves and by our refusal to grow up and embrace adulthood. It is we who accept the historical conditioning process through the search for outside validation and allow others to tell us what to think, meekly submitting to the injunctions of parents, teachers, society and religion.

It is we who refuse to let go of earlier matrices, tenaciously holding onto the past waiting for the love we never received as children. It is we who are unwilling to let go of the past and move fully into the present, finding our love and the fulfilment of our needs in the now and the conscious creation of our future. It is our decision not to grow up. It is our choice not to become the emotionally mature adult.

And it is precisely because we refuse to consciously think and create our own reality that the ego is forced to think for us. But the ego was not designed to think; it does not know how. So it blindly recreates the past and follows what it is told by external sources – hence the constant search for outside validation and the alliance with a significant other.

Remember, the ego's real function is to deliver data from the outside world via the senses to higher consciousness. That is what it was designed to do, to inform the conscious mind of external planetary conditions ensuring physical survival. Therefore, when asked to take charge it merely does what it knows best. It checks out what is happening outside and mimics those conditions within. The ego is not a creative force but an information processing system. It can repeat the past but it cannot create the future. This is the function of the conscious mind working in conjunction with the resident spirit.

As we refuse to think more and more, the negative ego and the forces of conformity, tradition, imitation and domination gain ever-greater control of our lives. Because we have forced the ego to take charge, this is the first act of domination, and hence we force the ego into a relationship of co-dependency. It knows no other way to relate to the world other than through what we have demonstrated to it. The ego is initially our servant, and only becomes the master through our abdication, but in that very act we have taught it how to manipulate, for we ourselves have created the forces of oppression which are the hallmark of co-dependency. As we get caught more and more in the past, trying to resolve the problem of unfulfilled needs and relating through the screen of that filter, the ego is forced to deal more and more with the present, for its function is to ensure the physical survival of the organism in the present. As we refuse to be responsible for our behaviour and act from past addictive patterns of fear, we give the negative ego more control, power and opportunity to dominate our lives.

The development of the ego mirrors that of the human infant. We are not born with a fully functioning mature ego. Like us it starts off weak, immature, vulnerable and ignorant. Like us it also needs the security of a safe matrix in order to grow and develop correctly. As mentioned, the activation of the senses and the patterning of knowledge evolve according to stage specific cues and needs. Because of unnatural child birthing techniques and the deprival of primary biological needs, this activation process is severely retarded. The ego's natural growth is impaired. It is not given enough raw data, or sensory stimulation to activate the reticular formation and other necessary inputs for its development. Added to this is that in this highly immature, vulnerable and weakened position, it is also thrust prematurely into a position of prominence which it was never designed to handle.

It is thus not even given the opportunity to grow to its own maturity, to develop its own functioning, for it is now too busy trying to do the wrong job. It never matures; it never becomes secure within the structure of consciousness.

The ego therefore has no choice. It has been commanded by its master – *you* – to do a job for which it is not equipped, nor ready. It must therefore pretend and manipulate, gaining ever-greater control of the system so that you, its master, will not see its inability to act or its inherent powerlessness. Feeling powerless, it seeks to cover this with the pseudo power of weakness: the false power of domination.

The ego believes that if it has control of everything, if it takes over the whole system, then it might just succeed or at least cover its incompetence. For there will be no one left to evaluate its work. Thus, the ego becomes negative and destructive, seeking absolute domination, which is classic co-dependency.

In the beginning, it is we who initiate the oppression, who rob the ego of its opportunity to mature, who make unrealistic demands upon it, who lay down the rules of limitation. But then in turn, it is the ego who turns on us and oppresses us with its limitations, who seeks to control and dominate us because it has no choice, because it cannot fulfil the task we have assigned to it.

As in all cases, the dominator becomes the dominated! We are caught fast in our own prison. The ego takes more and more control, making more and more promises and delivering less and less. As in all co-dependent relationships, the ego is caught in denial. It lies. It never tells the truth, and it seeks to manipulate reality to cover its inability to deliver. The negative ego then initiates a co-dependent relationship with another negative ego which enables it to play its game of pretence. If I have a dominating negative ego, I will attract a submissive negative ego out there in the world in order to play out my ego games. The whole point of the exercise is to find somebody who will buy my story, my rationalisation, my justification, and my excuses.

Co-dependency is basically a relationship pattern that allows and supports unconscious, addictive behaviours. It is a system of oppression and limitation that seeks to bind the significant other in a relationship of denial of the truth and the suppression of individual expression. The term 'co-dependency' implies that both partners fulfil this need in the other. It is a mutual agreement to hide from the truth and to accept each other's rationalisations. Co-dependency is really an entanglement, for it is a process of diminishing freedom and increased captivity, which limits the growth of personal potential.

On the other hand, love is a relationship that stimulates personal growth, fulfilment and expression, inspiring each partner to higher and higher realisation of inner potential. Co-dependency results in a diminished capacity to be oneself, to freely and fully express one's innate individuality. Love creates a supportive environment within which the individual gives ever-greater expression to their unique inner divinity.

The external co-dependent entanglement is nothing more than a manifestation of our own inner co-dependency with our negative ego. It is imperative to appreciate this fact. Every moment of life, every single act and decision is the exercise of free will choice. It is always a choice between love and fear: expression or repression, dominion or domination, responsibility or abdication, co-creativity or co-dependency.

Life is ultimately the choice between taking conscious, personal, sovereign, dominion and actively creating our reality by bringing the future into the present or allowing unconscious, addictive, behavioural patterns to dominate and control our unreality by bringing the past into the present.

There is no grey area, no middle ground. The human being was designed to operate according to the dictates of its own inner being and knowing. Like every expression of life there are specific laws, vibrations, frequencies or modes of behaviour that are appropriate to the human being. This is the original nature of humanity. It is not inherently evil but has been corrupted throughout the millennia of generations by a refusal to follow the natural wisdom of the biological plan.

To abuse the gift of free will, to choose to behave in ways that are inappropriate for a human being, must inevitably result in bondage, domination and co-dependency. In abandoning the right, privilege and responsibility of making our own decisions, we end up the victim of another's oppressive rules and dominating behaviour, addicted to the continual pursuit of outside validation and entangled in the mutual self-destructive web of co-dependency.

TWELVE: THE COLLECTIVE NEGATIVE EGO AND THE NEW WORLD ORDER

The real fall from grace was not in some mythological garden in ancient history. It is the daily enactment by each individual human being every time this choice is made to give away personal power. The original mistake – or original sin – was the initial act of demanding that the ego takes charge of our life. This is a very personal decision. The fall has no momentum of its own that we do not give it; it must be re-enacted every day by every individual human being.

Every time we relinquish our power of dominion we fuel the fire of the negative ego and create co-dependency. Co-dependency is not so much a form of external relationship as a way of relating to life, our personal life, our personal world. It is the distorted worldview that is the inevitable result of the deprival and unfulfillment of necessary primary, biological and emotional needs and the attendant feeling of lack of love in early infancy and childhood.

It is a very private and personal matter.

However, as we have seen, this distortion then becomes embodied over time in the historical conditioning process and becomes culturally encoded and passed from one generation to the next. With a diminished sense of self comes the over-identification with and over-dependency upon the external sources of validation afforded by the outside world. The inner individual dependency upon the personal ego externalises as the creation of the collective negative ego.

The collective negative ego is the summation of the total negative egos of all individual human beings throughout history. It is alike to the collective unconscious of Carl Jung. It is commonly referred to as the power of evil and it is essential to realise that this is a man-made construct and not the work of the Devil. Man is not the hapless and helpless victim of demonic forces but rather the willing victim of the abuse of his own free will.

The collective negative ego manifests as excessive conformity, imitation, herd instinct, authoritarianism, fascism, fanaticism, fundamentalism, totalitarianism and so forth. It is evident wherever the sanctity of the individual is sacrificed for the supposed well-being of the collective. It is usually most pronounced in times of war and social upheaval, when the individual self is viewed as subordinate to social progress. War is the absolute manifestation of the insanity and neurosis of the collective negative ego and the belief in separation.

This is why in these situations the individual human being is capable of committing atrocities to his fellow man that he would not normally consider or be capable of performing, and that he quite often looks back on in horror and disbelief. Much of the post-traumatic stress disorders associated with war veterans comes about because of the abhorrent and unnatural acts soldiers are forced to commit in the name of war. It is the power of the collective negative ego that has assumed control of the individual. We have all experienced being taken up by this collective current in one way or another, even if it is just the euphoria of a sports stadium or being part of a pack.

So there is this collective negative ego, and over thousands and thousands of years it has gained an increasing hold on planetary consciousness. As the individual abdicates more and more to their personal negative ego, it in turn, turns more and more to the collective negative ego for outside validation. Just as the personal negative ego seeks a co-dependent entanglement with the negative ego of a significant other in order to recreate the security of the mother-matrix, it also forms a symbiotic relationship with the collective negative unconscious rather than a direct sovereign relationship with life. Each and every time we choose to give our power to our ego we are indirectly feeding the stranglehold of mass consciousness.

Mass consciousness acts like the force of gravity. It holds us to the collective worldview or paradigm of the commonly accepted world picture. This is variously referred to as the consensus reality, the conventional wisdom, the mass thought-form, normalcy, humanity's common belief system or simply the *status quo*. Remember, it is not that long ago that the collective paradigm was that the world was flat and that the sun revolved around the earth. It took over 100 years for this paradigm to be changed from when Copernicus first put forward this radical idea in the sixteenth century. The collective seldom wants to give up its hold on the *status quo*.

Mass consciousness dictates what we all agree is the way the world works. The essential thrust of the biological plan is for the infant to discover and learn first-hand how in actuality the real world does in fact work. This is the building of the structure of knowledge that is the real growth of intelligence that allows the personal sovereignty of dynamic and spontaneous interaction with life in the present. The goal and sole objective of the collective negative ego is to seduce us into accepting the distorted world picture that it offers as a substitute for reality.

As primary biological needs go unfulfilled and unmet, the infant falls into pain and the autonomic response of repression. The collective ego stands ready and waiting to offer an alternative, substitute, secondary gratification to replace and placate the feeling of lack. Love is replaced by outside validation; dominion is usurped by domination; sovereignty of the self is eclipsed by the attempt to manipulate and control others. The primary motivating force of divine love is taken over by the secondary inhibiting force of fear. Fear gains in its dominance of the planet. The suppressive forces of the collective gain in their control over and suppression of individual self-expression.

The force of collectivity stands directly opposed to the force of individuality. The whole purpose and goal of nature, evolution and the biological plan is to produce the fully aware, conscious and sovereign individual, not a clone of the collective mass. Nature fulfils itself in individuality and in diversity! Every single expression of life is unique. Yet, the forces of conformity and imitation are intent on producing the type according to an accepted image. It is in this conformity and imitation that real bondage lies.

Fear produces imitation. It is the fear of being oneself, of expressing oneself lest one is rejected, ridiculed, humiliated. It is the fear of being different and thus separate.

With repression and the fragmentation of consciousness comes the distortion of the ego from its pure form and function of obedient servant to the inner commands of the resident spirit to that of an image-based, altered ego that is commanded by the gravitational pull of the collective ego and its forces of imitation and conformity. In its search for outside validation, the ego firstly sets up and then responds to this collective gravitation.

This force manifests itself in the creation of an image-based reality to which the individual must adhere. Life becomes dictated to and dominated by the things ones must do to maintain and upkeep this image. Life is no longer a spontaneous expression arising from the primary biological impulses from within but a contrived conforming to and imitation of what ones finds without.

In the rejection of love and sovereign dominion of the self, the ego begins to devise an image that is based on fear and domination. The ultimate image became one of power over another and that power eventually expressed itself in the historical journey of conquest and war: the conquering and enslavement of other peoples and the plundering and looting of the spoils of war. This was the birth of the collective negative ego. To maintain one's image one had to achieve, conquer, assert one's superiority, and display one's domination of others to the world.

Instead of deriving our sense of self from within, from who we are as a divine spirit, we began to derive our identity from this image projected to the outside world. This is no longer authentic, based on our own inner thoughts and worldview, but rather on the view the world has of us. Our sense of identity became externally derived according to our image of power and possessions. But this derived sense of self requires continual maintenance and feeding, which is why we have become such an acquisitive and exploitive society. The current world of the collective negative ego is based on establishing and protecting that sense of identity that is based on displaying power and possessions.

Outside validation now takes the form of societal ego strokes earned through being better than others, which basically means possessing more! We acquire possessions to bolster our sense of self. Our sense of self becomes what we possess rather than who we are. Our identity becomes entwined with owning the right house, driving the right car, wearing the right clothes, having the right mobile etc. We become slaves of fashion, which is nothing more than the force of conformity and imitation.

Since the very beginning there has been this dialectic connection between the conquering of others in war and the economic process. On the one hand, war has always justified and legitimised the pillage, the plundering, the rape and the robbery of the conquered people. On the other hand, the maintenance of an image-based reality and its necessity for the upkeep of large standing armies has also created the need for war in order to finance those armies from the spoils of conquest. At one and the same time economic growth became the direct cause and result of further war.

As sovereign nation states developed, trade and commerce led to imbalances in economic wealth. At first this would result in the borrowing of money to finance this growth and trade with the result that the debtor nation would have to repay the creditor the initial loan plus interest. When this proved difficult, the easiest thing to do was to invade the creditor nation, confiscating the required gold. For example, Babylon lent money to Persia, which was then eventually conquered because Persia could not repay the loan. In turn, Persia lent money to Greece to finance trade and to build armies. Sparta conquered Athens and transferred her debt to the conquered nation. In time, Alexander was forced to invade and conquer Persia to pay off the original debt and to finance his armies by confiscating the Persian gold. When the Romans found it impossible to repay their debt to the Greeks and maintain their armies, they sought the same solution by conquering Greece and looting her treasures and wealth.

As long as there was gold to be won, the wars continued: Rome invaded and conquered Syria, Carthage, Italy, Sicily, North Africa, Turkey, Algeria, Spain, Egypt, France, Morocco, England, Scotland, Arabia, Mesopotamia and Armenia. The collective negative ego was gaining a stranglehold on the lifeblood of the world. An image-based reality demands an ever-increasing flow of victory, achievement and gold to placate the altered ego and to finance its armies.

The negative ego is synonymous with the power of domination and the conquest of others – whether that be an individual person or another people. War justifies the pillage of the conquered people and the rape of their lands. The acquisition of stolen treasures becomes revered as the crowning accomplishment of the conquering hero. 'I came. I saw. I conquered.' becomes the battle cry of the victor. Whether it was the looting of the treasury or the enslavement of people or the rape of the land and its resources, war justified criminal and destructive behaviour. The stolen booty becomes the fuel of the inflated negative ego, proving its dominance and power.

Enough is never enough, for there is never any real satisfaction. It is a derived secondary need and therefore an insatiable lust for power and domination over others rather than the real need of power and dominion over oneself. It is essential to understand this connection between the collective negative ego and the eternal wars and battles that plague the planet. For it is just not in ancient history that this occurred. It is still occurring in every war to this very day. War is the fuel that keeps the economic machine going and allows the forces of collectivity to rule the world.

We spoke earlier of Luther as being instrumental in paving the way for the future rise of fascism in Germany. Luther's doctrine helped create a character-type or a collective ego that was susceptible to the seduction of a 'leader' or 'fuhrer' like Hitler who represents more than anyone else the insanity and depravity of the negative ego when left unchecked. This is called the authoritarian character structure because of its attitude towards authority. This type of person admires authority and is overly willing to submit to it and yet is desirous of being in authority oneself and having power over and having others submit to the self.

We return to our earlier concept of the 'holon' and note the point we have repeatedly made that the sadomasochistic person is both dominating and submissive; both the coward and the bully. It is significant that the collective ego of the authoritarian character type will manifest as an authoritarian political system in which the authority of the state (or the masses) takes precedence over the sanctity and rights of the individual.

Just as domination is the false power of the weak as a substitute for the real power of dominion, so too, the power of authority in such a system is the false authority of exploitation and manipulation based in fear rather than the real authority of benevolence and true leadership based in love. Real power and authority spring from an inner superiority of worth and are always associated with love, kindness, and admiration. This is a voluntary relationship that leads to the betterment of all concerned.

Artificial authority is image-based, centred on external appearance and invariably accompanied by fear, suppression, resentment and hostility. People are held by coercion and threat rather than a voluntary allegiance. It is a forced relationship that is imposed from above and maintained by the dominating forces of oppression and violence. Real authority will lead to individual growth and development and a happy populous, while authoritarian regimes inevitably inhibit and stifle individual expression and bring out the worst in people as the collective negative ego and the personal negative ego work in tandem to create chaos.

The collective negative ego is the antithesis of individual personal freedom!

Artificial authority is the means by which the collective ego keeps the individual ego of the self in check. It uses the tools of conformity, imitation, suppression, fear and intimidation to ensure that the individual adheres to the correct social images. This authority need not always operate through external visible means. Internalised authority can be an even greater force of conformity than any overt outer structure. Guilt, morality, religion, social custom and social mores are all forms of an internalised authority.

Although modern man is freer economically, socially and politically, he is also more dominated by these inner voices of the anonymous collective ego. Public opinion, common sense, morality, normality, peer pressure and social media and an infinite array of subtle suggestions and persuasions assault us daily seducing us to accept the *status quo* and conventional wisdom of the collective paradigm. As technology connects us at the speed of light it also weaves the world wide web around us entangling us in mass thought form.

As mass media and social media gain an ever-increasing hold on the psyche of the population, the subtle forces of conformity grow. We are continually being bombarded by images to which we should conform if we want to fit in, be accepted and be part of the 'in' group. As our personal identity becomes intricately interwoven with our image, it is essential we adhere to the right cues of mass consciousness. The derived self is constantly seeking ways and means of being accepted, of building its security, of fitting in, of being 'liked'; belonging to the 'right' group becomes paramount.

Moreover, there is a dangerous tendency to accept that which is heard or seen on mass media or social media as coming from authority, of being true. Our worldview and picture of the world is increasingly derived from electronic screens rather than dealing first-hand with life ourselves. Mass media propagates mass consciousness. We lose our ability to perceive for ourselves, to think original thought, to form our own conclusions and beliefs, to construct our own individual, unique worldview and to exercise intelligence. We go to sleep and become stupid. We forsake originality and live in a cued universe.

The individual ceases to think for itself, allowing its opinions to be formed by journalists and commentators who mouth the prevailing policy or the ideas of the fashion industry. Every political, social and important event is dissected and discussed ad nauseam in the media to the point where it becomes ludicrous. It is now much easier to mould public opinion and it is debateable as to whether the media does in fact reflect or dictate that opinion. Mass media is owned by the ruling oligarchy who have a vested interest in keeping the *status quo* safe and suppressing too much individual freedom of thought. The current debate on 'Fake News' and the independence of journalism goes to the heart of this question as to exactly who is manipulating whom.

The individual believes his thoughts, feelings, ideas, beliefs and opinions are his own, but in actual fact are carefully crafted by the ruling elite. Whereas a totalitarian regime will overtly suppress freedom of thought and opinion, we in the so-called free, democratic west are subtly seduced by carefully crafted messages that are publicly broadcast over and over again via mass media and social media. As our sense of self is dependent upon our sense of belonging, and our greatest fear is that of not fitting in, it is relatively easy to sell the desired message.

The media tell us what we want to hear – that all is well with the world so we should eat, drink and be merry. We should spend beyond our means and put it all on the house, meaning we should go into debt. The negative ego, in its insatiable thirst to not only keep up with the Joneses but to surpass them and be seen as number one, does not care about the reality of one's livelihood, income, or real wealth. It will borrow beyond its means to create and sustain the illusion of inflated wealth!

If the litmus test of the real self is living intelligently in the present, then that of the negative ego is either living in the past or the future. As we live beyond our means we are robbing the future to maintain the image of our deprived self. We desperately need to sustain the illusion. We tell ourselves we 'need' the latest car, mobile phone, fashion accessory or new house in order to be accepted, in order to reaffirm our false sense of self.

The image self is the negative ego. This is the guardian or filter that does not allow anything to access our inner consciousness that is not in harmony with its proposed image of the self. The problem with the image self is that it is insatiable because no amount of possessions or power will compensate for the inner lack. We are caught on a perpetual merry-go-round of more. We need to keep the image alive by constantly feeding it. Plus, we never really get to feel the satisfaction of our efforts and real achievements because the natural glory of the real self is suppressed by the altered ego.

This image-based self has been growing for tens of thousands of years through the exigencies of war and conquest and now through economic manipulation. Since the Napoleonic Wars, the economic machine of debt has taken over from brute force. The negative egos of the power-hungry have been fed by the Fed! The Federal Reserve Bank of each country, in its various names and guises, now prints money to finance the indebtedness of all the countries of the world. On both an individual and a collective level we are sinking ever more into indebtedness as a way of life that robs us of our personal sovereignty. One cannot be a sovereign being and be in excessive debt, for to owe beyond our means is to be beholden to and a loss of freedom.

We began this conversation by defining being sovereign as that ability to make one's own decisions free from the interference and influence of another. A country or nation can only be defined as sovereign if it is able to make its own laws. However, in this interdependent world, all countries and nations are now in debt and so have lost their sovereign freedom. We are already witnessing the imposition of draconian conditions upon indebted nations when they cannot finance their interest or repay their loans.

The ruling elite, working through the Reserve Bank system of the world, finance conflict and war in order to create national indebtedness and to bring sovereign nations under their control. Social movements, upheaval, revolutions and conflicts are engineered and plotted to bring about a One World Government where all individuals and individual nation-states are beholden to the ruling few. This is the antithesis of the goal of evolution and the biological plan.

With the demise of the gold system at Bretton Woods in 1944, paper currencies became worthless and able to be printed at whim to finance the growth of the conspicuous consumption of the masses and the territorial ambitions of megalomaniac leaders. The lust for absolute power has been fuelled and financed by this central banking system. As mentioned previously, Hitler represents the extreme example of the altered negative ego where he actually envisioned himself as the absolute ruler of the world or world emperor. In other words, he saw himself as the supreme being on the planet above everyone else. Yet, Hitler could not have risen to power without the financial backing of the ruling elite.

It is essential to realise that today, in the modern economic system no one – no individual person or nation state – is free from the manipulation of the ruling few who totally dominate all political, economic and social affairs. So even though on the surface there has been this outer movement towards personal freedom, in the shadows we are moving inexorably towards a New World Order run by the international banking cartel.

As individual nations borrow to finance war and economic growth, they in turn sell their freedom as a sovereign nation which means their ownership of gold, minerals and resources, land, control of borders and the ability to rule oneself. As individual countries lose their freedom, so too do the individual inhabitants of those countries. Once again, there is a reversion to the teachings of Luther and Calvin, whereby the masses are seen as unintelligent and unable to rule themselves and thus in need of the divine stewardship of the ruling elite who will save the people from their animalistic attitudes and self-destructive tendencies.

The New World Order is a Marxist concept of elitism which envisions a world ruled by an enlightened, wealthy and powerful oligarchy. Ordinary people are seen as dumb and unintelligent. And just as the negative ego acts in the individual structure of consciousness through the agencies of fear, suppression and repression, so too, this methodology is repeated on the world stage. The middle classes have to be held in check, suppressed and controlled via the media, education and the constant messages being promulgated throughout society.

Moreover, through this constant and subtle social indoctrination the people do gradually go to sleep, turning off their faculty of discerning thought and their ability to exercise free will choice. As long as we have our jobs to earn our wages, as long as we can come home and be mesmerised by the idiot box, as long as the economy keeps turning, we enter into that peaceful lethargy where we do not really care about the world. We live our lives through the television and through other forms of mass and social media which tell us what to think, how to behave and what to purchase so that we can be 'chic' and belong to the in-crowd.

We enter a psychic vacuum that allows and invites the forces of conformity and collectivity to enter and tell us what to do, which is anything but forming our own discerning and intelligent worldview and making our own sovereign decisions. And because the image-based ego has an insatiable appetite and needs constant reassurance and feeding, we need to work ever harder, going into more debt to fuel our inflated, false sense of self, and our social identity.

Sovereignty is absolute freedom from any and all extraneous influences and forces that own or control us. The average human being in any advanced, industrial, capitalist economy is anything but free. We are conditioned by an ever-pervasive social consciousness that dictates everything in our lives. Sovereignty, liberty, freedom and free will choice are all facets of the one crystal. Are we truly free to choose, to decide for ourselves? Are we able and willing to exercise that faculty and gift of free will? Do we possess our own unique structure of knowledge, our own world picture? Do we have our own values and principles? Is our personal corporate structure of consciousness alive and kicking? Does it work? Do we hold our altered negative ego in check or does it control our destiny?

Everything that we do and everything that we are, is the result of our choices. And we choose either consciously according to our own inner messages, beliefs, feelings, thoughts, attitudes and decisions or unconsciously, according to the external cues and messages of the social conditioning around us. Conscious choice facilitates personal growth and evolution. Unconscious choice breeds stagnation and being stuck in the repetitive boredom of the negative ego keeping us in a holding pattern of a life going nowhere but stuck in the comfort zone of mediocrity.

As we enter the epoch of Marshal McLuhan's global village, as the world wide web shrinks the planet, as we become electronically more interconnected, the risk of losing our unique individuality and sense of self increases exponentially. The collective negative ego gains in strength and influence and we become more socially dependent upon mass consciousness. As we attempt to satisfy the personal negative ego's insatiable craving for those possessions which reinforce our image-based identity, we become more economically dependent upon the *status quo*, needing our jobs, needing to fit in, needing financial security, needing to be an integral part of the economic machine, needing the positive ego strokes of societal approval. Only the foolish or the very brave would dare to speak up and buck the system! We all have far too much to lose.

The altered negative ego is the Antichrist! There is no absolute external evil apart from that created by man and his image-based identity ruled by fear, doubt and trepidation. We have created the evil and then created the fiction of the Devil to justify our insanity and aberrant behaviour. Evil is merely a choice and the abuse of human free will. Wickedness is the natural condition of the negative ego. The negative ego chooses destructiveness; the negative ego chooses domination; the negative ego chooses conquest and power over another. The negative ego chooses the co-dependent sadomasochistic relationship rather than the dignity, freedom and honour of love.

We choose to be either intolerant or to be compassionate. We choose to be either fearful or courageous. We choose to be either understanding or to wage war. We choose to either condemn or to forgive. We choose to either allow or to suppress. We choose to either feel or to repress. We choose to be fully awake, aware, alive, responsible and sovereign or we choose to go to sleep and be dominated and led.

We have moved on from the early days, tens of thousands of years ago, when we commanded our ego to take charge and created the evil of the altered negative ego. We then created the collective negative ego of war and brutality; the inhumanity and insanity that has ruled the planet suppressing the people and raping the earth. We are now entering the third and final chapter of One World Order where suppression and domination is no longer clumsy, overt and barbaric but subtle, sophisticated and unseen.

The goal of the negative ego is now complete world domination, not through force but through financial manipulation. This is still another form of co-dependency, of a social fascism where the elite will rule all the peoples and nations of the world and each and every individual human being will be enslaved by the economic machine. Just as in the past the wars were over gold to finance more wars and economic expansion, now the wars are all about black gold: the fossil fuels that sustain the world and are easily bought and owned by the ruling elite. Through the domination and ownership of central banking, currency printing and fossil fuels a co-dependent partnership has been formed between this elite and the world. The world is totally dominated by and beholden to the elite.

In the end, it is human greed that is fuelling the image-based ego and eventually destroying the planet and our home. As we have stressed, nature fulfils itself in the fully conscious, self-aware, sovereign human being. If we were to end up with no prospect for free will choice; if the ruling elite were to get their way of complete world domination it would truly be the end of the historical process, for there would be no purpose to life. The gift of free will choice and being a human being are two sides of the one coin: take one away and you abort the other!

Choice is the agency of evolution. Take away free will choice and you abort the evolutionary process. To be a human being with no free will is an oxymoron. We would become automatons, no better than robotic clones, all stepping in tune to the social conditioning of the New World Order. There is no spiritual purpose and no meaning to life if we completely abort this process and forsake our human destiny.

Evolution, learning, the structure of knowledge, personal growth and sovereignty are urgent concerns. To enlighten is to dispel the darkness of ignorance, to shed light upon and to overcome the negative forces of fear, superstition, ignorance and the belief in separateness. To be enlightened is to heal the division of separation and to fully understand and comprehend one's innate divinity and oneness with creation. In that wholeness one perceives the natural beauty and order of the universe.

There is no lack and thus no need for fear of 'not enough', and hence no need for greed. Greed is the outer manifestation of the inner emptiness and lack the negative ego feels because it is stuck in infantile matrices of unmet needs. As we become healed, as we become whole, and as we live consciously in the present, intelligently meeting and interacting with the now, the hold of the social conditioning and our dependence upon the economic machine wanes and we are free to be ourselves, to live our lives, to express our inner divine nature and to be who we truly are. As we wake up, individually – one by one – those courageous individuals willing to risk the journey to selfhood, subtly change the morphogenic field of collective human consciousness. Just as when one athlete breaks the four-minute mile, and many follow, so too, when one strong, self-aware individual achieves Personal Sovereignty, that person opens the psychic door for others to follow.

This does not mean we need to renounce the economic machine or become an ascetic recluse. But it does mean that we need to think for ourselves, broaden our minds and open our hearts and let the light of consciousness pierce the darkness of fear and separation. It means we need to stand up for what we believe in and renounce the co-dependent lie. It means we need to make our own sovereign decisions and exercise our faculty of free choice. It means we need to listen to and express our inner selves and stop listening to the injunctions of social consciousness. It does not mean we need to give up our jobs, but it does mean we need to give up the greed and lust for power of our derived and altered negative ego. It does mean we need to do our jobs with love and concern for the well-being of the whole. It means we need to reassert the supremacy of our resident spirit, taking back command of our corporate structure of consciousness and put the positive ego back where it belongs.

As more of us take this evolutionary journey, the future of humanity, the future of the planet, the future of our home – the Earth – takes a positive turn and lessens the hold of the collective negative ego. For the ruling elite are themselves the victims of their own negative egos and are caught in darkness and despair, wrongly believing that world domination and complete power over humanity will allay their deep inner lack of meaning and purpose.

In the final analysis, the meaning and purpose of life is to evolve, to become all that you can be, to express your own innate and unique inner divinity fully and to be yourself. Not to own all that you can own, not to dominate and have ultimate and unlimited power over every single man, woman and child on the planet, not to be consumed with fear and greed. But to be yourself, to do the right thing and to share the wonders of God's creation!

Life is a gift. Free will is a gift. Mother Earth as our home is a gift. Are we willing to risk aborting and losing all of these precious gifts and thus life itself for the myopic greed and power of an inflated and artificial negative ego that has no base in reality?

Part III: THE NEW HUMAN

Thirteen: Roadmap to Recovery

In Section I, we looked at the phylogenetic aspects of personal sovereignty in terms of the cosmological development and evolution of consciousness in its broader and universal context. We examined the corporate structure of consciousness, the inherent divine wisdom of the evolutionary plan and its eventual distortion and aberration, with the abdication of personal power and responsibility and the subsequent creation of the negative ego.

In Section II, we then traced how this malfunction – characterised as the mythological fall in the Garden of Eden – is culturally encoded and recreated in each of our own personal lives. How we willingly give away our power of decision-making and gift of free will rather than risk being at odds with the dictates of mass consciousness and being humiliated by being excluded from the mainstream of humanity's conventions and the *status quo*.

We abandon ourselves, turning our backs on our sacred individuality in order to 'fit in' with the profanity of the world. To be unique is to be different. And to be different is to be dangerous. We seek the comfort of conformity and the security of the consensus rather than risk the isolation and separateness of being true to ourselves.

Both of these sections are a looking back at the evolutionary and historical developments of what has already occurred in the past – both in terms of the original, divine, biological plan and the distorted human corruption of that plan.

Now we must look forward. For diagnosis is worse than useless if we do not have a cure. To merely indulge in doom and gloom without proposing a solution is to give into the very forces of darkness and fear that have created the problem in the first place. We need a roadmap, as it were, to create a future filled with joy and happiness, and to chart our course back to personal sovereignty, to living our lives authentically, to creating a full and meaningful sense of self taking back our personal power and replacing the altered negative ego with the resident spirit as supreme ruler of our being.

For humanity stands on the brink... but the brink of what? We stand at the crossroads at the beginning of the twenty first century – the new millennium. Do we stand on the brink of disaster, bringing ecological annihilation to the planet and to ourselves as well? Do we continue in our separatist state of the negative ego being disconnected from the biological plan and thus life and nature and each other? Do we bring destruction to not only ourselves but also to everything we touch? Do we continue our present rape of the planet, destroying its fragile eco-system, reducing its bio-diversity at the rate of myriad species per day? Do we continue to decimate the forests –– the lungs of the planet – and pollute the arterial waterways – the lifeblood of the bio-sphere? Do we continue the wars, the ethnic cleansing, the terrorism, the tyranny and authoritarianism? Do we allow the secret agenda of a small but powerful and hidden oligarchy to seduce us into economic slavery and mass-consumerism conformity?

Do we totally abort 4.6 billion years of preparation and evolution, throwing away our all too precious sense of self and beg others to make our decisions for us? Do we capitulate our responsibility and abdicate our power? Do we meekly give in?

Or do we turn the tide? Do we seek to redress the imbalance, restore the harmony, rescue the planet and rekindle the love? Do we roll up our figurative sleeves and do the necessary work to reclaim our dominion of the planet and take our rightful place in the Infinity of Being? Do we become the peaceful custodians of planet Earth, working in harmony with Gaia and her kingdoms? Do we earn the right to be here and to be accepted into the Intergalactic Federation of Responsible Beings? For as the I Ching says: '... what has been spoiled through man's fault can be made good again through man's work.'[41]

This is probably the most important question in our entire existence on both a personal, individual level and that of humanity. For it is not an exaggeration, nor is it hysteria to postulate that if we do not come to terms with these issues of personal sovereignty in the immediate future then our very survival as a species is severely threatened.

The biological plan follows and dictates certain laws of life. These laws describe the way in which life works, just as the law of gravity, for example, explains and describes how stellar bodies interrelate.

One can no more disobey the laws of life than one can disobey the law of gravity. One can only learn how to work with them. If we insist on going against the biological plan and the laws of life, it will be us who will suffer. The only real question is how many other species we will take with us and whether we will do irreparable damage to the planet before we go.

Either way, if we do not become the fully aware, self-conscious, emotionally mature and sovereign being that by now (in evolutionary terms) we ought to be, we will soon be an extinct species. It is only a matter of time! My personal feeling is that the biological plan of nature and God will carry on regardless, seeking its fulfilment through another species.

Is it not the height of arrogance and stupidity and is it not the hallmark of the altered, negative ego that humanity assumes it is the only 'intelligent' species on the planet and indeed in the universe? Have we now not witnessed first-hand the superior intelligence, social skills, emotional freedom, compassion and environmental adaptation of, for example, whales and dolphins enough to realise we are not as superior as our negative egos would like us to think?

There are now increasing examples of the animal kingdom's use of reasoning, intelligence and compassion. If anything does separate us from the animal kingdom, it is not our superior intelligence but our false sense of superiority and stupidity. For we are the only single species on the planet that is destroying ourselves and our environment. If this is the mark of a superior being, then God help us. What's the point of being at the top of the evolutionary tree if you are wildly chain-sawing it at the bottom?

So we need, as a matter of urgency, to find a way back to the intent of the biological plan. And as always, if one gets lost on a journey one must do several things. First, as we have repeatedly emphasised, we must have the nobility, the courage and the humility to recognise and acknowledge that one is lost. For it is only by having the courage to face the reality of the disorder that we have indeed created, over the last several thousand years of detour, exactly as it is, without the denial, self-deception, rationalisation or justification of the negative ego, that we can find the way home.

Second, is the acknowledgment that we ourselves have done this and that we continue to do it on an ongoing daily basis and that we are not the hapless, helpless victims of either a vengeful god or a satanic Devil. We are not being punished for a misdemeanour committed by our forebears long ago in a mythological garden. We are not a fatally flawed species and we are not powerless.

For it is only this combination of recognising exactly what is going on, linked with the acknowledgement that it is our own doing, that gives us the power and the ability to change direction. The third thing one must establish if one gets lost is exactly where and when one last knew where one was. In other words, one must retrace one's steps to the last place before getting lost. This is what has been established in Parts I and II. We needed to retrace our evolutionary journey both in the universal and the individual contexts in order to know exactly where and how we got lost.

Finally, one needs to determine precisely what the correct destination and path is so that one can plan a route from the present situation to that preferred outcome. In other words, if we are lost, we need to know exactly where we got lost, where we are now and where we need to get to in order to get back on track. Sometimes, as in this situation, it is impossible to go back and so one must forge a new path from the present to the future.

This is the challenge facing humanity. Having abandoned the biological plan tens of thousands of years ago, we now need to find our own way home. Once we find this path we must be prepared to follow it resolutely, perseveringly and valiantly for the voices of the negative ego will not be silenced easily and we will be accused of heresy just as Galileo, Copernicus, Leonardo and Columbus were.

We must be prepared to fight for what is right. We must assume the mantle of personal sovereignty as a knight dons a coat of armour – not the rigid armouring of the emotional plague of the negative ego but the firm and compassionate armouring of the warrior-sage.

The problem is that with so many generations of tinkering and violation of the biological plan we really have little or no idea of what a natural, self-realised, fully aware, spontaneous sovereign being looks like. How does a person behave who has and exercises personal sovereignty? What are their characteristics? What does their life look like?

I commenced this book in 1994, after finishing my book *The Art of Nourishment* and while it was at the printer's, completing sections I and II in a matter of months. Then all creativity (on this project) ceased abruptly and mysteriously. No matter how hard I tried, with what determination or resolve I intended to complete the manuscript, it just was not to be. It did not flow, and it did not happen. Then just as suddenly, in June 2001, exactly seven years later, this last section was written. It is now another 17 years later as the manuscript becomes a reality.

Looking back now, what I realise is that I was not ready to describe the qualities of personal sovereignty for I did not know them first hand. They were foreign to me, for I was still too trapped in my own co-dependency. It was only by confronting these demons within my own psyche and their out-picturing in my own world that I could recognise their origins, acknowledge my part in their creation and change those aspects of my character enough to glimpse the evolutionary horizon of personal sovereignty. It was the personal journey of the last twenty years that allowed me to experience first-hand the machinations and manipulations of the negative ego and to witness its destructive intent.

Thus, I would preface this section with the confession and the disclaimer that I in no way describe these qualities as a mission accomplished but rather as one person's attempt to envisage what personal sovereignty would look like, just as a science fiction writer might envision the future. I do not speak as one who has succeeded in making the transition, for as I have postulated repeatedly personal sovereignty is a new and emerging evolutionary quantum leap in human consciousness that as yet does not exist on the planet except for a few rare enlightened beings.

As mentioned earlier, changes are always made by a few courageous individuals willing to leave the pack of mass belief and mass consciousness and go out on their own, seeking new more expanded horizons. This is the work of the warrior-sage, the white knight, the map-maker and way shower, the adventurer in consciousness. But I have glimpsed this new world and I have tasted of its nectar. So, I do not speak as the authority but as the adventurer offering my hypothesis, my roadmap, as one suggested path to follow in order to find its reality.

Christopher Columbus did not set off to discover the new world as an authority but as an adventurer. He intuitively knew from the depths of his being – from his real self – that it existed. He had only to find it! So too, I know from the depths of my being – from my real self – that this reality of consciousness does indeed exist and that we can live and breathe from that space and that if we do, the magnificence and splendour that we will discover, will be equal on the inner planes to that of the discovery of the New World 300 years ago.

Personal sovereignty is the next evolutionary phase of human consciousness. This is not an external revolution like the agricultural, industrial, technological or information revolutions. This goes far beyond those material aspects of our reality. This goes to the heart of being human! This answers the pivotal question: do we choose, *en masse*, as a species, to survive? This answers the question of us all, as individual human beings – do we choose to be happy and do we choose to cease the fragmentation, the destruction and the domination of our own negative egos.

Do we choose to take back our power both individually and collectively? Do we choose to give up domination and assume dominion of the planet?

But before we can hope to achieve any of these things we must first become responsible for ourselves and for the personal reality that we create on a daily basis and for the impact we have on the world and on others in our lives.

This for me has been the journey of the last decade. It has been the most difficult and tumultuous and at the same time the most magnificent journey of my life. For it has taken me from the heights and joys of intimate love and sharing to the depths of self-doubt and self-reflection. It has forced me to confront firsthand the machinations, distortions, and manipulations of the negative ego and to witness its evil destructiveness. Again, I use the word evil not in any religious or judgemental sense but merely as a word to describe those processes which are fundamentally by their very nature opposed to the principles of life and creation.

Life is creative. Evil is destructive. For in life even the forces of decay and death are ultimately creative of new life. But evil simply destroys, tears down, attacks and leaves destitute all that it touches. It has no redeeming quality. The negative ego is destructive and if we as individuals are not vigilant and aware of its inherent nature, it will slowly but surely bring disaster and destruction into our lives just as the collective negative ego is surely destroying the planet. We are already witnessing the pain, suffering, desolation and destruction, the tyranny the negative ego has caused in our own lives, the lives of our loved ones, in humanity and on the planet.

I offer the following seven principles as a means by which we can counter the pernicious hold the negative ego exercises on all of our lives and find a way back to our real and true divine inner natures. For I do believe that there is a way home, there is a way out of this mess that we have created here and it is to hold to our heavenly nature and practise the virtue of its injunctions as revealed to us in our own individual, natural, primary impulses. If we are to live with personal sovereignty, we must practise these seven qualities:

    I   Personal Powah
    II   Inner Clarity
    III   Intention
    IV   Self-mastery and Functioning with Dominion
    V   Purity of Purpose
    VI   Self-love and Self-acceptance
    VII   The Joy of Self-expression

To be oneself and to be true to one's inner nature would seem to be the simplest thing in the world to do; yet, as we will discover in Section III, it is one of the most difficult.

FOURTEEN: PERSONAL POWAH

I have coined the word 'powah' to distinguish it from the word power, which has now many unfavourable connotations associated with it as power over someone else. The word 'powah', however, denotes true personal power that has nothing to do with another. Rather, it is our ability to do, to perform, and to take charge of our own lives. Whereas power is associated with domination, 'powah' is associated with dominion.

In the world of machines, we use the term 'horsepower' to measure the power or strength of a motor. In the world of electronics, we use the term 'amplitude' to measure the output of a device. In the world of computers, we use the terms 'speed' and 'memory'. In mechanics, power depends upon two things: the original design and the ability to function as intended, according to the design specifications.

We have all experienced the loss of power from a dirty spark plug or a wet distributer cap. We have all experienced the slowness of a computer or server when it labours under a virus attack. The simplest analogy for powah is a current generated by a battery or an electrical circuit. How much current or electrical charge – Chi or energy – our nervous system can carry depends on the synapses of our personal circuitry.

If the wiring is faulty, if the gating mechanism of pain has closed down many of the synaptic pathways and we are operating on only a small fraction of our potential current; if there are short circuits, then when the current reaches a certain voltage or amplitude the system will fail. True power comes from free-flowing circuitry and an uninterrupted current.

This is true power and majesty: the ability to be true to oneself. During my counselling sessions in *TaoTuning*, I was able to graph the comfort zones and the short circuits in individual circuitry. We all do have them. It is important to recognise and acknowledge our comfort zones and our electrical thresholds.

If one watches an animal in the wild, there is patience, calculation and precision, followed by precise action that is elegant in its execution. There is no hesitation, no doubt, and no lame vacillation.

Meditation is the means by which we increase the current-carrying capacity of the neurological circuitry – deep, slow, rhythmic breathing is the means by which we activate the biological circuitry. A subtle change takes place at a certain level of stillness. It is as if one changes stations from the 'yamma-yamma' of the negative ego's hard rock channel to the peace and tranquillity of the intuition's classical FM. It is real and potent as verified by numerous experiments with plants and their response to music and more recently with bio-feedback research done on meditators.

If one never achieves this state of inner quiet, one cannot hear the sounds of silence: the still small voice of god within. For if the ego's incessant chatter and noise of the left brain is not silenced, one cannot receive and pay attention to the more delicate broadcasts of universal intelligence which are picked up by the intuition of the right brain. It is vitally important to understand this functional division of labour between the two brains with its attendant implications.

Not all thinking is intelligent! Not all intelligence operates through conscious left brain thought. These are not mutually exclusive functions, but they are definitely not concomitant.

Because the negative ego has by now usurped such total and complete control of the corporate structure of consciousness, the left brain is permanently turned on, producing an incessant chatter of veritable mental diarrhoea. This thinking is automatic, reflexive, unintelligent, repetitious and dumb. If you become adept at watching your mind by strengthening the observer (which is the real and intelligent part of you) you will observe its repetitive nature, its stupidity and its propensity for destruction.

We have come to believe that we – meaning that superior intelligence that makes us human and gives us our unique individuality – reside in the thinking, reasoning left brain. Nothing could be further from the truth! For if we honestly examine the functioning of the thinking brain we will see very quickly that it is anything but intelligent. Rather it is cumbersome, slow, self-doubting, superstitious, judgemental and filled with negativity. It is inherently unhealthy and thus unintelligent. Remember, I have defined intelligence as the ability to respond to the challenges of life in the now in a creative future-oriented way.

In this society, we have come to value the logical rational brain above all else. As emphasised in Section II, the cultural encoding of the fall does everything possible to discredit the intuitive mind. However, we need to return to the primary thrust of the biological plan and its intention for humanity as a self-aware, fully conscious sovereign being. As already mentioned, each animal species activates specific holographic representations of the overall intelligence of the planet that allows it to act with instinctive certainty and facilitates that precision and mastery that is such an eloquent part of the nature kingdom.

However, there is no option or choice to adopt another hologram or behavioural pattern, no free will choice. One species cannot tune into the innate biological intelligence of another. It is a closed circuit ruled by instinct and evolutionary hereditary. A mouse cannot become a lion – nor can it roar.

Mankind, on the other hand, is this open-ended potential with no limitation. That is why we are as a species continually pushing back the frontiers of mental discovery, physical performance, emotional expression and artistic creativity. As a species we never stop overcoming our own limits and setting new records or entering new dimensions. This aspect, which probably more than any other separates humanity from the other species on the planet, depends upon open circuitry. As explained in Section II, the human neonate is the most helpless of all animals and depends upon its parents for the longest period of time, precisely because it needs to build this open ended holographic intelligence.

Animals have personal power because they listen to and trust their own inner nature implicitly and without faltering. Thus, they exhibit that surety and self-confidence that so many humans lack. But they do this precisely because they have no other choice. They cannot disobey that inner navigational system of instinct. They still reside within the mythological Garden of Eden, pre free will.

However, once Adam and Eve ate of the forbidden fruit, learning of the knowledge of good and evil, understanding the duality of free will choice and gaining the power of the gods, humanity was no longer constrained by the inevitability of biological programming via instinctive responses. We became free. This is the gift of free will – the ability to choose. But the real question is: to choose what?

And the answer is to listen! To obey! To follow!

Animals have no choice but to listen, follow and obey their inner nature – to be true to themselves and accede to their instinctive response. There is no choice being made, there is no decision, there is no doubt, there is no quandary.

We, on the other hand, are faced with unlimited potential, a sea of endless possibilities and infinite choices from which to choose and create our own personal reality. We do not have the surety of instinctive response compelling us to act according to prescribed behaviour. And as we discovered at the beginning, that sea of potential is expanding exponentially as the geographic, social and economic constraints around us lose their hold on our culture and our individual psyches. For example, some human beings have now purchased tickets to the Moon on private spacecraft. Not so long ago, this choice was simply not available.

So how do we decide? How do we choose from this infinite sea of potential? How do we know what is right for us? And this is where the paradox – which is both a blessing and a curse – of being human, lies.

For we can only know what is right for us by being true to our own inner natures and by listening to our own inner voice, the voice of our intuition which has taken over the function of the primary navigational mechanism of the system from instinct. However, to do this we must silence the ego. We must be able to hold the noise of the thinking brain in abeyance long enough to allow the more subtle injunctions and guidance of the intuition to be heard. We must be able to receive the broadcasts of universal intelligence which prompt us and lead us on our path.

Powah comes from strength and all strength must be sourced. The source of strength can either be within or without. Many people are strong within the context of a given situation. This is the basis of the clan mentality of the collective ego, of the gang, the crowd, the army, the political or religious group. The individual feels strengthened when surrounded by and aligned with the ideology of the mass. Both the atrocities of war and gang rape are examples of the false inflation of the yin principle, which is inherently weak of itself but feels strong when supported by the encouragement of others.

But this is not real and true strength. It is false and artificial precisely because it is dependent upon a source from without. In fact, this is the complete opposite of personal sovereignty. This is the grip of mass consciousness from which we are only now just emerging in evolutionary terms.

Similarly, many people feel strong within the context of a marriage or personal relationship. This is the essence of co-dependency. All sadomasochistic relationships are examples of weak individuals finding strength in an alliance with another weak individual. All bullies are cowards and all cowards are bullies. It is just that they exhibit characteristics of either end of the polar extremes. If the source of one's strength is without, in one's relationship to an ideology, a group or another individual, then one is inevitably doomed to the vicissitudes of the fate of that other. One will either be strong or weak, happy or sad, motivated or despondent according to the accord or discord of that alliance. In other words, one needs an ally in order to feel complete.

We will be examining this concept of the 'ally' in much greater detail later on, but for now it is essential to grasp the significance of the concept. For it is true that no one is an island and that we are all interrelated. We return to the concept of the 'holon' introduced in Section I. The significant point is that many of us can operate as the part of a larger whole but not as the single sovereign entity. How many of us can truly make decisions for and by ourselves? How many of us really know what we truly want? How many of us ever experience any degree of real autonomy?

I am not saying that all alliances or that the influence of the mass over the individual are always wrong or destructive. Many noble and altruistic goals are achieved because of many people coming together to work for the common good. Indeed, this is the story of humanity's evolution. We have evolved purely and simply because of the division of labour, the specialisation of tasks and the cooperation of individual members of a society for the common good of all. This cooperation enabled the first beginnings of agriculture and herding, which eventually led to the subsequent sociological and technological developments of history.

No, it is not that holding together, *per se*, is right or wrong but rather upon what that holding together is based. If this is a union of weak individuals looking for a source of strength outside of themselves then that union will eventually degenerate into religious fundamentalism, political authoritarianism, the vigilante group or simply the gang. Even in marriage and intimacy, love will ultimately deteriorate into some form of co-dependency if it is not based in inner truth and mutual respect.

The point being that the individual will eventually lose his or her sense of personal powah and sovereignty to the group. The individual will feel strengthened by its association with the larger body but will gradually lose its sense of individuality and self. The process of conformity will eventually obliterate any sense of authenticity.

If on the other hand, it is the union of strong individuals seeking to ally themselves with other strong individuals in order to achieve something significant for which they themselves, of their own strength, may not have been able to achieve, union and cooperation can be wholesome, enjoyable and fulfilling. Indeed, there is no greater joy than working collaboratively with others to achieve an altruistic goal and objective. However, the individual holon must hold onto their sanctity and sovereignty as an individual unit of that group. The group must also hold and respect the sanctity of the individual. There can be no diminishing of the individual for the sake of the group.

And this is the point of demarcation. In all authoritarian structures, the individual self is seen as lesser than the collective self. The will of the individual is subjugated to the will of the collective. Individual needs are sacrificed for the so-called common good. But in the end, the law of entropy ensures that all end up worse off except for the ruling elite. We have only to witness the rape and pillage of the common wealth of all states that have been through the communist, socialist, authoritarian mould of the last fifty years to verify this tendency.

In all sovereign social structures, the individual sense of self is enhanced and ennobled by its association with the collective. One is a part of something larger, but one does not sacrifice one's authentic self for that alliance. One is able to remain true to the self; the self is honoured in its integrity. There is no conflict of interest between the goals of the individual and the goals of the group because both are based on what is right. It is this sense of rightness that is ultimately the only true and sovereign source of strength.

For if something is right then it is right for all. This is the glory of God, the omniscience of divine intelligence, the benevolence of the universe. The universe works in perfect harmony. Ultimately, all the cycles of life and death, the workings of the seasons and the spinning of the celestial orbs cooperate in such a way that 'Life Works'!

Life Works! This is why it is so vital to grasp this concept of evil, or 'live' spelt backwards. Wherever we look, from the most microscopic to the far reaches of infinite space, life works. And life works precisely because it follows the laws of life. On the other hand, wherever we look where the negative ego operates, life does not work. There is eventual pain and destruction that is not regenerative, that is not cyclic, that does not create new life. In nature, all processes of death and decay lead to the eventual creation of more, new and better life. Where humanity destroys, life ceases.

Life operates according to certain principles and laws. It is being in harmony with these principles and laws that gives this sense of rightness. It is being in harmony with this rightness that is the only true source of strength and thus powah.

All plants and animals in nature exist within a continuum of being – a group or set. Let us call this group 'the wild'. In the wild, all species compete for food and survival with one species living off some other. Yet in both the plant and animal kingdoms there is an inherent harmony and longevity – a viability that ensures the long-term survival of the whole: the ecosystem of the planet. The sanctity of the individual – both as a species and as an individual member of a species – is maintained. No two animals, no two plants, no two leaves and no two cells in nature are the same. There is no conformity, no imitation, no copying, no envy, no jealousy, no better than or less than. There is no comparison!

Oranges are not better or less than apples. Roses not better or less than camellias. Lions are not better or less than tigers. Elephants are not better or less than mice. We all may have our personal preferences, but each is a sacred part of the web of life and each species respects the others' right to life. None takes more than it needs, as so eloquently stated by Elton John in *The Lion King*.

It is only humanity that causes destruction and the extinction of species because we transgress and break the laws of life. It is only humans that compare themselves to others, coveting, envying another's possessions or qualities, denying our own richness and unique authenticity.

In the wild, the individual exists within the group consciousness but does not lose itself or feel lesser than the group. No single species suffers for the group. On the contrary, the group exists to support every single species and every individual member of the wild.

The source of an animal's or plant's strength is its instinctive obedience to and allegiance with the laws of life. This is the mythological Garden of Eden. It is a state in which the individual does not have free will choice to disobey the laws of life and thus is aligned with that biological process. It is this alignment which generates strength and powah. The lion's strength, the elephant's might, and the whale's majesty all come from their being in harmony with life. There is no discord, no self-doubt, no short circuit in the bio-currents of power that courses through their being.

But with humanity's eating of the forbidden fruit comes the knowledge of good and evil – the knowledge of the gods – the existence of duality and the ability to disobey. And what also comes is self-doubt! With self-awareness comes self-doubt. This is the mythological representation of the fig leaf: 'the awareness of their nakedness.' This is not a sexual, physiological or genital reference but rather a psychological reference of their awareness of self-hood. An awareness of oneself as a separate individual, an awareness that one has emerged from the group consciousness of 'the wild' of the garden and that one now stands on the brink of the journey of individuation and the evolution of consciousness. This is the birth of that awkwardness of being self-conscious.

With self-awareness comes self-doubt – the short circuiting of the currents of life and an interruption of the inner source of strength with an eventual loss of personal powah. Cut off from the instinctive connection with 'the wild', we now embarked on the journey of co-dependency with our negative egos and each other and our subsequent loss of powah.

Powah is intimately connected to alignment. That connection is either involuntary and instinctive as in 'the wild' or volitional and conscious as in the fully mature, self-realised, sovereign individual. Between these two polar extremes is the painful journey of adolescence – of awkward self-awareness, self-doubt and lack of powah as we transit the continuum.

The only way to reconnect with our inner powah is to realign with the natural harmony of the principles and laws of life, by regaining clarity.

FIFTEEN: INNER CLARITY

So, what is clarity and how does it function?

Clarity is being clear. It is that unobstructed vision that enables one to do what is right with instinctive certainty, decisively, free from doubt and hesitation. Once again, we come to this dialectic of freedom: freedom *from* the debilitating force of doubt, giving the freedom *to* make a conscious decision and act. Free will choice is a process that must follow certain steps if it is to be successful. The steps are as follows:

- ❖ AN OPTION:
  One must be faced with alternative courses of action or behaviour lest one has no real choice. There must be at least two paths or alternatives to choose from.

- ❖ REFLECTION:
  One must be able to identify and recognise those alternatives and be able to evaluate their relative merits and weaknesses.

- ❖ DELIBERATION:
  One then enters into some form of deliberation of the probable outcomes and consequences of each choice against some predetermined goal or criteria that one desires.

- ❖ SOVEREIGN CHOICE:
  Eventually, one must make a conscious, free choice and choose one path – not one from default by not choosing. Many people, unable to choose consciously, wait until life or destiny or external events make the choice for them. Others listen to the advice of others, allowing themselves to be influenced into a particular path. This is not what we mean by sovereign choice.

- ❖ DECISION:
  Having identified the options, reflected, deliberated and chosen, it is then necessary to make a decision – to follow through with some action, even if that action is merely an internal change of attitude or behaviour. The process of choosing fulfils itself in the process of decision. Without a decision there is no sense of completion.

- ❖ EXECUTION:
  That decision must somehow make itself show in reality. It is of no consequence making a decision and then subsequently changing one's mind and vacillating backwards and forwards. There needs to be an element of resolve and determination – a sense of achievement, of going forward. The decision must lead to some tangible change in one's world inner and outer.

- ❖ MONITORING:
  Having made a decision, it is then necessary to watch carefully for some time how that decision bears the test of actuality to see if any adjustments need to be made – to evaluate the consequences.

- ❖ RECOGNITION:
  We need to recognise that we have made a decision, that we have chosen a path and give ourselves some reward, some acknowledgement, some praise or recognition that we did, in fact, do it so that we are empowered by the exercise rather than weakened by the deliberation and indecision.

Admittedly, this is a fairly laborious structure and only intended to be used as a template and not a definitive rule, but it does give us a sense of the components involved in the decision-making process. And to a greater or lesser extent, depending on the seriousness of the decision facing us, we do go through either some or all of these steps. Obviously, the choice as to what to have for lunch does not exact the same intensity as say the choice to select a new house or job.

However, what is essential to understand is that like any sport, art or skill, the decision-making process is a discipline that must be learnt, practised and cultivated if we want to get good at it. Because the average human being avoids making definitive decisions it is generally not a skill or practice we are good at. Therefore, we do need to break it down into its constituent parts until we develop proficiency. Moreover, as we get better at making decisions, as we exercise our personal sovereignty, this decision-making process becomes faster and more intuitive. We just *know* in the depths of our being without too much deliberation or reflection.

Just as an elite athlete or performer needs to initially practise the steps of a routine consciously, deliberately and carefully and then eventually hand the process over to the autonomic nervous system, so too, we need to initially practise making small and deliberate decisions until we develop the intuitive certainty of knowing what our inner self chooses without too much deliberation or reflection.

However, if we are to understand the traps and weaknesses of exactly where we do get stuck or at which stage of the process our reluctance lies, it is important to break it up into its constituent phases. As previously emphasised, this is the process of intelligent conscious choice. If there is any breakdown in the process choices will not be effective. If for example, one labours the reflection and deliberation process pushing it too far, one will lame the power of decision. If one is unable to reach a definitive conclusion one will be unable to act. If one does not reflect at all, acting impulsively, the choice may not be intelligent nor right.

Thus, clarity is this ability to choose, to decide for oneself what is right and then being able to act on that decision. Just as powah is rooted in strength and strength in clarity, so too, clarity is rooted in knowing. Without knowing there is no clarity, no surety, no strength. Inner strength and powah come from that definitive state of knowing what is right for the self. To thyself be true! Ultimately, it all begins with developing true intimacy with the self.

And just as doubt is the short circuit of powah, confusion is the nemesis of clarity. Confusion is an inability to choose between alternative options and thus an inability to decide and move forward.

Inability to decide because of self-doubt leads to inability to act. Everything remains in lame vacillation.

Confusion paralyses and debilitates: the paralysis of analysis! Confusion leads to indecision and eventual stagnation. Confusion comes about because we cannot get clear; we cannot find our way; we cannot choose and decide exactly what is right for us as an individual. We do not have access to that inner state of intuitive certainty and knowing that is such an integral part of strength and personal powah. And most, if not all self-doubt, comes from the fear of being wrong, the fear of humiliation, and the fear of another's judgement.

This happens when we are disconnected from the inner circuits of our being because of self-doubt. For a self-doubting person, the process of decision-making is an incredibly painful experience and one to be avoided at all costs. So, a self-doubting person just does not make decisions because they cannot get clear. They procrastinate, deliberate, vacillate and give their powah away to another so that the other – whether that other be a person, a religion, a belief system or ideology, a group – will make the decisions for them and thus 'save' them from their confusion and the anxiety of having to make their own decision.

If the decision-making process is a painful and laborious one, then far better to give away one's sovereignty and depend upon another to make one's decisions, rather than do it oneself. This is also particularly relevant if one has found from experience that one's decisions are not usually right.

In other words, if powah depends upon strength, strength upon clarity and clarity upon this quality of rightness, then without rightness the whole structure collapses. This is exactly what has happened in the evolutionary process. As we left the Garden of Eden's instinctive certainty and rightness, without the necessity of making free will choice, we entered the domain of personal free will where we needed to exercise that all too precious gift, now consciously choosing for ourselves what was 'right' for us.

However, by renouncing that gift, abdicating control and forcing the negative ego to assume the role of decision maker for which it was neither designed nor intended, the whole process collapsed in upon itself. The limiting forces of fear and doubt penetrated too deeply into the mechanism of consciousness and we lost our clarity, becoming more and more lost and confused.

So, we need to examine this quality of rightness more closely, for it is obvious that many choices appear to be right at the time but prove subsequently to be wrong with the benefit of hindsight. So too, many of the most heinous atrocities throughout history have been committed under the guise of being right. For in how many conflicts do both peoples or sides passionately believe they are right? Most wars are fought in the name of God or at least a belief in the superior wisdom or rightness of their cause.

What is this quality of rightness in the sense that we are using it? For it has little to do with the petty ego's sense of 'I am right and you are wrong' and everything to do with Universal Truth. The former is nothing more than just the boastful posturing of the falsely inflated, self-righteous ego. The latter is nothing less than the divine will of God expressed through the principles and laws of life.

As I mentioned in *The Art of Nourishment* there is a Universal Law – The Tao – running throughout the universe. This law is the will of God or the Divine Intelligence of Creation. This one law then manifests in all the countless laws that regulate life and is the way of the universe referred to as The Way, The Path, The Truth, and The Light. Call it what you will, it does exist and is universal in its application and in its jurisdiction.

It is important to mention at this point that this has nothing to do with religion. This law is not personal or subjective and has nothing to do with God in Heaven. It is merely a function of the living universe; the way things are; a part of and why Life Works. It is not a prescriptive law that one must follow or be punished. It is rather a descriptive law, like gravity, that operates universally and objectively.

As we are just beginning to discover through our wholesale destruction of the planet, there is no escaping these universal laws of life. Even Christ's edict 'to do unto others as you would have them do unto you' is a very basic and profound statement of the law of life.

On the personal level, each and every being has a personal law which guides it from within. This is the biological plan: that inherent wisdom passed down through the ages that we inherit at birth and gives us access to the codes of life. This personal law is unique for all of us and describes who we are. To know and to follow this personal law is clarity and the path to a successful life.

We return to the notion that at our core we are not inherently bad or fatally flawed but divinely good. We have received from mother nature, from the biological plan, from the 4.6-billion-year evolutionary process, an intrinsic ability to know what is right for us. We just need to be able to tune into and listen to our divine inner nature.

Man has received from heaven a nature innately good, to guide him in all his movements. By devotion to this divine spirit within, the self attains an unsullied innocence that leads it to do 'right' with an instinctive sureness, with a sense of certainty, with that power of conviction that bespeaks authenticity and authority.

However, humanity no longer has the absolute instinctive certainty of 'the wild'. We must develop our own individual ability to listen to and obey the dictates of our own inner knowing and to choose what is right for us consciously. This is the whole point of being human – this is the destination and fulfilment of the evolutionary journey.

> Yet, not everything instinctive is nature in this higher sense of the word, but only that which is right and in accord with the will of heaven. Without this quality of rightness, an unreflecting, instinctive way of action brings only misfortune.[42]

Thus, the plot thickens. We no longer have automatic access to the biological codes as in the wild or the Garden of Eden. We must exercise free will choice, yet we cannot just act instinctively and without thinking, plus, we now have the distracting forces of self-doubt and fear robbing us of inner clarity and causing confusion. The ten thousand years of the 'fall of man' cultural encoding and social conditioning all create confusion and bewilderment.

For it is vital to realise once again, here, that the cultural encoding mechanism tells us on a daily basis and from every quarter – from parenting to religion, from social media to mass media, that we cannot trust ourselves; that we are inherently wrong, flawed, fallible and failing and that we need the injunctions of religion, society, and civilisation to 'save' us from our bestial natures. In other words, if we do listen to our inner selves we will be wrong. If we do act from inner impulse, we will be destructive. If we are true to ourselves, then we will be rejected by others.

Nowhere are we encouraged to believe in ourselves, to obey the dictates of our inner being, to listen to the still quiet voice of God that resides within, to have faith in our free will choice decision-making ability and to decide for and by ourselves, free from external influence and persuasion.

With the incessant noise and din of the pressure and pace of modern living and with the perpetual broadcasts of mass media and social media conformity, how can we possibly find the silence to listen to our inner beings? Added to that is the destructive pernicious influence of the negative ego deliberately trying to lead us astray. Is it any wonder clarity is such an elusive thing?

For to achieve clarity one must be still! One must silence the 'yammering' of the negative ego's left brain and enter into that state of inner quietude. One must be composed, serious and reverent if one wishes to acquire that clarity of mind needed for coming to terms with the confusion of external daily reality and its innumerable impressions. One must be content and at peace with oneself. The negative ego is never at peace with itself but is always comparing.

This is why all the great mystery schools and all religious training involve some aspect of the practice of contemplation and meditation. Without the ability to concentrate one cannot focus and achieve clarity. We must be free from the din and confusion, the turmoil of outer life in order to be free to access the peace and tranquillity of inner silence, bringing order out of chaos.

For it is only in this state of inner composure that we silence the dominance of the negative ego and allow the spirit to speak through the intuition. It is through this process and this process only that we can go back to a correct functioning of the healthy state of consciousness where the ego is the servant and the spirit is the master.

It is only through the discipline of concentration that we enter the meditative state whereby the lower, noisy, beta brainwaves of the rational thinking bio-computer make way for the higher, more subtle, alpha brainwaves of intuitive awareness.

It is a personal choice! And in many ways, it is our only choice: to listen to the ego with its constant demands for attention and gratification or to listen to the Tao with its call to do what is right. Just as when we turn on a television or radio we choose which station to listen to, so too, we are continually making a choice every moment of our lives: who will we listen to; who will we follow – our ego or our Tao?

For we each have a very personal law of our being which is our own Tao: the way that is right for us as a fully aware, self-realised, sovereign individuated being. And it is this law which we must obey if we are to make the right choices. It has absolutely nothing to do with religious morality, societal norms or conventions or the injunctions of mass consciousness. It has absolutely nothing to do with any other human being, no matter how close or intimate. It is a purely personal affair between the individuated self and the creator as prescribed by the dictates of our own Being and revealed via our own Tao through the process of meditation and inner reflection.

One must take the time to get to know oneself. One must set aside time for peace and solitude with no mass media noise, no electronic screens, and no significant other present. One must befriend oneself in order to know oneself.

This is Clarity. This is how we 'know' what is right for us: free from doubt, free from fear, free from the influence of the negative ego and free to follow courageously, decisively our own inner being. This is the only way to know. No amount of consultation, advice or external discussion can ever replace this inner process. It is a vital and fundamental prerequisite of personal sovereignty.

We either listen to the broadcasts of the collective negative ego through the daily bombardment of the mass media or we listen to the broadcasts of Divine Universal Intelligence through the daily discipline of quiet inner stillness. We are either restless or at peace. We are either confused or clear. We are either agitated or calm. We are either our ego or our Tao; we cannot be both at once.

Ultimately, there is no choice, for this is the only choice: to listen to and obey our inner divine spirit or to listen to and obey our negative ego. To do what is right or to do what is wrong.

It is all a question of alignment and spiritual attunement. Eventually, we enter that state of the mystics that is referred to as 'choiceless awareness' where we are so attuned to the will of God that we have no choice. This is what Christ referred to when he said, 'not my will but thine be done'.

We have arrived at the end of the process. We have re-entered the Garden of Eden but not as an unconscious creature compelled by instinct to obey but rather as a sovereign being choosing freely and consciously to do the will of God, to do what is right.

I feel it is important here to clarify the meaning of the phrase 'the will of God', lest it be misinterpreted as some form of evangelical or religious admonition. Nothing could be further from the truth. I am not using the term 'God' in any religious or even spiritual sense. This is definitely not to be confused with fundamentalism or pre-determinism. God is most definitely not an old man in Heaven with a beard! God is most definitely not a glorified image of man.

I like to use the analogy of a sphere. Think of an apple, an orange or a ball. If God is the centre of the sphere and each individual being is a point on its surface, then there is one and only one radius from that point to the centre. That is your individual personal relationship with God. That radius is your path, your Tao, and your way home. There is no other way! And God is purely the centre of the sphere, with absolutely no religious connotations.

And no matter how close any two points on the surface of the sphere may be, no two radii are the same. Each and every person must determine their own path, find their own way, discover their own Tao. To know what is right for us, to know the will of god, to find our way, to make our choices, we cannot look outside of ourselves. We must find our own way, make our own choices and decisions and travel along our own radius to the centre. All else is distraction.

Similarly, the will of God is not some form of commandment or religious edict or a morality or scripture. God does not sit in Heaven in judgement. The will of God is purely and simply your path, your way, your Tao. It is objective and universal in its application. Ultimately, there is no absolute right or wrong, or good or evil in a linear judgmental sense. We urgently need to demythologise this whole religious concept, so we can take back our personal powah and begin to take life seriously. While we continue to create external mythical creatures of God and the Devil, we will continue to throw away our personal powah and sovereign dominion.

It is only what is most appropriate, most correct for you at any point in time as an evolving consciousness on your own way home. There is an optimum path and that path is your Tao or the will of God – the way that is right for you and nobody else. The Universal Law or Absolute Will of God does operate through the spiritual practice and laws of life that govern our existence. And it is these laws, these principles that must not be transgressed if we would have that quality of rightness in our lives. But these principles are not moralistic. They are the scientific laws of life; the way life works.

So to be clear, to have clarity, to be right, we must both adhere to the universal laws of life and obey the individual law of our own being. The former is impersonal, universal and absolute. The latter is personal and individual and relative. The former generates an infinite field of possibility for the evolution of life. The latter generates a finite and limited field of potential for our own individual evolution. The two together create the field of probabilities from which our choices and alternatives arise.

To have Clarity is to understand the backdrop or the context of our individual path against which my individual choices must make sense. In other words, we must have a sense of our individual purpose. We must have an inkling or an appreciation of the meaning of our lives. Without this higher understanding of the specific purpose of this individual lifetime on the planet earth, we cannot achieve that inner clarity that gives us the certainty to act with surety and conviction.

If we are lost amidst the turmoil of outer confusion and fall prey to the influences of distraction that abound in social consciousness, our own negative ego will combine with that of the collective unconscious and lead us on a merry dance that takes us anywhere but down our own radius home. We will be constantly seeking on the surface of the sphere rather than looking to the centre. We cannot make clear decisions and are thus forced by default into co-dependency with both our own negative ego within and significant others without.

We have no real sense of who we are or why we are here. We lack a spiritual purpose and the true meaning of our lives. It is therefore impossible for us to create a clear intention of where we are going. We thus fail to create the context which is so essential to correctly set up the criteria for making intelligent successful decisions which are right for us. To be able to make an intelligent choice one must have relevant criteria against which one makes those decisions.

SIXTEEN: INTENTION

Personal powah is the combination of both ability and a willingness to use that ability. Powah depends upon inner strength and that strength must be sourced either from within the self or from without in one's relationship to something external. True powah has very little to do with power over another or domination, but rather with an ability and a willingness to take dominion of one's own life – to be responsible for one's own self, one's decisions and the impact of those decisions on others.

We have discussed the connection between powah and strength and uninterrupted circuitry; that self-doubt renders one powerless and weak and in that state of weakness, we often seek an alliance with another in order to gain strength, but at the price of personal sovereignty. An alliance based on weakness invariably leads to what I call the LCD phenomenon – the lowest common denominator. A chain is only as strong as its weakest link. In a union based on weakness, the lowest will always eventually gain control and usurp power by default.

In the final analysis, strength depends on clarity and an understanding of one's place in the Infinity of Being. In other words, one must develop a spiritual or higher perspective of why one is here and what is the purpose of this lifetime. For it is only with this perspective and within this context that we can develop a set of realistic criteria with which we can make intelligent choices.

It is extremely difficult to make choices and come to a resolute decision if one lacks appropriate criteria. For example, in choosing a new car one must know the criteria of purpose – pleasure or business, how many people will it carry, what is its use and funds – how much does one wish to spend both in its purchase and its upkeep. These criteria narrow the set of possibilities to a more limited and manageable set of probabilities.

I always found in my counselling work that it was impossible to deal with a specific personal issue or problem unless one examined the broader context of the spiritual purpose of a person's incarnation on the planet in the first place. Precisely why we are here, determines many decisions.

One could say that the process of gaining clarity is the development of a set of spiritual criteria against which one makes the decisions of life. I have a saying: 'decisions determine destiny!' We do create our own reality. But also in a very real sense – destiny determines decisions. For our destiny is not something predetermined in the Lutheran and Calvinistic sense by an all-powerful, remote and vengeful God in Heaven, but rather by ourselves as an ever-changing, evolving construct created by us.

Our destiny is our direction and the path that we chose to travel as a fully conscious spirit before incarnating as a human being. It is self-willed. It is our intention for this lifetime. Obviously, in the birthing process and in the subsequent cultural encoding of the fall in our infancy, we lose this perspective and this clarity and then the injunctions of the negative ego and the gravity of mass consciousness take over, creating further distraction and confusion.

Intention is the fine line between success and failure. A person with strong intention will invariably succeed. A person with weak intention inevitably fails to achieve their objective. Thus, intention is a vitally important quality and aspect of personal sovereignty – strong intention is synonymous with strong will. But as mentioned earlier this is not to be confused with will power.

Whereas choices and decisions deal with the specific circumstances in our lives – the nuts and bolts of daily reality – intention sets up the overall direction. Where do we want to go? What do we want to achieve? It is akin to a meta-decision: an overriding quest that guides our individual decisions. For often in life one must do something – choose a path – that seems to lead away from one's central objective. Part of being real is being flexible!

And this is precisely one of the main differences between intuitive awareness or the language of spirit and the rational, logical bio-computer of the negative ego. Spirit can be gentle, flexible, patient. The ego is rigid, inflexible and restless. A person of strong intent can bide his time, having the strength and the patience to wait for his destiny to create the appropriate opportunity to act. The restless negative ego, on the other hand, is always weak, impatient and impetuous, wanting it all at once, immediately. The ego is not willing to wait for the right time to unfold.

Spirit knows that it must weave and tack, taking different courses and paths of action to achieve its goal but never loses sight of its original objective. The negative ego in its stubborn obstinacy and rigidity does not possess this wisdom or flexibility. It always tries to force its way to the goal, striving vaingloriously to execute its petty will at whatever cost.

Spirit is willing to compromise – not in its principles – but it is willing to meet the other half way. The negative ego is hard and unwilling to compromise. It always insists on getting its own way and on winning at all costs. Spirit is always detached from the outcome – open and receptive. The negative ego exercises extreme attachment to its wants and desires and experiences acute pain, disappointment and frustration if its designs are thwarted or not realised. If thwarted, it immediately becomes hostile, defensive, judgemental and critical. The other is always made wrong.

The negative ego uses will power to gets its way. Spirit uses the powah of intention to firstly generate the wave that then becomes the way or Tao most suited to its nature and purpose. The negative ego acts prematurely and without inner preparation and thus the going is always hard, fraught with obstacles and necessitates the use of the petty will. From this comes the consensus reality viewpoint of the cultural encoding that life is hard, life wasn't meant to be easy, life sucks, life is a bitch, and that if you want something you have to work really hard to achieve it, you have to force your way to the goal – survival of the fittest and the meanest.

All of these are statements of the fact that the human condition is invariably at odds with the natural organic processes of life, the biological plan, and the law of life.

Remember 'evil' is 'live' spelt backwards. Evil is the opposite or counter flow of life. The law of life as manifest in the biological plan describes the inherent wisdom and natural flow of life. By going against this flow and by turning our backs on this wisdom, we are fundamentally at odds with and against life. We spend our lives trying to swim upstream and then wonder why we are exhausted and why nothing flows. We are the only species to do this. We are the only species to resist the natural flow of evolution, the natural laws of life's processes.

It is not that life is hard *per se*. It is just that our orientation or direction sets us against the flow. We are trying to swim upstream and finding it difficult whereas the rest of nature easily and effortlessly goes with the flow. It is vitally important to grasp this point for this is the point of separation. We are not talking about external, worldly, material success as an ego personality performing on the world stage. We are talking about our success as a spiritual entity enrolled in this Earth plane school of life.

For our spiritual purpose is never to become rich or famous or even to change or 'save' the world. Our purpose is not even to become a doctor, a lawyer, a mother, an author, an artist, etc. Although all of these may be a subset of our purpose and valid aspects of our soul journey and lesson for this lifetime, they are the means to achieve the higher purpose and not an end in and of themselves. All of these are temporary aspects of our life's journey. They are an integral part of our purpose but not the ultimate soul purpose.

Our only purpose is to evolve towards progressive perfection, to become more of who we are, to realise more of our destiny, and to become the fully actualised, self-aware, conscious and sovereign Being that is the thrust and intention of the 4.6-billion-year biological plan on planet Earth. Our purpose is to grow and develop!

It is not our worldly success that is important. It is our spiritual quest to become better people – a more consciously evolved human being. And this has nothing to do with the competition and comparison of the negative ego. This has nothing to do with being better than or less than another. This has to do with being better than you were yesterday. It is being the best that you can be. Not winning, not doing, not conquering, and not competing with another. It is all about your personal best as a being.

All of mass consciousness revolves around comparison and competition – what others think. What anyone thinks of you is none of your business and totally irrelevant for your own personal growth. Life is a very personal affair. It is our gift; it is our life and we need to learn how to appreciate that gift and how to live our lives consciously, gratefully and with joy. It is what you think, how you behave and how you evaluate your own progress as a spiritual warrior that truly matters, not what the world thinks of you.

Because we have turned our backs on the inherent divine wisdom and natural flow of the biological plan and law of life, we are in an inner state of conflict. In conflict with nature, in conflict with life, in conflict with each other and in conflict with ourselves – we live in a constant state of inner opposition and cannot therefore relax. We are in a perpetual war zone! The negative ego needs to use the force of its own will precisely because it does not have access to the superior codes of the corporate structure and hence strength of consciousness and it cannot engage the Tao – the flow, the way of creation.

The powah of intention is a completely different way of living and of creating. Intention is an inner volition that engages the divine power of the universe before acting. Intention generates the wave.

The negative ego must act on its own limited power because it stands alone, isolated, separated and cut off from the universal currents of cosmic power. These currents are obviously of infinite potential and unlimited power. Intention is the way we gain access to the infinite storehouse of that potential power. Intention is an inner mechanism whereby the individuated consciousness aligns itself with universal consciousness and rides the wave of chi effortlessly.

Just as a surfer rides a wave on the ocean by being in the right place at the right time and exerting just the right amount of effort to get onto or 'catch' the wave, so too, the spiritual warrior rides the waves of life. Ocean waves are generated by a whole host of stellar and planetary forces – the moon, the tides, etc. The waves of our own life are generated by a whole host of spiritual (or unseen) and temporal variables that can best be described as our personal Tao. This Tao is our way, our path, our destiny, and our direction. It is as totally personal and unique for each and every individual as is our face, our personality, our fingerprint, our DNA and our soul. It is yours! It is precious! It is the gift of life for without this Tao there is no wave, no fate to carry you through life.

And the only way to access its power (which is awesome) is through your intention. This is why intention is so incredibly important. It is the carrier wave of spiritual growth. For even though it may go under any number of names and descriptions, it is ultimately your own personal living breathing relationship with God, Goddess, All That Is.

Intention is a process of attunement! We described in Section II the holographic principle of creation whereby each individual species activates a limited set of biological programs that are specific for it. We saw that the power and majesty of the animal and plant kingdoms comes from their unswerving obedience to and compliance with the biological plan or the Law of Life. They are true to themselves; they do not doubt. But they have no choice.

We, on the other hand, must consciously choose to align, to attune, and to live in harmony with the laws of life. We must also consciously choose to listen to our inner natures, we must consciously choose to do the right thing, and to obey the will of God as revealed to us individually and specifically through the law of our own being – our Tao. This is our first and foremost intention from which all else follows. This is the root, the solid foundation upon which a truly successful life stands for without this quality of rightness, this clarity and this alignment there can be no real growth, and no spiritual success.

Our intention is our choice of direction. Which way do we intend to go? What is our intention for this lifetime? And our first choice, as explained earlier, is: do we consciously choose to align with, to be in harmony with, to attune to the universal currents of the cosmos and the divine principles and laws of life? This is the overriding choice and decision we must make at each and every moment of our existence. For we are always either seeking attunement, listening to the voice of spirit through our intuitive awareness or seeking self-aggrandisement, listening to the voice of our negative ego through the linear thinking brain.

Is it our intention to obey the creative will of God as revealed through the biological plan – the evolutionary process, or is it our intention to obey the destructive will of the negative ego? Intention is not about becoming a doctor or a movie star or making lots of money. Intention is about what you intend as a conscious being to do with the primary gift of life and the secondary gift of free will choice.

- What is your intention for this lifetime?
- What is your intention for your spiritual journey?
- What is your intention for your self – for your personal spiritual growth?
- What is your intention for your gift back to the world?
- What do you intend to give back to life?

The gift of life is given freely but it does place upon us an obligation, a responsibility, to give back by becoming more of who we are, by becoming all that we can be. Intention begets becoming. If we do not set our intention strongly then what becomes of us depends upon chance and external influences. Just as in sailing, if one does not set the sails firmly, the sails will just flap in the breeze and the boat will drift aimlessly. Intention is the course you chart as a sovereign being. It is not that in becoming God we lose our individuality (remember, this is the hallmark of the authoritarian collective) but that we express it more eloquently, more elegantly. As we become stronger and clearer about who we are, we express that divinity more passionately and more fully. We become more self-realised, self-actualised, self-aware, more conscious and sovereign. We become more of our selves. We become more authentic.

Without a strong intention, we become more homogeneous, more conformist, more intimidated by the collective force of the cultural encoding. We lose our individuality, our uniqueness and our sovereignty. We become less able to think for ourselves, to make our own decisions, and to listen to the inner voice of our spirit. We become lost, losing our selves, losing our inner divine wisdom, and losing our connection to the universal currents of life. We give up the direction of our own lives.

Without the spiritual foundation of a clear and powerful intent we compare ourselves with others, degenerating into competition, envy and jealousy, separating ourselves from the flow of life, believing in our own weakness, evil and inadequacy and then abrogating responsibility to our ego. In this state of separation and isolation, fear and doubt set in. We are no longer strong, no longer powahful. We become weak and in this weakness seek the co-dependent alliance of the negative ego and others.

Intention is the beginning and the end, the Alpha and the Omega. Intention is not just a decision, for decision without resolution will amount to nothing. Intention is a POWAH! Intention has commitment, resolution, determination. Intention is an act of will.

Intention elicits a response from the universe. A strong intention generates a strong wave. A strong intention enables one to wait and to listen, so that one is in the right place at the right time. Intention empowers one to put forward just that right amount of effort necessary to catch the wave. Intention gives one the discipline and training, the skill not to fall off.

Intention is the link between the seen and the unseen worlds. Pure intent engages the Tao and vanquishes the negative ego. The negative ego is corrupt and cannot coexist with a purity of intent. Pure intention is not based on the petty personal whims and desires of the ego but on concerns that are universal, on firm and correct principles. Intention works for the good of all. Pure intention springs from a pure heart and not from the mind. The heart and the intuition work together as the voice of spirit. If one listens to these voices, then one's intention is pure and engages the benevolent forces of creation.

We discovered in Section II that the biological plan has its own evolutionary intent that has been developing for approximately five billion years on this planet. In Section I, we examined the evolution of consciousness over umpteen billions of years. We also discovered that nature fulfils itself in the creation of the fully aware, conscious, sovereign being. Thus, there is a cosmic thrust, the Big Bang if you like, the desire for God to know itself through creation, which has its own intention. This intention is quite obviously infinitely powerful and very strong. We are calling it the way of the universe or the Tao.

And then of course, there is our own personal, finite thrust or intent which is by comparison extremely weak and vulnerable. So, the real question is, if there is this primary, all powerful, universal thrust, is it not wisdom to align oneself with it, in other words, to go with the flow? Let go and let God! More to the point, is it not the height of humanity's folly and stupidity to think that as an individual evolving consciousness, one can go against this current and win. Obviously not!

But when we look a little closer and really get clear is this not exactly what we are doing? For if we are honest, does it make any sense for nature to work for 4.6 billion years to create a species that in the infinitely small time frame of 10,000 years, has all but created havoc and the near destruction of the myriad species that comprise the biodiversity that ensures the survival and continuity of life on the planet, and has almost destroyed the delicate biosphere within which we all live? Does it make any sense for nature to complete itself in a being that is so at odds with the inherent harmony of the law of life that it is threatening the very processes of nature and of life itself? It certainly does not.

And if we look at it from a purely selfish point of view, from the myopic, self-centred, arrogant and conceited point of view of us as the dominant, superior species on the planet, does it make any sense to create a species so at odds with itself, that wars, starvation, poverty, crime, unhappiness, fear, loneliness, alienation, separation and illness are the norm rather than the exception? Are we happy? Are we really so superior? Are we shining examples of the finished product of 4.6 billion years of work, trial and effort and evolution? Are we in fact, the most highly evolved species on the planet as our egos would like to have us believe?

As we shed our evangelical mythology and explore nature honestly, the answer is obviously: 'no!' In fact, we are the only species to demonstrate such self-destructive and other-destructive tendencies. Moreover, it is only one part of humanity that exhibits these characteristics and that is the part dominated by the negative ego! There are many so-called 'non-civilised primitive' peoples that do live in harmony with each other and nature exhibiting none of our 'civilised' ills. Modern humanity stands singularly apart from the rest of creation, not because of its evolutionary superiority but precisely because of its devolutionary tendencies.

So, the second question is: if we as a species and as individual units of consciousness are so at odds with the evolutionary thrust and intent of the 4.6-billion-year old biological plan on this planet, which intention will win? Are we really so arrogant, blind and stupid that we truly believe we can go against this tide? Humanity is always trying to subjugate and dominate 'the wild' nature and we always lose. For we either destroy habitat or nature wreaks havoc. Global warming, pollution, weather abnormalities and so on are just the beginning of nature's fight back against our wayward and aberrant ways. When nature really performs it is quite obvious who is the stronger and more powerful.

In any contest, ultimately, it is not the more skilled who wins but the one with the stronger intent. For intention is the fine line between success and failure. If we pit the destructive intent of the collective negative-ego or mass consciousness against the creative intent of the universal currents of life, which do you think will win? Whose side do you choose to be on?

For this is now an intensely personal question. The hour of reckoning draws near! Each and every one of us must of necessity exercise our personal sovereignty and make a free will choice. Is our personal intention aligned with that of the negative-ego or that of life? To make no choice is to choose by default and abrogate responsibility and that is the choice of the negative-ego, for as we have repeatedly explained that is where the whole dilemma began.

It is now time to take back our powah and assert our sovereignty. As David Suzuki once said, 'we are either part of the problem or part of the solution.' We must make a choice. It is either a conscious, intelligent choice of knowing or an unconscious unintelligent one of unknowing.

SEVENTEEN: SELF-MASTERY AND FUNCTIONING WITH DOMINION

So, let's say we have strengthened ourselves, making sure that the source of that strength is within so that we can assume our Powah! And we have taken the time to reflect, to meditate, to contemplate and to arrive at Clarity. Moreover, our resolve is strong and we have set our intention. Our heart is pure.

What then? For we all know it is not that easy! Many of us have travelled thus far, many, many times only to find our realities dissipate before our very eyes. Or we have achieved a measure of success, creating love, light and beauty in our lives only to see it dissolve once more into chaos and confusion. Many of us do get our lives to work for a while but then it all seems to go wrong; we reach an impasse and are unable to go forward.

Often, we set out with the purest and noblest of intentions, only to witness the destructive power of the negative-ego (either our own, another's, or that of the collective) usurp control and destroy what we intended to create.

The point is, this is not the Garden of Eden. We no longer live in paradise but on the plane of duality. The fruit of the Tree of Knowledge is the knowledge of good and evil. It is not just that we become self-aware but that in order to really receive the gift of free will there needs to be a choice and that choice is primarily the choice between good and evil, between the principles, processes and laws of life or those that are against life, between flowing with the Tao or going against the flow. This choice implies and necessitates a plane of duality, lest there would be no real choice.

Negativity and evil does exist! The Earth plane is a school and there are lessons to be learnt. The forbidden fruit of the Garden is the knowledge of the creator gods and once eaten we embarked on a journey to become co-creators with the gods. The Earth school is no less than an apprenticeship or traineeship of godhood. We are learning to become co-creators! And creativity as we know is a highly evolved skill. We have to earn the right by accepting our responsibility and learning the creator codes.

We do all create our own reality: this is precisely the gift of free will – to choose and create what we will. And we either do that consciously, knowingly, with awareness and wisdom or unconsciously, unknowingly with ignorance. We do so with every breath, at every moment of our existence.

The journey of the evolution of consciousness and personal sovereignty is this development from ignorance and self-delusion to enlightenment and self-awareness. It is the graduation from an unconscious, instinctive, habitual mode of behaviour, of being the victim, to a conscious, intuitive, spontaneous mode of being the victor. The graduation point, or the test we must pass is responsibility! We must take responsibility for our lives. We must take back our power and become the supreme authority within ourselves. We must be able to take complete ownership of this thing called the SELF. We must have and exhibit Personal Sovereignty.

The challenge of creativity is responsibility and the challenge of responsibility is ownership! We began by defining sovereignty as supreme power, autonomy, being the controlling influence. So, we can only be sovereign when we are willing to take responsibility for the creation of our lives, when we are willing to claim complete ownership of our daily reality. As long as there is someone else to blame, we are not sovereign.

For power without responsibility is manipulation and responsibility without power is foolishness. Only strong personal powah linked with true responsibility enables one to take dominion of one's life. Most of humanity is caught either in the former or the latter: arrogantly manipulating or being the foolish victim. Neither is a state of sovereignty.

To be sovereign is not to control or manipulate – that is a position of domination not dominion. To be sovereign is not to blame or to hold another responsible for one's state but to accept one's own co-creativity and responsibility in whatever befalls one. Co-dependency with either the negative ego, a significant other or an external ideology is the transference of our own personal power, creativity and responsibility onto that other. It is a denial of our own ownership in the creation of our reality and it is an abrogation of our authority. We are throwing our self away.

Creativity is a skill that must be learnt and acquired. It is precisely why we are here. It is the real meaning behind the myth and story of the Garden of Eden. We were not cast out of the garden as punishment for our sins but rather as a grand and glorious opportunity to evolve, to aspire, to become co-creators with God, Goddess, All That Is.

This implies and involves work, for as in all cases the only way to learn is by trial and error. We need to learn the mechanics of creation, the laws of the manifestation process: precisely how we do create our own reality. What are the raw materials; what tools do we use and what are the recipes and formulae? What are the dynamics? These are complex and involved questions and worthy of the most rigorous and scientific endeavour.

Indeed, it is odd that the history of humanity, especially in the last scientific technological age is characterised by our exploration and understanding of how things work. We have assiduously discovered and uncovered the laws of Physics, Biology, Thermodynamics, Nuclear Physics etc. We have prodded and dissected just about everything from the stellar bodies of outer space to the microscopic components of atomic structure and the cells of our body.

Yet, we have never understood nor studied life! We do not understand ourselves. We have never seen fit to devote our seemingly infinite resources of time and money to delve into and discover the mechanics of creation. We still ridicule the science of Metaphysics, which is probably the greatest area of research and study there is. We fly to the moon and outer space, yet we will not travel into the inner dimensions of our own beings. We are technologically advanced but lack the shamanic wisdom of the so-called primitive cultures. We are all too willing to look without, yet all too reluctant to look within!

We still clamber clumsily and awkwardly through our daily lives creating as much, if not more, distress, illness, unhappiness and mayhem as we did 500 or 5,000 years ago. Our growth and understanding of the creation process in terms of our own personal lives is as archaic and steeped in superstition as it was in the Dark Ages. Our inner spiritual and psychic progress has definitely not kept pace with that of outer scientific and technological discovery. We are spiritual children playing with the forces of creation – nuclear energy – in a very dangerous and foolish way. We have the ability but not the necessary responsibility. This is the urgency!

Why do we have this absurd fear of studying the one thing we are here to learn? For with all our scientific knowledge of zoology and ecology we are still decimating the biodiversity of the planet. With all our knowledge of geology, the weather and so on, we are still killing the ecosystem of the planet. With all our medical knowledge of biology we are still killing ourselves with stress, ill-health and disease. The number one cause of death in the advanced industrial nations is post-operative infection or complication. It seems the more we learn, the less we know. The more knowledge and data we accumulate, the less wisdom we have. The more we explore, the less secure we become. The more we do, the less we are.

We are here to learn and to master the process of creation: to become co-creators of life; to make our personal lives work; to live harmoniously, happily, effortlessly and easily. And it is precisely because we refuse *en masse*, as a collective species and as sovereign individuals to learn the delicate process of co-creativity that our lives do not work, that we get it wrong time and time again, undermining our belief and faith in ourselves thus creating doubt, indecision and the paralysis of fear.

It is hard because we make it hard by our stubborn refusal to cooperate with life, to obey the principles and laws of life and because of our alienated mentality. Indeed, we exist as aliens upon the planet. We view nature, 'the wild,' and life as something foreign, alien, frightening, and threatening; something to be dominated, conquered, subjugated and controlled. We live in a constant state of war and conflict with our environment and with life itself.

We see the world as a scary place that must be dominated and defended against. We go about our lives protecting and safeguarding ourselves against a future that we perceive as threatening, unsafe and dangerous. We live in a constant state of fear and unrest. We do not cultivate a co-creative relationship with life but instead develop a combative and destructive mentality. It is important to realise that this attitude is not just towards the planet or nature in 'the wild' but also towards our fellow brothers and sisters, ourselves and our futures. We are totally dominated by fear and anxiety and the surety that things will go wrong if we do not guard and defend against the inevitable.

How many of us have as our primary, basic belief that things will go wrong, that just when you have everything worked out, and just when your life is working, something will go wrong? How many of us truly believe that we are not worthy, that we are not good enough, that we are fatally flawed and are being punished for our sins by a vengeful reality? How many of us sincerely believe that we deserve to suffer?

These are all inevitable results of the aforementioned cultural encoding of the fall in our daily lives. We are constantly surrounded by this global belief system. And just as a fish cannot taste water or we cannot smell air because we exist within that medium, so too, we cannot perceive the significance of this belief system because we are imbued with it. It has become as commonplace and as accepted as the air we breathe. We live within the metaparadigm and so do not even know it exists. It totally dominates our worldview and belief about who we are.

The point being that belief precedes experience. Attitude and belief create reality. Our beliefs are one of the major building blocks out of which we do construct our daily lives. So that if we do ascribe to this societal belief system that says that life is scary, ugly and cannot be trusted, that is exactly what we will manifest on a daily basis. But in our rational-scientific model this does not make sense. Belief does not precede reality but arises out of observation. Then why the double-blind experiment? Why, especially in the field of nuclear physics, is the behaviour of sub-atomic particles influenced by the beliefs and expectations of the observer?

The fact is we do indeed create our lives out of the belief system we hold. In fact, external daily reality is there to reflect and illustrate to us, to demonstrate exactly what beliefs we do hold.

> All beliefs have energy systems that act like birthing rooms for the manifestation of belief. Within these energy systems are currents that direct your life experience. You are aware

of these currents either consciously or subconsciously and you allow them to carry you into the realm of experience that best exemplifies your true belief system.[43]

So, the answer to the question asked at the beginning of this chapter and asked by every human being since the beginning of time as to why things go wrong, is that we are on a journey of discovery, a learning experience. We are students of life, seeking to learn the knowledge of the gods – how to create, how to be creator gods. This is the gift of life, the gift of free will. But like all knowledge it must be acquired and while learning we make mistakes.

The real question as in all learning is: do we choose to learn quickly by dint of serious study and application, learning from our mistakes, minimising the pain and discomfort of the learning process, or do we choose to learn slowly by not acting maturely, and refusing to take responsibility for our mistakes and thus prolonging the learning period by repeating our errors?

For this is a very real and pertinent question. If one enrols in a university and then foolishly refuses to study and learn the prescribed curriculum, one can only expect to fail and repeat. One cannot attain mastery of the subject or faculty. So too, if one enrols in the University of Life, in the faculty of the Earth School, and then stubbornly refuses to learn and master the curriculum of the school, which is the manifestation process, can one really expect to manifest anything in one's life but disaster? It is very simple.

The evolutionary journey that we have described and the end result of the biological plan, which is the development of the corporate structure of consciousness, fulfils itself within the fully aware, conscious, sovereign being, capable of taking dominion, earning its right to be a co-creator of life. As we have said, nature fulfils itself in the birth of the individual and the individual fulfils itself in the birth of creation. The whole process fulfils itself.

We willingly left the Garden of Eden in order to earn our right to be co-creators with the gods. We willingly entered the Earth school, the plane of duality of good and evil, in order to master the process of free will choice, so that we could consciously choose to align with the forces of creation, to obey the Laws of Life, to listen to our own inner divinity and intuition.

As in any situation, we had to earn our stripes before we could be given our command. And once again, we have been given a choice: to create with domination or dominion! We may choose to see the world as the enemy, as a scary place to be controlled and conquered, or to see the world as a friend, an abundant place to be enjoyed and played with. We may see the relationship between ourselves as an individual unit of consciousness and the consciousness of Life as a conflict, a competition, a war to be won at all and at any cost, or to view that relationship as one of cooperation, mutual support and co-creation.

Do we seek to control, manipulate and dominate or do we choose to allow, comply with and take dominion? Do we believe in a vengeful, wrathful God exacting punishment and suffering for our sins or do we truly believe in the divine benevolence of the universe?

Do we choose to humbly accept our station as the student of life, modestly seeking our education and fulfilment through mastering the manifestation process by learning the Laws of Life; or do we choose to arrogantly assume that we know it all, that we are the superior species on the planet, asserting domination because of our divine right to rule?

Do we choose to listen to the cultural encoding of the collective negative-ego which tells us that the world is ugly, that humanity is destructive, that people are bad and evil; or do we choose to listen to the broadcasts of universal intelligence via our intuition which tells us that the world is beautiful, that humanity is creative and that people are basically good, caring and loving?

Do we choose to foster and care for – to nourish – our Spiritual Self by becoming all that we can be, by aspiring to become more of the God within us by learning to become co-creators; or do we choose to foster and care for – to nourish – our negative ego by doing all that can be done, by conquering all that can be dominated, manipulated and controlled?

Do we choose to be the divine husbandman, the real caretakers of the planet Earth, reaping the benefits and enjoying the wealth we create; or do we choose to be the conqueror, raping and pillaging the earth until there is no more to take?

Do we choose to take or to give? For the negative ego is always caught in the infantile 'not enough'. If Piaget's stage-specific needs remain unmet, a part of our neurology and a part of our awareness is caught back there in the past trying desperately to get those needs met. That aspect of consciousness uses its creative power to recreate those situations that occurred in infancy hoping for a more successful outcome.

This is why and how we keep attracting the same types of lovers, the same types of relationships, and the same types of circumstances into our lives. We are continually caught in the creative/destructive loop of re-creating our childhood past in the present. We allow our negative ego, caught in its infancy, to rule and take charge of the creative processes of consciousness. We do not move on or learn our lessons but are stuck on a merry-go-round going over and over old ground.

We become desperate because we can see that our lives are not working. We operate from a place of wanting and needing; we become needy and, in that neediness, seek a co-dependent relationship with a significant other. We feel unworthy, losing self-love and self-esteem and ending with nothing to give. We blame the world, our parents, our children, our spouses, our bosses, the government, the system, God. We blame anyone and everyone but ourselves! We refuse to take responsibility and to heal our own wounds, to meet our unmet needs, to nurture the inner child and silence the negative ego.

By abrogating responsibility, we choose to nurture the negative ego rather than the spiritual self. By taking responsibility for our lives, we assume complete authority, take ownership and exercise dominion. We move out of the neediness of the ego and into the compassion of the real self. We have compassion both for ourselves and others.

In this state of compassion, we are able to both give and to love. Firstly, to give to and to love ourselves. By nurturing the inner child, giving ourselves the time to heal, and doing the inner work necessary to discover and meet those childhood unmet needs. By taking responsibility for the healing process so that we can bring all units of consciousness back into the present and joyously create the future.

By dealing with and healing the past we can be fully present! And the point of powah, the place of dominion, is always in the present. Intuitive awareness can only operate in the stillness and silence of the eternal now – the present moment. The negative ego lives in the past or the future – in any place but the present. This is why meditation as a personal discipline is so essential for spiritual growth as it enables us to access present time within which the negative ego has no sway. By bringing our attention, our conscious awareness into the present we are more able to engage in the co-creative process of actively generating our future according to what we desire.

It is all a question of amplitude. The louder the cry the more it is heard. Remember we create our lives both consciously and unconsciously. Some aspects, for example autonomic bodily functions such as breathing, digesting food etc. are better left to the unconscious. But as we discovered in Section II, traumatic experiences in childhood that are denied access to higher consciousness via the gating of pain result in a degree of unconsciousness. These wounds reside in cellular memory having a potency and valency of their own and desire to be healed. They have as much access to the creator codes as you do. And quite often their cries are stronger, meaning their creative power takes precedence over yours.

In other words, you desire to create X. You get clear, strong, powerful and set your intention. Let's say on a scale of one to ten in the creative process your amplitude is four. But let us also say that on an unconscious level you also desire Y in order to heal the past and the amplitude of that desire is six. Which one will win? Moreover, you now have set up two waves in the ocean of consciousness corresponding to the desires of X and Y. As in all wave theory, the third wave generated by these two will have components of both and will subsume or predominate both, creating Z.

You will not cleanly generate the reality you consciously desire until you willingly take responsibility for healing the past and allow these wounds access to higher consciousness without having to engage the manifestation process. Healing does not need to interfere in the creation of the future if it is allowed access to the conscious mind in the present.

However, healing can only occur in the present when allowed and facilitated by the spiritual self. As long as the ego is in charge it is not prepared to acknowledge that healing even needs to occur. Remember, the negative ego denies, rationalises and justifies the neurotic behaviour which is the rerouting of pain. By recognising and acknowledging our neurosis we heal the pain and become whole.

In this wholeness and state of compassion, we can cleanly generate the future we desire by exercising dominion and not trying vaingloriously to dominate our reality. By loving ourselves enough we can heal these wounds and satisfy any stage-specific unmet needs in an inner meditative process rather than in the compulsive neurotic acting out that occurs in the outer manifestation process.

Our unmet needs only need to clamour for attention by wreaking havoc in our lives when we are not listening, when we deny them access to consciousness. As a neonate with a fragile and delicate nervous system that could not safely carry the current of pain, the gating mechanism is a necessary part of survival. The trauma is denied access to the conscious mind. As an adult, however, it is our duty and responsibility to allow these currents full access for integration and healing. It is via this healing process that we become more fully conscious. It is via this integration that we no longer need to dominate, to control, to manipulate or have power over that scary world that frightened us as a child.

Once acknowledged, heard and integrated, the unresolved pain loses its valency and becomes quiet. As a child we may be frightened of the dark. As a child we may be frightened of many imaginary fears and monsters and see the world as a scary place. But as an adult one would hope to outgrow such childish fantasies and see the world in all its beauty and splendour.

Similarly, the negative ego in its childish fantasy and because it does not have access to the higher creator codes of spirit, imagines that it needs to take control via domination, manipulation and having power over life. The negative ego must work hard at making life work, precisely because it is out of its depth and not designed for the job. It has not the inherent intelligence to learn the principles of manifestation and master the co-creative process. Therefore, it can only pretend, promise and fail. It is like a two-year-old trying to write a PHD thesis.

As long as we allow the left brain or bio-computer of the ego to assume control of the corporate structure of consciousness and attempt to manipulate the creator codes, our creativity will be severely limited and flawed. It simply will not work. Life will be seen as hard and not to be trusted and the self as unworthy and undeserving. Our experience will indeed verify our initial belief. Our domination of life and the planet will continue and escalate until either one of us is destroyed. For is this not the inevitable outcome of any conflict?

On the other hand, if we forego the dominance of the ego, if we take back our powah and responsibility, healing our wounds, integrating our consciousness, becoming whole and sovereign, then we enter into dominion. Functioning with dominion we do not need to control but can, rather, allow! Rather than working hard at making our lives work, we can relax into allowing the co-creative process of evolution and the biological plan to take over. We can work easily, effortlessly, gracefully. We can have fun and enjoy the journey. We can play with life, with the world, with creation. We can trust ourselves, our inner divinity and the divine benevolence of the universe. We can feel supported rather than threatened by life. We can feel safe and secure to experiment and experience – to learn joyously, and playfully.

In the place of dominion and compassion we can also love and give to others. There is no need to take. There is no neediness, but rather a contented joyousness that seeks to give generously to others. We are not only supported by life but we in turn support it. We come to realise that love, life and God are nothing but different facets of the one prism – different names of the one thing – a new holy trinity.

Our attention is focused in the present and we co-create our future effortlessly, joyfully, easily and confidently, generating the waves in the Tao that bring to us the opportunities for action. We allow the process because we trust our own inner divine creative powah. We can wait patiently for the right time because we know the powah of dominion always works. There is no doubt, no fear, no hesitation. No short circuits exist within our circuitry because we have healed and integrated our childhood wounds that caused the short circuits in the first place. We are willing to believe in ourselves and in the divine process of creation.

Thus, there are basically two ways of acting or two modes of being. And this is the crux of personal sovereignty for they are mutually exclusive. You are either one or the other. The one I am calling 'acting with dominion' and is an expression of personal sovereignty; the other I am calling 'acting with domination' and is an expression of co-dependency.

For it is vitally important to realise that what we hold onto holds onto us; what we are attached to is attached to us; and what we dominate eventually dominates us! Dependency is always a two-way street – this is why it is called co-dependency. It becomes like a tug of war. The more one pulls, the more one is pulled. There is only one solution and that is to let go! Totally, unconditionally and unilaterally! And immediately!

EIGHTEEN: PURITY OF PURPOSE

Acting out of domination is the assertion of will power: the petty will of the ego. It is an attempt to assert oneself over reality. It is our personal, petty, thinking self's intention to get its own way – to force life to operate according to what we want. And as we have already discovered, the wants of the ego are ground in the past. It is always an effort to recreate some childhood situation in an attempt to satisfy some unfulfilled infantile need. But precisely because these needs are stage-specific and can only be fulfilled in childhood, the ego is bent on a self-destructive and futile journey of trying vaingloriously to assert its will.

This never succeeds and is what I call the primal paradox. The primal paradox is that you always end up with exactly the opposite of what you set out to get if you operate from the ego. And this is one of the main characteristics of egoic action: there is always an ulterior motive. One always does in order to get! It is never a pure action. The ego is always motivated out of its unfulfilled needs and wants. The ego always wants more.

The ego acts in order to get something: more wealth, more fame, more recognition, more approval, more power over others, more attention etc., and because there is an ulterior motive there is always a hidden agenda. There is always dishonesty, duplicity and complication.

Moreover, because egoic action is an assertion of the personal will there is always the necessity of force. We have to use our personal will to make it happen. We have to coerce, bully, manipulate and this is always associated with fear, anxiety, agitation and restlessness for there is always doubt and uncertainty as to the eventual outcome; whether we will achieve what we set out to do which is really to satisfy the ego's unfulfilled wants and needs.

Egoic action comes from a place of neediness and thus powerlessness. It is doomed to failure and repetition. For egoic action increases our level of frustration and feelings of 'not enough', necessitating an ever-increasing attempt to allay these feelings. This is why neurotic behaviour is always compulsive and escalating in the sense that we always need more of whatever it is we are chasing to allay the inner insecurity. Addictions always escalate to the point of complete domination and ruin of our lives. They end up controlling us in an ever-decreasing spiral of self-destructive behaviour.

This is how the ego operates!

On the other hand, acting out of dominion is the allowance of the divine will. There is no assertion; there is no attempt to dominate and control but rather the cooperation and co-creation with the forces of the universe. Thus, there is no need to use force in an attempt to make things happen prematurely.

As in our analogy with the surfer, we align our personal energy wave – our Tao – with the energy currents of the universe – The Tao – and effortlessly ride the wave of success. The Tao is not rooted in the past but is fully, consciously aware in the present. Thus, it is able to respond intelligently to the demands of the situation – it is able to respond, which is to be response-able or to take responsibility. When a part of our consciousness is locked away in the past, we are not fully conscious in the present. A part of us is unconscious and to that extent we are incapable of acting responsibly or of taking responsibility for our actions and our creation. We are unable to respond to the here and now.

One of the main differences between egoic and Taoic action is that where the former is ulteriorly motivated and dishonest in its intention, the latter is pure. By pure, I mean it is appropriate to the demands of the time. Again, there is no moral, religious or mystical connotation here; it is simply a statement of fact. Are we fully present and thus pure or is our intention adulterated and thus weakened? We act because that is what we want to do in that present tense, not because we want to achieve something in a future tense to relieve a need from a past tense: 'we do each task as time and place demand and not with an eye to the result.'[44]

We are innocent, pure, free, unadulterated, coming from that space I call the Joy of Self Expression. We act because that is what we want to do in that space/time continuum, in that moment. The creative force of the universe flows through us and influences us to act appropriately; there is no egoic interference. We are in harmony with primal innocence, with the biological plan, with the divine will of God, with our inner natures, with the intention of our spiritual self. No matter what you call it or whichever way you look at it, it is one and the same thing – the Tao!

The Tao moves through creation. The Tao is the way of the universe expressing itself in every moment, in every situation. It is the way of success. It is the evolutionary process. It is the biological plan. It is the blueprint, the design, the formula. It is the Divine Intent. It is the One Law running through end and beginning that manifests as the principles and laws of life which regulate the way life works.

If we act in harmony with these laws, if we act from our Tao, then success, peace, happiness and good fortune are assured. If we act from our ego, in conflict with these laws, then we create the destructive chaos and confusion that we are now witnessing on the planet and in our own personal lives. And just as the Tao is the divine will of God or the intention of the universe, so too, the personal Tao is our own individual intention. We are not in any way preaching or advocating a return to some form of pre-determinism. Taoism is not a rehashed version of Lutheranism or Calvinism. Nothing could be further from the truth.

For it is just as wrong for the universe to dictate its will to us as it is for us to dictate our will on another, whether that other be another person or the forces of creation. It is absolutely vital to understand that we do create our own reality. We do generate our own waves. We do determine our own destiny. It is just that we can generate those waves in harmony with the universal currents or at odds with them.

This is the essential difference between domination and dominion; egoic and taoic action. Egoic action seeks to force its will on creation, to get its own way just as the petulant child seeks to enforce its will on the family through tantrum and tyrannical behaviour. Taoic action seeks to align its will with the greater forces of creation, not to get its own way, but to express The Way through its own individual creativity. The greatest artists, composers, musicians, authors, leaders and statesmen do not seek to impose their will through their work but rather to reveal the glory of God, of life, through their individual expression. A Beethoven or a Van Gough does not compose or paint in order to become rich or famous but because the Tao of their Being flows through them and impulses them to create. Their creativity is their own unique individual expression – it is their gift to life and to all of us who can appreciate their discipline and self-sacrifice.

There is no domination, no coercion, no manipulation in this mode. Rather there is the co-creative partnership of the individual and the universal bringing into being something that did not exist before. This is what I mean by a pure act. When we come from innocence, we come from that pure space of spontaneous joy and creativity. Anyone who has momentarily 'lost themselves' in the pursuit of any form of creativity, sport or hobby knows this joy, this rapture. Time ceases! We become totally immersed in our creativity, in the now. The tyrannical hold of the negative ego is cast aside and our intuitive, pure 'self' comes out to play.

Even the word 'play' implies this lightness of being, this childhood innocence before self-conscious thought and ulterior motivation destroy the true spontaneity and freedom of the carefree act. Egoic action is always contrived and is designed to achieve an ulterior purpose. Taoic action is always innocent and is designed to purely and simply express life moving through itself. Whether the result of that creation is a Mona Lisa, or a child's sandcastle on the beach, or young animals frolicking in the sun or a majestic old growth forest does not matter. Creativity does not create to beget but to BE!

Although there very obviously is a superior, divine intelligence orchestrating this vast and beautiful creation, as evidenced by the biological plan of the evolutionary process, the end result is not ulteriorly motivated. God does not have a hidden agenda. The universe is not going somewhere in order to get there. The universe just *is*! As we discovered in the very beginning, the Big Bang is the original divine explosion of love, of God seeking to know itself through creative expression. We are that creative expression. We are God smelling the roses. The gift of free will is to express our own joy, our own creative essence in whichever way we consciously choose, to embark on our own journey of self-discovery and to get to know ourselves via our own creativity.

It is just that we also need to choose whether we are going to express that self in harmony with the principles of the universe and the laws of life and align ourselves with the Tao or whether we are going to express that self in opposition to the forces of creativity. Are we going to listen to the intuitive promptings of our creative, higher, inner real self, or the selfish machinations of our destructive, lower, outer unreal personality? The one is an expression of self-love and leads to the joy of self-fulfilment; the other is an outpouring of self-hate and leads to the despair of frustration and self-destruction.

NINETEEN: SELF-LOVE AND SELF-ACCEPTANCE

And so we enter the sacred inner sanctum of our beings. For ultimately, all of these issues of personal sovereignty revolve around one aspect and one aspect only. On the deepest level, in our innermost heart and soul, do we really love ourselves? This is the question we each must answer. And answer alone and in all honesty.

For it does not matter what others say or how much one is loved by others. One can only receive the love, one can only *be* loved to the extent one loves oneself. On our imaginary scale of one to ten, if one loves oneself to the level of four, then that is all the love one will allow in, no matter that the other is loving one to the power of ten. A thimble, a cup, a jug, a bucket, a bath, a dam, a lake, an ocean can only contain the amount of water they can hold. So too, a human being can only feel and express the amount of love they can contain in their heart.

And one can only love oneself to the extent that one accepts oneself. This is why Piaget's stage-specific needs and the thrust of the biological plan are so necessary to understand. For if we are not accepted – totally, thoroughly, completely, and unconditionally – as a young child, we will grow up not accepting ourselves. We will find ourselves lacking, wanting, and not good enough!

It is this feeling of 'not good enough' that is the fuel of the negative ego. It is this feeling of not being good enough that generates its own waves or energy currents of restlessness, insecurity, neediness, lack, inadequacy and so on. For each of us this feeling is as unique as our face and our fingerprint. Just as we each have our unique personality, so too, each and every one of us has a unique matrix of unmet needs that becomes this feeling of 'not good enough'. And so, we spend our lives trying to become good enough, trying to get that attention, that approval, that recognition, that praise, that acclaim, that outward success that we think will allay this deep inner feeling that something is wrong with me.

Thus, the return to the mythological belief in original sin and that the human race is fatally flawed and so by deduction, I am too. I am not good enough of myself. I must earn my salvation by hard work, self-denial and using my will power – the will power of my egoic thinking mind – to suppress and sublimate my natural spontaneous impulses. It is absolutely vital to grasp this concept for it is the ultimate catch-22 and the paradox of the human race.

The more I use my egoic will to enforce its way upon my world, the more I depart from purity and innocence. The more I depart from my spontaneous natural self, the more my world falls apart, thus proving that I am not good enough. The more my world falls apart, the more my belief in the world as a scary place that needs to be fought off and defended against increases. The more I abandon my real self and believe that I am not good enough, that the world cannot be trusted, the more reliance I place on my ego to take control. The more the negative ego takes control, the more I dominate and manipulate. The more I dominate and control, the further I move away from dominion.

Thus, the cycle becomes self-perpetuating in a never-ending downward spiral of self-doubt, self-hate and self-destructiveness. All because in the beginning I was not unconditionally accepted and loved for who I was – a child of God, a being of the universe, as pure and as innocent as any newborn is. It is interesting that in the first moments of life nearly all parents and people do spontaneously, totally and unconditionally accept and love their newborn. We all marvel at the miracle of life, at the purity and innocence of the newborn, at the sanctity of their being. Somehow, we do recognise the essence of their resident spirit before the social conditioning masks the inner purity. It is only later, as the personality of the child develops and the pressures of the life of the adult take hold that the cultural encoding aborts the natural evolutionary process of unconditional love and acceptance.

Animals in the wild retain their natural spontaneity because they are not psychologically or emotionally rejected by their parents. As parents seek to enforce their egoic will on natural childhood behaviour, the innocence and spontaneity of the neonate is lost to a contrived performance that is more acceptable and comfortable within the cultural norm. As children we learn very quickly to 'perform'. The less spontaneous love and affection are forthcoming, the more the child performs in order to get approval, attention, praise, etc.

This causes the primary split between spirit and psyche. The soft voice of spirit, via intuition and natural creativity is lost to the louder injunctions of egoic needs to fit in and be accepted. Authenticity is sacrificed for conformity; creativity is replaced by imitation; natural spontaneity gives way to cued behaviour; the self-confidence and self-assurance of the infant becomes the self-doubt and awkward hesitation of the young child.

And the most tragic of all – love dies! The child no longer trusts itself, seeing that its natural inclinations, those spontaneous impulses of the biological plan, only get it into trouble, causing the loss of parental love. By now, its major stage-specific need is to be loved and accepted exactly for who it is. It is this need that is used, manipulated and toyed with by the parents to get what they want: an obedient, conforming child.

The child perceives very quickly the opposition between its primary evolutionary impulses and the satisfaction of its need for love and acceptance. The latter is so strong and vital for the security and survival of the child that it has no choice but to quash its natural tendencies, learning to distrust and disown its inner world for the sake of conformity to the outer.

In a word, the child becomes separated from its *real self.* It denies the validity of its inner intuitive world. It comes to the only logical conclusion which is: that it is wrong, flawed and not good enough. It also no longer loves and accepts itself unconditionally. This does not happen in one instant of time, but the decision is made nonetheless. For all of us it happens at different moments, in different ways and in different areas of our psyches. For each of us the split is unique, but the end result is that we stop loving ourselves. Rather than totally accepting the primary impulses of our inner divinity, we come to the conclusion that we are fatally flawed and need to earn our acceptance, earn our 'salvation', earn our place in the world by being 'good'.

Being 'good', however, becomes a full-time job for the child. For it must deny its natural inclinations, its spontaneous creativity and its emotional nature. It must seek to conform, to comply, to obey, and to fit in. It is basically at odds with itself and the stronger this primary, natural self, the more difficult the child's life will become. Those who surrender sheepishly and easily are seen as the model children. Those whose spirits are harder to break are seen as delinquents or dangerous elements. They are dangerous indeed, because they threaten the conventional wisdom of conformity and the *status quo*.

The basic result of all of this is a fundamental confusion between right and wrong, and good and bad. What the child inherently feels to be right and good is being labelled as wrong and bad. Moreover, rather than inappropriate behaviour being discerned, and the child being taught that *that* particular behaviour is wrong or inappropriate, the child is chastised for *being* a bad boy or a bad girl. The child is not bad – their behaviour may have been inappropriate in that given situation and they may need to be disciplined and corrected but their very beingness should not be invalidated in the process.

Correct parenting teaches right from wrong without invalidating the child. Correct parenting teaches self-discipline and self-love. Correct parenting guides the child to find that true balance between fitting into society and honouring its own essential nature. Egoic parenting only reinforces the original split and fuels the feeling of 'not good enough'. The child searches for behaviour that is deemed 'good' and this becomes its *modus operandi* for the rest of its life. For some of us, this is helping mother with the housework and hence we become the dutiful servant. For others, it is doing well at school and so we become the intellectual authority. For others, it is being the entertainer, and so we become the centre of attention. For others, it is caring for a sick parent and so we become the caretaker. And so on.

The important point is that naturalness, self-love and self-acceptance (which are our birthrights) are replaced by a counterfeit self that is filled with self-doubt and self-loathing and that fundamentally feels not good enough. This feeling of 'not good enough' then gives birth to a myriad form of neuroses based on the *modus operandi* of the false personality.

To be able to come from a space of dominion, to be able to harness the powah of one's Tao, to be able to act in harmony with the universal laws of life, one must, first love and accept oneself totally and unconditionally. This means healing the split and coming to terms with this feeling of 'not good enough'. Perfection is progressive. We have already established that fact. The universe is continually unfolding. Evolution *is*! The only constant in the universe is change. We also, as individuals, are constantly evolving and changing. It is not that we are or will ever be perfect in a completed, final sense. This form of perfection is the voice of the negative ego.

But we are good enough! The whole problem revolves around the word 'enough', not the word good. Good enough for what? More is never enough! This is the nature of compulsive, neurotic behaviour. More money, more power, more fame, more sex, more alcohol, more drugs, more attention… these are never enough. It is always a vicious downward spiral. So too, more good! In trying to satisfy the unmet stage-specific need of the child for unconditional love and acceptance by performing in the present we set up an insolvable equation. We are attempting to meet the demands of a past need from a parent by neurotic behaviour in the present. No amount of drinking milk or alcohol, no amount of smoking cigarettes, today, will relieve the unmet needs for breast milk and affection at the age of two months! No amount of fame or fortune, today, will alleviate the unmet need for acceptance as a two-year-old.

It is not that we are either good or bad as in the myth of the garden, but rather that we feel not good *enough!* It is the enough we need to look at and understand. For we are good enough. Life is good enough. There is always enough. The universe provides abundantly.

Each and every one of us has different capabilities, talents, intelligence, beauty and so on. Each of us has different strengths, assets, and wealth. But each and every one of us, just as each and every plant and animal, is an equal child of the universe. Each and every one of us is worthy and good enough! This is Christ's parable in the sermon on the mount: God, the universe, nature, cares for and looks after all.

The feeling of not being good enough is a feeling of unworthiness: it is primarily a lack of self-worth, a lack of self-acceptance. We do not feel good enough to be accepted, to be loved just as we are. We feel we need to do more in order to gain acceptance and approval, in order to gain love. This is the basis of the ulterior motivation of the negative ego. The ego acts in order to get. There is always a pay-off and there is always a hidden agenda.

But this is not love! We do not love people for what they do, but for who they are! We love their beingness. Real love recognises another's essence – their heart and soul. If we love another for their doings – for their fame or fortune – this is not real love. That is not to say we cannot be inspired by another's actions or that inappropriate behaviour should be condoned. If a loved one acts incorrectly, we may need to walk away and love from a distance. But we still love.

Love and acceptance have nothing to do with behaviour and nothing to do with performance. One cannot win love by performing better, trying harder, or by being good enough according to some arbitrary definition of good. 'If you do this I will love you', is not love but co-dependent manipulation. Performing in order to get love will only result in frustration and disappointment.

We cannot get our inner, unmet, and past needs satisfied in our external present. We must satisfy them from within. We must love and accept ourselves. We must establish within ourselves that we are good enough: that we are not lacking or flawed. We must treasure our own worth and build our own esteem. We must cease the performance – the dance of approval seeking – and come to the realisation that we are our own masters. This is personal sovereignty. This is being the fully conscious, aware, mature adult. As a child we need our parents' unconditional love and acceptance. This is the thrust and intent of the biological plan and it is a personal tragedy for each and every one of us that we did not get it.

But as adults, we now need our own unconditional love and acceptance, not that of our biological parents or that of any other substitute we may wish to elect. We are the source of our own fulfilment. The more we seek outside validation, the more we are doomed to feelings of not good enough, neurotic behaviour and self-serving co-dependency.

TWENTY: THE JOY OF SELF-EXPRESSION

The more sovereign we become, the more we heal the primal wounds of inner separation, the more whole we become. In this wholeness there is inner peace and contentment. From this space there is the joy of self-expression and an orderliness that regulates that expression. Egoic neurotic behaviour is characterised by a compulsivity that is both restless and unquenchable. More is never enough to the addict. There is an inner insatiable desire that is only fed by gratification. Indulgence breeds itself. Neurosis knows no moderation and is always associated with excess and exhaustion. There is no balance; no self-love.

Compulsive neurotic behaviour always ends in self-destruction!

On the other hand, the whole of the universe demonstrates an orderliness that endures. All of nature obeys the cycles of the seasons: the rhythm of life. This is one of the key principles of life: it never exhausts itself. This pleasure is left for us. The Tao moves through beginning and end in a movement that is eternal. It uses time to move forward and to achieve. Time is its ally and its servant and not a tyrant to be feared. All things happen in a natural unfolding and orderly sequence of events. All things come to he who is patient!

Taoic movement is gentle, rhythmic, patient and effortless. Taoic movement harmonises itself with the greater currents of the universe and thus does not spend itself prematurely hastening that which is not ready. It never hurries or is restless, agitated or impatient. Taoic movement is thorough, doing what needs to be done, taking the time to do each task properly. Because it is not agitated, it is calm and serene and therefore successful.

The Tao knows that movement and stillness are polar extremes of the one continuum. Thus, movement begets stillness and stillness begets movement. Both are in balance and there is a harmony of action and non-action. Taoic movement knows when to stop, when to rest, when to desist, when to retreat, when to withdraw. There is no conflict, no attempt to dominate or enforce its will over reality. Everything is in its just measure.

This is all a form of self-love and self-acceptance. For it is when we do not accept ourselves, feeling not good enough, that we do not accept what is going on around us and try to force the situation to change, using our egoic will power. When we are in a state of self-love and self-acceptance we know that everything fulfils itself in the perfection of time. There is no need for desperation or anxiety. Rather there is a calm patience that is the source of that inner strength and powah we spoke of earlier.

When one moves in harmony with the universal currents there is a destiny that lends power to one's life. There is an effortlessness that needs no great expenditure of personal energy. There is no need to fight a friendly world! One attunes to the divine benevolence of the universe and is carried by the tide of the Tao, just as the surfer is carried by the waves of the ocean. There is a harmony of individual and universal effort which is always the recipe of great success.

It is this divorce of the individual and the universal which creates the feelings of separation, loneliness, fear and alienation in the first place, necessitating the co-dependent alliance with the ego. Most modern-day ills and diseases spring from this excessive movement characterised by haste, restlessness, impatience, anger and eventual exhaustion. We deplete our own energy resources, vaingloriously trying to achieve our neurotic desires without the natural rhythm and tempo illustrated by nature.

Even when at rest we are not at ease. There is still that restlessness and ill-at-ease feeling that is the symptom of not feeling good enough – that sense that everything is not okay. Rest is seldom deep relaxation. Sleep is seldom recuperative. We live on our adrenalin. We suffer constant exhaustion and tiredness. Our lives lack the natural balance afforded by a life in harmony with the seasons and in rhythm with the day/night cycle and circadian clock.

There is a constant tension in our lives and in our relationships and a constant sense of frustration and unfulfillment that comes from 'keeping up with the Joneses'. We always want more, feeling we have not accomplished enough. We fill our lives with activity, haste, hustle and bustle to keep us from feeling and being.

We have become human doings rather than human beings. Most of us have forgotten how to just *BE*! The feelings that come up when we do relax are too painful to face and so we retreat into further compulsive addictive behaviour, rather than allow the past trauma to surface, connect to present consciousness and be healed. Because we were not unconditionally accepted and loved as children purely and simply for who we are, rather than being judged on our behaviour and performance, we have all come to reject those parts of ourselves that we each consider undesirable or not good enough.

Because perfection is progressive and more importantly, because this is the plane of duality, we all have positive and negative sides. Everything in the manifested universe consists of both yin and yang – the dual poles of creation. Western philosophy and religion view this duality as good and evil – another manifestation of the better than / less than of the ego's perspective. Those parts of ourselves we consider negative or evil, the shadow, we reject. Most of the inner chatter of the left hemisphere, rational, thinking brain, or the voice of the negative ego, is based in self-criticism.

If you strengthen the observer and really watch and listen to your inner dialogue, you will witness this propensity for self-deprecation. We are constantly admonishing, criticising, evaluating and denigrating ourselves and our performance in life. We are continually building and reinforcing the shadow self as being 'not good enough'. Each of us has our own area of perceived deficiency, whether it be our bodies, minds, physical prowess, courage, sexual attractiveness or indeed just our lovability. There is always at least one area of life in which 'we' find ourselves lacking and deficient.

As long as we reject the shadow it reigns victorious. There is a spiritual principle or law of life which states that what you reject, you attract, and that what you resist, persists. This is because we are giving those states energy with our focus and attention. Those parts of ourselves that we do not fully embrace become the fuel that attracts misfortune or opportunities to heal. For it is only by embracing ourselves 100 per cent, totally and completely, that we can become whole and healed.

It is only from this place of wholeness that we can act with personal sovereignty. For those areas of 'perceived' lack will become areas of weakness, our Achilles heels, where we will be prone to be influenced by and dependent upon another. Remember, it is because we did not have enough faith, confidence and trust in our own ability to govern ourselves in the first place that we assigned our egos to take charge.

Wherever you feel vulnerable, wherever you feel deficient, and wherever you do not recognise and accept your own ability to perform, you will enter into situations of low self-esteem and attract others who will treat you poorly. You will attract people and situations into your life – externally – to mirror the way you treat yourself within. If you put yourself down and are self-critical, you will attract others who do the same. If you rob yourself energetically, through self-criticism and self-loathing, you will attract others who will rob you of your dignity and wealth. If you do not feel attractive and lovable, you will attract situations of abuse and degradation. And so on.

The outer is always a mirror of the inner.

So, to act with personal sovereignty one must first, totally and completely – 100 per cent - love and accept oneself, exactly as one is. No emotion, feeling, strength or weakness is any better or worse than any other. Everything just *is*! Moreover, denial is the handmaiden of the negative ego. You cannot change what you deny. The ego works through rationalisation, justification, excuse and blame. It is only when we have the courage to truly face ourselves exactly as we are, without any self-delusion or denial, and embrace the shadow self, that we can integrate it into our personality and release the full spectrum of *SELF*.

To live with personal sovereignty is to be true to the self. To be true to the self means we must *know* the self fully, frankly, without any form of self-deception or illusion.

One of the main causes of ill-health and disease is this rejection of parts of our self that we deem inappropriate or 'less than'. The feeling of not being good enough always manifests in specific aspects of our character, psyche and body. There are always parts of each that we find lacking. It is these areas and the rejection of them that eventually fall prey to disease. It is those areas of ourselves that we are in a space of dis-ease with that eventually become diseased.

Moreover, it is this rejection of self that causes the restlessness, haste, hurry, anxiety and nervous tension that is such a characteristic of compulsive, neurotic behaviour. We can never really relax for there is always something to do in order to allay that feeling of not good enough. Whether that activity seeks to make the self 'better' by working harder or 'fixing' things or to escape the pain by self-destructive addiction to abusive substances does not greatly matter. Both are just two sides of the one coin of self-rejection.

Thus, egoic action never ceases. It knows not when to desist. It has no natural rhythm. It is not in harmony with the great laws of life, which posit rest and action as two polar extremes of a natural balance. Egoic action is characterised by impatience, rudeness, agitation, anger and an excessive use of force. It is the ego's attempt to control and manipulate through domination. It is harsh.

Taoic action is soft and gentle, but it is far more effective. There is an old Chinese proverb which states: 'the sage does nothing, but nothing remains undone.' What this means is effortless effort. Everything is done in the goodness of time, at the right time. There is no need for force, no need for anxiety. For both come from a fear of failure. The Tao never fails, just as intuition is never wrong.

Nature moves unerringly. The universe just *is*! The Tao moves with elegance and grace: an economy of energy that is breathtaking in its awesome certainty to our petty human intelligence. All of nature exhibits both rest and action, expansion and contraction, sympathetic and parasympathetic behaviour. Balance, harmony, grace, stillness and quietude. These are the hallmarks of nature and the Tao.

So, personal sovereignty involves reaching a level of clarity and intention whereby one's personal intention is so totally at one with universal intention that all behaviour is effortless. I call this the level of 'effortless intention'. When one's focus of clarity reaches this level of impeccability, there is no self-doubt, no self-criticism, no self-delusion, no self-deception, and everything just flows. There is no struggle. There is no need to fight a hostile universe because there is no resistance. There is no need to control, manipulate or dominate because one has creatively generated the necessary cosmic waves of with one's inner intent *before* one makes a move or takes any action.

Moreover, one has waited patiently in strength and determination for the right moment – that most auspicious moment when all forces are in harmony. One works with the propitiousness of the time, rather than trying to force the fulfilment of some egoic will and desire. One rides on the wave generated by the powah of one's will rather than struggling to enforce by one's will power. In this effortlessness there is no waste of energy. Life is not hard but easy. One is not in conflict with life but in harmony with its laws and principles. *Life works! Life flows!* One is at ease, content, tranquil, at peace with oneself and the universe. One accepts oneself, where one is in life and the greater majesty of its glory. There is no conflict, no struggle, no resistance and thus no frustration and no tension.

For it is ultimately resistance, frustration and tension that kill us. We spend our all too precious lifeforce fighting life! This is the greatest tragedy. By ignoring the divine thrust of the evolutionary, biological plan and abdicating control to our ego, we have stepped out of tempo with the rhythm and movement of life. By adopting a 'superior than' attitude of arrogance and domination, we have separated ourselves from mother nature and the laws of life, believing that we know better and that we are exempt from their jurisdiction. By believing in a mythological fall and that we are fatally flawed and encoding that 'story' into our cultural heritage, we have rejected ourselves and our humanity. We are a species at war with ourselves, our brothers and sisters, our fellow species, our environment and the earth that sustains us. Thus, there is no peace to be found anywhere.

One cannot be at peace in a war zone. What little peace remains in the surviving pockets of wilderness, we are rapidly destroying. This is why wilderness preservation is so vitally important for our well-being and longevity as a species, for it is here that we hear the silence. It is here that we can still make contact with the divine essence of nature. It is here that we can *be* ourselves, free from the nagging feelings of not being enough, and free to *enjoy!*

For to really enjoy one must be. Egoic action leads to pleasure and satiation. This pleasure seeking is ultimately self-destructive and brings boredom. Taoic action leads to joy and happiness. Joy is uplifting and brings fulfilment. The former is a vicious downward spiral. The latter is an elevation to ecstasy.

One of the greatest tests of personal sovereignty is its inherent harmony and balance. If decisions are sovereign they lead ultimately to joy, fulfilment and good fortune. These are the hallmarks of the Tao. If decisions are co-dependent they lead to sorrow, frustration and misfortune. These are the trademarks of the negative-ego. The former are an expression of self-love and grow out of self-acceptance. The latter are a symptom of deep inner self-distrust and self-rejection.

We have observed that one can only receive love or be loved to the extent that one loves oneself. So too, one can only love and accept others to the extent that one loves and accepts oneself. Indeed, the same mechanism as mentioned in the last chapter is totally relevant here. Those aspects of others – those annoying idiosyncrasies that we criticise and hate in another – those traits that 'really get up our nose', are invariably the very characteristics of our shadow that we reject and deny.

For once again we come up against that principle of life that what we reject we attract. What we deny in our own psyches manifests in our outer world in the characteristics of the significant others that we pull into our orbit. It is merely a principle of attraction that works in much the same way as the law of gravity. What our negative ego denies, the universe presents, so that we can deal with it and recognise its reality.

As the fundamental principle of life is evolution, all life seeks to fulfil itself in full expression. Therefore, those parts of our self that we deny access to consciousness, that are unconscious, seek to make their connection and integration into the light of day. The shadow seeks the light and wants to be embraced. As mentioned previously, the child does not have the neural circuitry to carry the excess current or amplitude of the intense pain of emotional rejection by its parents. This rejection goes underground into cellular memory and musculature armouring. But with emotional maturity and physical growth to adulthood, these shut-off loops of circuit seek to gain access to the main bio-computer and be healed through integration.

However, if because of fear, we resist this healing process and avoid the truth through the rationalisation and justification of the negative ego, life presents it to us in our daily lives. This has two vital consequences for intimacy and love. On the one hand, to the extent that we are unconscious and caught in the past, we cannot give ourselves fully to the present moment of intimacy and embrace. To the extent that we are divorced from our feelings and emotional nature, to the extent that we are numb, we obviously cannot love freely and openly or give ourselves fully to the other person.

On the other hand, because of the principle of attraction and life's desire to heal and integrate all parts of itself, we will attract partners who reflect our shadow and thus push our buttons. This is why so many relationships get bogged down in neurotic conflict and hostility. By not embracing and accepting our own self we cannot embrace and accept another. Those aspects of our shadow that we deny are the very characteristics that attract our partners and we are left with a relationship with our shadow externalised in another.

This principle or law of life manifests in many of us marrying our fathers or our mothers depending on which part of our psyche is being denied and seeks healing. We will find that we 'fall in love with' a fantasy of our own projection only to be rudely awakened to the fact that we have married someone who is exactly like one of our parents. And it is not always the parent of the opposite sex. Men do not necessarily marry their mothers, nor women their fathers. We all have unresolved issues with both parents, and our partners may reflect one or the other or be a composite of both. The principle at work here is that life sets up a recreation of unresolved childhood trauma so that we can relive those experiences, feel those feelings and integrate them into consciousness. This is the healing process that is a fundamental principle and law of life.

However, for this principle to become effective, we must act with courage, determination and honesty. These are not characteristics of the negative ego. To the extent that your ego is in control of your life, then to that extent you cannot recognise what is going on and heal. Instead, one blames the other, both partners sinking deeper into denial. It is all their fault. Thus, conflict and enmity usurp love and intimacy and the alienation and separation of the ego are perpetuated.

Many relationships end up in a seesaw of little boy/mother and little girl/father with both partners seeking to get their unfulfilled infantile needs of the past met in the present relationship. This is an unconscious contract of co-dependency with an oscillation between one party playing the child and the other playing the parent. It has often been said that there are six people in any intimate relationship: the two lovers and both sets of parents. How often do we find ourselves acting just like our own mother or father even though we swore as emerging adults we would never be the same?

What is important to understand is that if we have an aspect of ourselves that is rejected and not integrated it will become an area of weakness in life. It becomes a short circuit in the currents of powah and leaves us unable to make effective sovereign decisions in that particular area. We will attract a partner or ally who is strong in that area and thus give over our power in that arena, furthering the original weakness.

For example, let us say one had an overbearing, critical and dominant father that as a child one could never please. One grows up feeling 'not good enough', deficient and defective in that arena of performance. One distrusts oneself and one's decision-making ability and so seeks to ally oneself with a significant other who is strong in that area. One attracts a recreation of that dominant father in one's partner – one marries one's father. In marital life, one will become suppressed and 'allow' the other to take over and be the main decision-maker. One gives away one's power; one loses strength and is no longer able to operate with sovereignty by being true to oneself.

One cannot operate from a place of dominion. Whether one is being dominated or dominates, it is still a place of domination and not dominion. Thus, we have the origins of a classic co-dependent relationship. Moreover, rather than recognise and acknowledge what is really going on – that we have willingly given away our power and abdicated responsibility yet once again – we will blame the other for being an emotional bully and dominating us. This only makes us feel weaker and more dependent.

Another example is the over-solicitous mother who is too protective and emasculates her children by not allowing them to be adventurous and learn from trial and error. This person will grow up fearing making mistakes and thus avoiding decision-making. They will seek out a 'protective other' to shield them from the painful anxiety of making decisions. This other will then become the over-protective and dominating mother of childhood.

Wherever we reject and criticise in ourselves, that area will develop into a weak blind spot that will then attract a stronger ally to compensate for that weakness. To the extent of that weakness we will throw ourselves away, giving our power of dominion to the other. Moreover, we will not take the responsibility necessary to heal and strengthen that area of weakness, which was our evolutionary intent in the first place. We repeat the initial mistake we made with our egos, seeking another to take charge of our lives. We refuse to develop strength and competency in that area and further our dependency on another, whom we perceive to be 'better than' our self. Weakness, self-criticism, self-loathing and the feeling of not being good enough are perpetuated.

This is the stereotype of many relationships and is to a certain extent a component of all of them. This is not true intimacy and love. Sovereign relationships seek to fulfil the freedom, self-reliance, independence and the autonomy of the individual within the context of an equal union. It is not that to be sovereign we need to be alone, but rather that we need to be able to make our decisions on our own; that we can be true to ourselves! It is not that to be sovereign is to be beyond influence, but that we should not be too easily influenced or swayed by another against our own inner judgement.

We can only give what we already have. To be truly loving and to give of ourselves we must have access to that self. If we are in need, self-denying or unconscious, we cannot give ourselves fully to another. If we come from a place of neediness then we will seek another to meet our needs, to fill our emptiness. This is not love but co-dependency. We often mistake our attachment and dependency for love. We believe that because we need the other person we are in love, where we are really only in need.

Conclusion: THE LIBERATED SELF – THE NEW FRONTIER

Twenty-one: Sovereign Love and Real Relationships

Taoic love gives freely. Egoic love gives in order to get. Taoic love is unconditional and accepts the other fully, for themselves, just as they are, in the present. Egoic love is conditional and judges the other's performance against preconceived criteria according to one's inner expectations and upbringing – the background of the past. In this way an egoic co-dependent relationship replaces that of parent and child with the child seeking the approval of the significant other as a parent substitute. This is not real love.

Real love comes from the spirit: from the heart and soul. Unreal love comes from the ego: from the thinking mind and the insecure psyche. Real taoic love seeks the betterment and well-being of the other. Unreal egoic love seeks its own satisfaction. In a mature sovereign union, both parties give generously and unconditionally. Thus, there is always more than enough. In an immature co-dependent union both parties seek to take from the other and so there is never enough.

If the universe began with the Big Bang, or the explosion of God's love seeking to know itself through creation, then all love is a form of this seeking to know. True love seeks to learn all there is to know about oneself and one's beloved through the intimacy and security of that love. It is open-ended and free. Free from fear; free to be oneself. Co-dependency seeks to control and dominate and to mould the other into a person of its own fashion and design. There is always fear of loss and an inability to express oneself openly in the relationship for fear of ridicule, rejection and criticism.

Real relationships are open and honest, seeking the true revelation of each other's inner psyches. Unreal relationships are closed and dishonest with both seeking to placate the other's tyranny and oppression. Egoic relationships use the very weapons of negativity to deepen the childhood wounds and consolidate the hold of the negative ego. Taoic relationships offer the safety and security of love to heal the wounds of the past so that both parties can more fully express their inner love within the union in the present.

Love is kind, generous, warm, comforting. Co-dependency is cruel, mean, cold and threatening. Love creates a safe haven, a matrix for growth and personal expression. Co-dependency creates a nightmare of insecurity, a dangerous terrain of personal inhibition and anguish. If life starts in the matrix of womb, then it ends in the matrix of a loving and supportive union.

Obviously, these are polar extremes of the continuum, and to a greater or lesser extent both are components of all relationships. No union is either totally loving or totally co-dependent. As this is the plane of duality, positive and negative exist in all things. The point is that personal sovereignty is a new evolutionary movement and we are only now just beginning to learn how to express our real and true selves within the context of an open, equal relationship. The tide is turning away from the sadomasochistic, dominant-suppressive co-dependent form that has so characterised the past to a new, open, mature, more loving form of equality.

It is therefore important for us who are the pioneers, the way-showers and the map-makers in this movement to know the terrain, and to grasp and understand the dynamic and dialectic of the phenomena. The more we heal the past, the more fully conscious and present we become, the more able we are to enter into loving, real intimacy. The more we are in denial and the more we are stuck in the past trying to get our unfulfilled childhood needs met, the more we enter into destructive co-dependent enmeshments.

Each and every relationship holds the seeds of both just as every garden holds the seeds of flowers and weeds. It is our sovereign choice whether we will water and cultivate the flowers, pulling out the weeds, or whether we will allow the weeds to take over and strangle the love. We can, however, only make this choice if we are clear and not in self-denial. Real love demands truth and honesty. Both parties must have the courage to express their feelings, their points of view, honestly and openly without fear of loss or the withdrawal of love. Both parties must give the permission and the safety for this frank expression.

Love must not be a tool or a weapon to be given and taken back according to one's pleasure or displeasure. Real love demands strength: the strength to express one's personal powah and to be accountable for one's own behaviour. It demands impeccability! If one is cowardly or weak, one will allow the other to take over and dominate, to take control. One must be vigilant. Too many relationships end up in a power struggle with both parties seeking to assert their will over the other, over the relationship. This is domination not dominion. Love and dominion go together just as co-dependency and domination do.

If one is needy and depends upon the other's approval to allay one's feeling of not being good enough, then one will throw oneself away for the sake of the alliance. One will lose one's dignity, and hence one's personal powah. If one depends upon an inner accord with a loved one, if one cannot stand strong and sovereign in a difference of opinion, then one will lose the source of that strength. One's source of powah will be without rather than within. In this way one loses strength, powah and sovereignty. One will be unable to stand one's ground for fear of loss. One will give in too easily and be unable to negotiate.

Often, we cannot abide confrontation because it brings up the feelings of inadequacy and powerlessness that we felt as a child in a hostile environment filled with domestic conflict. The shadow self feels frightened and vulnerable and we try to assert our power from this place of weakness and powerlessness only to end up in a state of siege and permanent conflict. Many households deteriorate to this place of unspoken animosity and power play, where both feel imprisoned by the other's expectations and injunctions.

Love and freedom are one. Love can only be love if it allows true personal expression and facilitates inner spiritual growth. If there is any form of oppression or stagnation it is not love but co-dependency. What happens is that we initially fall in love not with the real person but an image that we create ourselves. We project our parent, our needs, and our desires onto the other and then expect them to live up to this image. When their performance fails to match our expectations, as it must over time, we become disappointed, disillusioned, and hostile and seek to control and force the other into our mould via criticism and domination. Thus, the co-dependent power struggle begins. Just as the negative ego is an image-based identity, so too, these unions are image-based and not real.

Sovereignty demands that we be totally responsible for our own reality creation and leave the other to be totally free from our manipulations and free to be responsible for their creation. This is an incredibly significant component of sovereign love. For it demands two things: one, that we be strong enough to take charge of our own lives; and two, that we be strong enough to resist unwanted interference and influence. We can and indeed we must discuss, dialogue, debate and negotiate, especially those issues that affect the common well-being of the family. But eventually each must make a sovereign choice. There can be no blame, no buck passing, no justification, and no excuses. There can be no manipulation, no threats, no ultimatums, no control, no oppression and no guilt. How often in intimate relationships do we hear the comment: 'You made me do it'?

The essence of sovereign love is mutual cooperation and co-creativity between strong and equal individuals, regardless of gender or station. Ultimately, we are all equal as human beings. We each have equal self-worth. Respect for oneself and respect for the other are the foundation upon which we build a sovereign union. Respect for oneself means that one knows and trusts what is right for the self and can express that truthfully and honestly. Respect for the other means that one listens attentively to and hears the other's point of view, especially if it is contrary to one's own.

Indeed, it is this difference, this opposition of viewpoints which creates a healthy relationship. If two people agree on everything, then one of them is unnecessary. Opposition creates the necessity to build a bridge, and often the outcome is a union of both perspectives and is a better solution. Antithesis gives rise to synthesis, which incorporates both points of view. As John Bradshaw points out, it is this ability to 'fight fair' that is such an essential component of a healthy relationship.

Love does not seek to dominate or smother. Smothering mother-love is unhealthy and merely another form of co-dependency. The person who thinks they always know best is suffering from delusions of grandeur and egomania. This is just another face of the negative ego.

Many people dig their heels into their position because the ego does not know how to compromise. The ego insists on getting its own way. The Tao is willing to meet in the middle. The ego is ruled by fear and fears that if it moves from its position it will show its vulnerability and its weakness. It hides its incapability behind a façade of self-assurance and rigid self-righteousness. Those people who are always 'right' are totally under the control of their negative ego and are afraid of genuine discussion, dialogue and compromise.

To be sovereign and know what one wants does not mean to be pig-headed. Quite to the contrary. To be sovereign means that one is so inwardly strong and sure of one's personal powah that one can incorporate another's point of view or perspective without compromising one's real self or one's principles. Intimacy is always about give and take. Love is always about loving and being loved. The dance of intimacy demands that at times we stand firm in our position and at others we give up our ground and meet the other half way. There is no rule except that if it is always one way it is not love.

Another important principle or law of life is that one does not injure. If it hurts, it is not love. To injure is to transgress, to cross the boundary of another's sovereignty, to violate their being. The ego meddles and is injurious. The Tao never goes where it is not welcome. Real love is sensitive to the moods, the needs, and the nuances of the beloved's feelings. It moves carefully, cautiously, wisely. Egoic love is insensitive, abrupt, harsh and arrogant. It seeks to enforce its will regardless of another's feelings, for it is always 'right'.

Real love is attentive to the needs of the other. The ego seeks attention for itself. The ego is filled with its own self-importance and its own self-delusion of grandeur and seeks to be the centre of attention. Taoic love forgets the self in its service and kindness. True kindness cares not for recognition nor reward but acts from its inner heart in innocence and purity. There is no ulterior motive. The ego always looks to the pay-off. The ego talks incessantly about itself and its vain accomplishments. The lover listens to the beloved to learn about their being. The ego boasts enthusiastically in order to assert its superiority. The lover shares modestly in humility to increase closeness and bonding. The ego makes a difference between itself and others. Lovers feel a oneness.

Thus, sovereignty does not breed isolation; the ego does. Being sovereign and taking responsibility for ourselves enables us to give more fully from our real and true self. For by becoming sovereign we become the emotionally mature adult capable of giving and receiving love. The ego, stuck in an emotionally immature infantile past, cannot truly give and receive love but seeks to be taken care of instead. Taking care of is not love. It is a spiritual robbing of responsibility. When we truly care for another we empower them to take care of themselves. When we become a caretaker, we take away the other's dignity and sovereignty. To love is to care but not to care-take.

In all my years of counselling and business consulting, I found this issue of personal sovereignty within relationship to be the number one biggest challenge. For we are all still experimenting with this newfound freedom. Freedom from oppression leading to freedom to be ourselves. Not many yet know how to do this. It is an emerging skill in an evolutionary sense. One or two generations ago there was no real personal freedom within marriage or within business. There was invariably a dominant partner or boss and a submissive partner or employee.

With women's liberation, gay liberation, same sex marriage and more enlightened workplaces, it is now time for us to explore this dimension of personal freedom. The ideal obviously is to be true to oneself within the comfort of a loving relationship and within the context of a secure job. To be true to oneself and true to the other. Ultimately, it is not about women's liberation or gay liberation but really about the liberation of us all, as individuals, from all types of oppression – political, financial, sexual, emotional, psychic and psychological.

Each and every being is a spark of divine consciousness and is right and worthy just as it is, in its own integrity. There is no 'better than'; there is no normal; there is no criteria for average. There is no perfect figure, height, shape, colour, race etc. There is no 'better than' social position, class, or amount of wealth, etc. We all live our own lives and each life is as unique and as valuable as any other.

When one becomes truly sovereign, embracing the shadow-self, and loves and accepts oneself just as one is, without judgement, criticism or condemnation, then one can extend that same generosity of spirit and love to others. When I can allow myself to just be who I am, then and only then, can I allow others to be who they are.

This is real unconditional love. This is the Tao. For the Tao in nature accepts all beings equally. There is no 'better than' in nature. There is no feeling of not being good enough in the wild. All beings co-exist in the garden sharing equally of God's bounty. There is an inherent order and harmony. There is no co-dependency and no oppression. The strongest and mightiest of predators do not oppress nor victimise their prey. They merely eat their fill and leave the other species to their lot.

When we are sovereign we are secure within ourselves. In that quiet security there is a freedom and in that freedom there is an allowance. We allow ourselves and others to *be*. There is an end to restlessness. There is an end to striving. There is an ending of anxiety. There is no competitiveness, no threat, no fear of loss and thus no need to dominate, control, manipulate. In this space of freedom true love is born. For love is not just something we feel for a significant other. Love is a state of being that we share in many ways with many different people, animals, plants, things and our own God. Love is something that grows out of this quiet freedom and blossoms in our lives in many different forms. It is like a beautiful full and blooming camellia or rose which is pregnant with colour and lots of wonderful flowers.

There is the love of our partner, of our children, of our parents, of our friends, of our pets, of our home and family, of our garden, of the earth. There is love of ourselves and the love of God. And then there is *love!* A love not centred in anything. A love that needs no object. A love that just *is*. A love that comes as a cool breeze on a summer's day. A love that keeps us warm when the world betrays us. A love that is a feeling of contentment and transcends the vicissitudes of fate.

This love is the source we spoke of at the beginning of this section. It is this love that is the only true source of strength and personal powah. It is this love which sustains our spirit and nourishes our soul. It is this love which is the energy of the universe, the grace of God, the chi of the Tao. We observed in Section II, that one of the main thrusts of the evolutionary process through the biological plan is the creation of intelligence. Intelligence is here defined as the ability to creatively respond to the challenges of life in a future oriented sense. It has nothing to do with repetition or rote learning from the past but rather an ability to meet the reality of the present. Evolutionary change is a prime example of this living intelligence – it is constantly adapting to and meeting the present in creating the future. It is living in the now.

In fact, if we observe the process of evolution down through the ages, it is in a constant state of adaptation and change. We see all species, everywhere, developing over the millennia to better respond to the challenges of life. The more we study and learn, the more we are amazed at the intelligence and complexity of life. This is one of the glories of bio-diversity on the planet.

In contrast, the ego, or more specifically the negative ego, is dumb and repetitious. It is caught in the past. If the real is open-ended, the unreal is closed. One of the overriding characteristics of life is its propensity to learn, to grow, to develop and to change and adapt. Nothing is static or stagnant. Change is everywhere. Life constantly evolves. On the other hand, the world of the ego seeks security, comfort, conformity and reassurance through eliminating change and suspecting the unknown. We fear change! The whole point of domination is to gain control over life in such a way that one can manipulate change to one's own advantage and to allay the unknown.

However, this is contrary to the principle of life. Life needs to be open-ended in order to explore freely all avenues of possibility. Bio-diversity ensures the exploration of all of these avenues by converting the possible into the probable. It is vitally important to understand the power of the past to deaden the future. Krishnamurti always spoke of the rational thinking mind's tendency to come from the background of its own thinking, to filter the present through the past. We do neurologically filter and decipher external daily reality through the mental constructs of our belief system. Remember, belief precedes reality. We can only perceive that which we are neurologically receptive to. The neuro-receptors are conditioned by our belief structures.

The rational thinking brain of the ego is conditioned by and operates out of the background of the past. We are all constantly evaluating our perceptions against an arbitrary set of inner criteria that we ourselves have created. We are all conditioned by our cultural and personal biases, prejudices, fears, beliefs. We are limited by our own definitions of what is possible.

The more these limitations take hold the more circumscribed one's life and attitudes become and the less freedom one enjoys. We have all met and know the type of person whose life is ruled by fear, bigotry, limitation or prejudice. Such a person knows no freedom and has no freedom of choice because they are dominated by the past. Again, we see that a person who seeks to dominate their reality ends up in being dominated by it.

Sovereignty demands, as a fundamental prerequisite, an inner state of spiritual, psychological and mental freedom. This means in very specific and concrete terms that the past must verily be the past. One learns and is enriched through and by one's experiences. This is exactly how evolution and intelligence work. One learns from the past and takes that learning, that wisdom into the present to determine the future. However, if we operate out of the past, assuming that what happened before will necessarily happen again, then we are denying the spontaneity, creativity and freedom of the new which are all principles of life. We are unable to respond to the present creatively, generating the future with intelligence.

For real intelligence is the subtle yet profound combination or synergy of the learning and wisdom of the past meeting the challenge and truth of the present to actively create the new and unknown future. This is the excitement of life. This is the joy and the wonder. Every morning heralds a new day. Each and every day we are born anew and given another chance to live. Without this alchemical process there can be no evolution. Life stagnates!

How many of us get caught in the rut of a life that has no newness, no excitement, and no change? How many of us operate out of the background of the known, doing what we have always done, afraid of the unknown? Afraid to risk the new path? Afraid to let go of the security and continuity of the past? For as we have seen, life, the Tao and love are all synonymous and an aspect of love of life is a sense of joy, excitement and adventure. 'Life is a daring adventure or nothing at all.'[45] If we never risk, we never gain.

To be filled with a sense of awe and wonder, to be curious and explore our lives, to welcome change and meet it with a sense of personal powah, to have faith and confidence in one's own ability to master the unknown and create new life – these are all characteristics of the sovereign being. These are all facets of a love of life. For without a sense of excitement, life becomes dull and boring. A life that is repetitious and caught in the past of its own background soon entropies and becomes lifeless: we become the walking dead.

This again is why wilderness is so vitally important for the biodiversity of the planet for it is the living laboratory where life recreates itself. It is here, in the wild, that life most fully explores and expresses itself. If we ever enter a pristine forest we immediately sense this wonder, this excitement, this teeming Chi and this magnificence of life. This is why we feel invigorated, refreshed, renewed and revitalised.

Wilderness is the source and the storehouse of the earth's Chi. As we encroach upon and destroy that wilderness we deplete the earth's energy and risk our own survival. The Big Bang explosion of God's love is not something that happened in a past tense, umpteen billion years ago, or in a seven-day wonder and which is now winding down to its conclusion. Life explodes in every moment. Life recreates itself anew in every second. It is just whether we are awake enough to sense it. This is the image of satori, Samadhi, enlightenment. This is the culmination of the evolution of consciousness towards which we are all going. We need to touch that newness, to actively experience the birth of creation in every moment. This is the art of Zen, the practise of the Tao. I am always reminded of a song by Cat Stevens: 'Morning has broken, like the first morning / blackbird has spoken like the first bird / fresh from the dawning, fresh from the word.'

A similar thing often happens to us when we go on vacation. We are filled with that sense of newness, excitement, and wonder which does rekindle the fires of passion for life. It is this newness which restores, regenerates and rejuvenates our vitality and love. This is also why we say: 'a change is as good as a holiday.'

How often do we sink into a state of despair, lethargy, depression and exhaustion because the rut and routine of life take over and extinguish our buoyancy? Everything seems hopeless and we feel helpless. There seems to be no way out and we cannot operate creatively. We have no real freedom of choice and we feel imprisoned by the obligations of our lives. We perform our daily duties perfunctorily without joy, without love, and without creativity.

This is not life. This is not personal sovereignty!

Life is not a prison but an opportunity. The fear of the negative ego and our desire to dominate life have left us spiritually bankrupt. We spend our lives making money to allay our insecurity and end up with no time, no joy, no effervescence. We trade time for money. We squander life force for security. We reject the new for the known. We end up spiritually destitute with our worldly riches. We are afraid to relate because our experience is that of co-dependency not sovereign love.

Life can be a grand and glorious adventure of the joy of self-expression. One can allow one's resident spirit to take charge of the corporate structure of consciousness, and befriend one's positive ego, re-engaging its services as servant and lead a fully conscious, self-aware life exercising sovereign dominion and being in harmony with the universal principles of life. In the words of ancient Chinese Taoism:

> ...the fate of fire depends on wood; as long as there is wood below, the fire burns above. It is the same in human life; there is in man likewise a fate that lends power to his life. And if he succeeds in assigning the right place to life and to fate, thus bringing the two into harmony, he puts his fate on a firm footing. All that is visible must grow beyond itself, extend into the realm of the invisible. Thereby it receives its true consecration and clarity and takes firm root in the cosmic order.[46]

The thesis of *Personal Sovereignty* is that humanity has lost its way; the fire is running out of wood. We are living on borrowed time and robbing future generations of their inheritance rather than passing on a richer and more glorious world. No one would argue the fact that the planet is poorer today than it was 100 years ago.

If we return to our analogy of the 4.6 billion-year old planet being a forty-six-year-old human, the last one hundred years is but a heartbeat in which we have successfully squandered our fate, our destiny, our riches and inheritance but most importantly, our divine gift of free will.

We need to re-align our fate. We need to recognise and acknowledge the fate and destiny of humanity to be the divine husbandman, to take dominion of the planet and cease its domination and destruction. We need to take back our personal control of ourselves, our lives and our destiny. We need to start to take responsibility for the lives we lead and for the impact our behaviour has on other beings – human and non-human. We need to become responsible planetary citizens of planet Earth.

We need to become sovereign beings exercising our free will judiciously and with ultimate care for all living things and the principle of life. We need to cease the illusion of separation and become one with All That Is – the only definition of God that makes sense.

NOTES

[1] Arthur Koestler, *The Ghost in the Machine*. Picador Pan Books, 1975.
[2] Eric Fromm, *The Fear of Freedom*. Bantam Press. 1981.
[3] Ibid.
[4] Ibid.
[5] Agresara, *The Eternal Resurrection*. Sidgwick & Jackson, 1965.
[6] Lao Tsu, *Tao Te Ching*. Penguin Classics, 1970.
[7] Dr Arthur Janov, *The New Primal Scream*. Sphere Books, 1992.
[8] Carl Jung, *Memories, Dreams, Reflections*. Vintage Books, 1963.
[9] Ibid.
[10] Ibid.
[11] Ibid.
[12] Ibid.
[13] Ibid.
[14] Ibid.
[15] Ibid.
[16] Ibid.
[17] Ibid.
[18] Ibid.
[19] Dr Arthur Janov, *The New Primal Scream*.
[20] Bartholomew, *I Come as a Brother*.
[21] Ken Carey, *Starseed*. Harper, 1991.
[22] Bartholomew, *I Come as a Brother*. High Mesa Press. 1986
[23] Richard Wilhelm, *The I Ching*. Routledge & Kegan Paul. 1970.
[24] Ibid.
[25] Ibid.
[26] Ibid.
[27] Ibid.
[28] Ibid.
[29] Ibid.

[30] Ken Carey, *Starseed*.
[31] Ibid.
[32] Ibid.
[33] Eric Fromm, *The Fear of Freedom*.
[34] Ibid.
[35] Ibid.
[36] Ken Carey, *Starseed*.
[37] Joseph Chilton-Pearce, *Magical Child*. Bantam Press, 1980.
[38] Ibid.
[39] Ibid.
[40] Ibid.
[41] Richard Wilhelm, *The I Ching*.
[42] Ibid.
[43] Project Wingmaker, *Ancient Arrow*. Wingmakers LLC, 1999.
[44] Richard Wilhelm, *The I Ching*.
[45] Helen Keller.
[46] Richard Wilhelm, *The I Ching*.

ABOUT THE AUTHOR

Author, entrepreneur, business owner, environmentalist & keen gardener, Adrian Emery has devoted his life to creating a new philosophy called *LifeWorks* based on understanding the laws, principles & codes that make life work easily, effortlessly & successfully. Life is a gift & we are here to enjoy life & be successful: it is our birthright.

He has developed a coaching modality called *TaoTuning* designed to assist others to find their life purpose or ikigai & attune to the flow of their inner destiny & fate, establishing their life on the firm foundation of cosmic principles.

Adrian has now retired to *Sennikatan*, a spectacular garden built over the last 50 years to demonstrate we can regenerate the Earth, to write & prepare others for the coming planetary transition to a new world. He has also created *rusticspirit* as a spiritual retreat for guests to come & experience the stillness.

For all enquiries: www.adrianemery.com

www.ingramcontent.com/pod-product-compliance
Lightning Source LLC
Chambersburg PA
CBHW032031290426
44110CB00012B/759